Targets of Terror

Targets of Terror

Contemporary Assassination

Laura N. Bell

ROWMAN & LITTLEFIELD
Lanham • Boulder • New York • London

Published by Rowman & Littlefield
An imprint of The Rowman & Littlefield Publishing Group, Inc.
4501 Forbes Boulevard, Suite 200, Lanham, Maryland 20706
www.rowman.com

British Library Cataloguing in Publication Information Available

Library of Congress Cataloging-in-Publication Data on File

ISBN 978-1-78661-391-2 (cloth)
ISBN 978-1-5381-5403-8 (pbk.)
ISBN 978-1-78661-392-9 (electronic)

For Clifton

In Memory
Velma V. Spangler (1933–2019)
Aunt and friend

Contents

Acknowledgments

The author wishes to acknowledge funding from West Texas A&M University. Funding from both the Foundation Development Research Grant (2017) and the Killgore Research Center (2019) contributed to the development and completion of this project. The author wishes to thank Dr. Iliyan R. Iliev, the faculty, and students at the School of Social Science and Global Studies at the University of Southern Mississippi for valuable feedback during the early stages of this project. Additionally, the author extends her appreciation to the *Studies in Conflict & Terrorism* journal for graciously permitting the inclusion of a previously published article. Finally, thank you to the one who provided important feedback and support along the way. You know who you are.

List of Tables and Figures

TABLES

FIGURES

Chapter 1

Introduction

Assassination is an act of political violence. There are no *nonpolitical* assassinations. Assassination is inherently political—the one losing their life to an assassin is not a random target but rather they are selected because they hold some manner of influence in political life. This distinguishes assassination from murder. Murder occurs frequently, and the United Nations Office on Drugs and Crime estimates that worldwide as many as 464,000 people were killed in 2017 alone.[1] Homicides are driven by nonpolitical criminal activity, personal motivations, and/or grievances. Assassinations are driven by political motivations, such as attempting to alter the policy of a state by changing its leadership or attempting to interfere with elections by deterring citizens from voting or participating as candidates.

Most people can recall from their knowledge of history at least one or two impactful assassinations, whether it is the assassination of Julius Caesar on the ides of March; Austrian archduke Franz Ferdinand, which sparked World War I; or U.S. president Abraham Lincoln at the end of the civil war. More recently, many will recall the killing of U.S. president John F. Kennedy in Dallas, Texas, or that of Israeli prime minister Yitzak Rabin after a peace rally in Tel Aviv. Yet, what most do not realize is the frequency or the manner in which assassinations occur, particularly since the mid-1970s.

There are assassinations that make international headlines, such as the 2016 shooting of Russian ambassador Andrei Karlov during a speech at an art exhibition in Ankara. Karlov was killed in retaliation for Turkey's actions in the Syrian civil war and relations with Russia. Less international attention is given, however, to the killings of clerics in Yemen or local electoral candidates in Mexico. In Afghanistan, the Taliban unsuccessfully targeted a U.S. general in a 2018 attack which killed three senior Afghan officials,[2] and Al-Shabaab is likely responsible for the 2017 killing of peace activist Seyduna Hajow in Somalia.[3] These latter assassinations typically do not make international headlines and sometimes not even national ones.

Contemporary assassinations are most often used in campaigns of violence and typically are not stand-alone events. Assassinations are only one of several tactics utilized in pursuit of specific goals, such as hindering democratic processes or disrupting peace talks between states or groups. The use of assassination in these broad campaigns of violence, which I will now refer to as terrorism, is not wholly unique to modern history. What is unique is the *extent* to which assassination is used as part of terrorist campaigns in recent decades. From 1977 through 2017, nearly 10,000 individuals have been assassinated in terror campaigns around the globe.

It is important to emphasize the nature of contemporary assassinations. The environment within which today's assassinations occur is significantly different from the well-remembered assassinations of the past, such as Kennedy or even the attempt on U.S. president Ronald Reagan in 1980. Thus, what I refer to as leader assassinations (such as Kennedy) and terrorist assassinations should be delineated. Additionally, the use of assassinations by sovereign states (i.e., state-sponsored or targeted killings) should be delineated as well.

For example, Israel is known for targeting and eliminating members of groups who threaten its security, and the United States uses drone technology to target terrorist enemies in the post-9/11 era. The argument that I make here and have made in prior work, is that before assassinations can be studied empirically, we must understand that not all assassinations are the same. I suggest three categories of assassination are appropriate—leader, terrorist, and state-sponsored. Overlap certainly exists and sometimes the absence of clear information may understandably challenge proper placing into these assassination categories. An in-depth discussion of all three categories is not within the scope of this book, but this explanation should help clarify for the reader the aim and focus of this project, which rests solely on terrorist assassinations. The definitions of both assassination and terrorist assassination are detailed further in the following chapter and therefore I will not offer too much discussion here. In short, a terrorist assassination is one that occurs during a broader campaign of violence when the victim is targeted due to their role in political life.

The intent for the remainder of this introductory chapter is twofold. First, the aim is to provide a brief overview of the historical norms of assassination. This will aid in understanding the nature of contemporary assassinations and second, the structure of the remainder of the book is explained in an effort to establish expectations for the reader.

AN OVERVIEW OF ASSASSINATION NORMS

The term "assassin" is traced to an eleventh-century group, sometimes referred to as the Order of the Assassins. Debate surrounds the origin of the word, derived from the Arabic word *hashishiyyin*, which Ford[4] states is closely related to another Arabic word which refers to users of hashish. Therefore, many have ascribed the use of hashish to the first known professional assassins, but Ford argues this is misplaced. What *is* known about the group is that it was formed by Hassan-i Sabbah, a Persian, who abandoned his Shi'ite faith for the Ismaili faith. He used the group to target elite Sunni's and spread the word of the Ismailis.

In 1090, Sabbah's group besieged Seljuk land in northern Persia, claiming it for their home base of operations. Sabbah's intent was to convert as many people as possible and to target those of influence who opposed Sabbah, such as Nizam ul-Mulk. Ul-Mulk, a prominent Sunni leader and scholar, was reportedly the first target of the assassins and was stabbed to death in 1092. Multiple murders were attributed to the group (death by dagger was the modus operandi of the group) and a similar group was formed in Syria— Sunni and Christian leaders were targeted and terrorized in the region from the Mediterranean Sea to Persia for nearly 200 years before the Mongol and Mamluk invasions in Persia and Syria, respectively.[5]

By the sixteenth century, assassination became an acceptable way of conducting politics and especially acceptable as a way to rid the world of tyrannical leaders. John Stuart Mill, the nineteenth-century British utilitarian philosopher, argued that it was indeed virtuous to assassinate a tyrant. The killing of an oppressor protects the masses and spares thousands from unnecessary hardships—repression, torture, and even death. Tryannicide was considered by many to be a morally acceptable alternative to war and widespread conflict in which large numbers of people would likely suffer and/or die. Yet, what of the targeting of those who were not tyrants? In the mid-to-late nineteenth century, a new international norm began to emerge in which assassination was no longer viewed as just or moral, and prohibitions against assassination were established.

Attempts to codify assassination norms began with the first official prohibition in the Lieber Code, written during the U.S. Civil War. In Section IX of this code, Article 148 prohibits the targeting of any individual for death and declares assassination to be a barbaric practice. Adopted by President Lincoln in General Orders 100, the Lieber Code served as a template for The Hague Conventions of 1899 and 1907, which also prohibit assassination in Article 23(b). The Organization of African Unity Charter condemns assassination and other prohibitions are found in the 1977 Convention on the Prevention and Punishment of Crimes against Internationally Protected Persons, Including Diplomatic Agents.[6]

In the United States, the 1976 Church Committee investigation into the activities of the U.S. intelligence community uncovered evidence of U.S. involvement in multiple plots aimed at killing Fidel Castro of Cuba and Patrice Lumumba of the Congo. Executive Order 11905 was then issued by President Gerald Ford, which states that involvement in assassination plots by anyone working on behalf of the U.S. government is strictly forbidden. The ban has since been renewed by presidents Jimmy Carter and Ronald Reagan and is still in effect today via Reagan's 1981 Executive Order 12333.[7]

For more than a century, the act of assassination has been an unacceptable tactic in the conduct of politics. Yet, as the data shows, these acts of political violence continue with abandon. In the late 1800s and into the 1920s, the anarchist movement assassinated several world leaders, including King Umberto I of Italy and King George I of Greece. In 1910, a plot by anarchists was uncovered that prevented the likely death of Emperor Meiji of Japan. Those who seek to alter or overthrow existing political systems or remove those who are in power will not operate within the boundaries of accepted norms and laws. Thus, terror organizations employ this method of political violence often and it is this category of assassinations—terrorist assassinations—upon which this study focuses.

CONTEMPORARY ASSASSINATIONS

The use of assassination in terror campaigns since the 1970s has at least two unique characteristics. One of which is the frequency of these events—nearly 10,000 people have been assassinated as part of terror campaigns from 1977 through 2017[8]—and another is the target of these events—local leaders, law enforcement officials, and others who were not targeted with any significant frequency in the past. Although outside the data range for this project, U.S. intelligence estimates that as many as 1,200 local officials were assassinated in Vietnam by the Vietcong in 1969 alone.[9] Thus, contemporary history is ripe with terrorist assassinations carried out by groups such as the Vietcong in Vietnam, the Shining Path in Peru, the Euskadi ta Askatasuna (ETA) in Spain, and the Taliban in Afghanistan.

The targets of terrorists in these assassinations include an array of victims from members of royalty to diplomats to political party leaders. Examples include the targeting of Saudi prince Talal bin Abd-al-Aziz who was killed in November 2003 by Islamist extremists in a bomb attack while hunting in the Algerian desert. Nayyar Iqbal Rana, a Pakistani diplomat stationed in Jalalabad, Afghanistan, was shot and killed near his home in November

2017. Khalaf al-Ali, the second secretary of the Saudi Arabian Embassy in Bangladesh, was also shot and killed in March 2012. The Taliban is likely responsible for the death of a local development council member in December 2017 in Afghanistan and officials suspect Abu Bakr Unis Jabr Brigade is to blame for the shooting and killing of Libyan deputy minister of industry, Hassan al-Droui, in Sirte in January 2014.

Other examples include the attempted assassination in June 2009 of Ernesto Cornejo, a congressional candidate in Mexico for the National Action Party, and/or the killing in Ukraine of the Crimean Christian-Liberal Party leader, Yevgeniy Podanev, in June 1994.[10] It is evident, even from this small sample of cases, that terrorist assassinations are widespread and more frequent than most realize. Yet, neither scholars nor popular nonfiction writers have made these acts of political violence the focus of study, at least not to any extent adequate for developing an understanding of these events. This book is intended to change that or at least be the beginning of the change. While one study alone cannot devise a complete understanding of terrorist assassinations, or any other event for that matter, this text is intended to jumpstart in-depth conversations about the repercussions of terrorist assassinations and the importance of terrorists' target selection.

PREMISE AND EMPIRICAL AIM

The premise of this project is that the targets selected by terrorists for assassination matters. A multitude of targets is chosen as part of terror campaigns and includes state prosecutors, election officials, intelligence officials, police security forces, journalists, military officials, religious leaders, political party officials, government officials, and diplomats. Scholarly examinations that focus on target selection are somewhat paltry,[11] but in a study of terrorism directed toward diplomats from the United States, Milton[12] reveals interesting data.

First, Milton's study finds that the type of groups who choose to target U.S. diplomats shifts from one decade to another, and in the 1970s and 1980s, the groups targeting diplomats were more diverse. By the 2000s, Milton finds that the five groups who most often targeted diplomats were religious in nature—such as al-Qaeda and the Taliban. Geographically, the descriptive data indicates that the 1970s were the most dangerous for diplomats in the Middle East and North Africa region (40% of the attacks against diplomats in the 1970s occurred there). In the 1980s and 1990s, Latin America was the most dangerous (52% and 40%, respectively, of the attacks) and in the 2000s, the danger shifted back to the Middle East and North Africa region (42% of the attacks). In the 2010s, the danger shifted to South and Southeast Asia (63% of the attacks).

One of the interesting findings from Milton's research is that there is an increase in the likelihood of a U.S. diplomat being attacked when stationed in countries where the United States sends foreign aid and where there is an existing military alliance. His research suggests that the lethality of attacks on U.S. diplomats may have different driving factors, such as the freedom levels that exist within the country of the attack. Altogether an extremely interesting study and one which advances our understanding of target selection, likely the most relevant point to be made from Milton's study, is that both empirical and theoretical examinations of terrorist target selections are possible and may yield important insight. He notes the potential that exists for furthering our understanding of terrorism simply by disaggregating the data already in existence.[13] I could not concur more.

In fact, the aim of this project is to engage in the disaggregation of data from an existing source and examine political institutional changes over time after terrorist assassinations, across target types. Using existing, yet refined, data on all the targets already discussed plus a few more, this study seeks to enhance our understanding of political changes in the aftermath of assassinations, according to chosen target. Are the assassinations of intelligence officials, for instance, more likely to result in political changes to authoritarian regimes? Do the killings of prosecutors or politicians have differing impacts on political changes? Using survival analysis methodology, the span of time after a terrorist assassination to a change in political institutions is measured with the aim of delineating differences in the likelihood of political change within states over time. Qualitative analyses, by way of case studies, sheds light on the environment and context within which these assassinations occur and the resultant outcomes. This mixed methods approach provides nuance that a single study (either quantitative or qualitative) could not offer.

STRUCTURE OF THE BOOK

The reminder of the book proceeds as follows. Chapter 2 is designed to provide the reader with an understanding of the evolution of the definitions of both assassination and terrorism. By highlighting the definitional challenges, the challenges of empirically studying assassination and terrorism are highlighted. This chapter also provides an overview of previous research regarding terrorist assassination and explains why these acts of political violence are relevant to the advancement of terrorism studies. The importance of target selection is introduced to the reader as is the data source.

Chapter 3 details the primary data source, the Global Terrorism Database, and explains the process taken by the author to refine the existing data. Other data sources utilized in the project are introduced and explained, such as the

Polity IV project, and a detailed explanation of the target categories is provided. Some descriptive data is included in this chapter as well, such as the geographic distribution of terrorist assassinations.

Chapter 4 introduces the reader to the quantitative method used throughout the book—survival analysis—and is taken from an article previously published in the *Studies in Conflict & Terrorism* journal. Revised data is used to replicate work from the prior article and thus, quantitative models are presented and explained as part of this chapter.

Chapter 5 is the first of what I refer to as the case study chapters. This chapter examines the terrorist assassinations of government officials and presents survival analysis models for several subtypes of government officials including diplomats, election officials, government personnel, intelligence personnel, heads of state, and international peacekeepers. The empirical approach is to examine changes by regime type—comparing authoritarian, mixed, and tumultuous regimes to democratic regimes. In this chapter and the ones that follow, models test not only for the likelihood of political institutional change in the aftermath of assassinations of government officials but also for the direction of these changes. For instance, are states more or less likely to shift toward authoritarianism or democracy in the wake of these events? Chapters 5 through 9 aim to address and answer this question. Qualitative case studies enhance understanding and assist in answering the questions posed here and thus, a discussion of the context and events that transpired in the aftermath of the assassinations of Indian prime minister Indira Gandhi and British military attaché brigadier Stephen Saunders is included in chapter 5.

Chapter 6 examines the assassinations of those who are politically active—politicians and political party leaders. Survival analysis models test for the likelihood of political change after the killings of politicians and influential political party members, as well as the direction of the changes. The case studies in this chapter are that of former Lebanese prime minister Rafik Hariri, a politician, and a series of attacks by the Shining Path on local candidates and party members in Peru in 1989.

Chapter 7 examines attacks on law enforcement officials and includes the subcategories of judges/attorneys and police security forces. As is discussed in this chapter, prosecutors and court officials are often targeted in terror campaigns as are members of police security forces. The case study of one police chief in Spain, Joseba Pagazaurtundúa, is discussed and a combined case study of a deputy chief justice, Aza Gazgireeva, and Judge Eduard Chuvashov in Russia is included. Survival analysis models are presented examining the likelihood of political institutional shifts, as well as the direction of these shifts, for both court officials and police security forces.

Chapter 8 examines the political impact of assassinations of journalists on regimes. As an informal public institution, the media have an important role to play in societal and political processes. The subtypes of newspaper, radio, online, and television journalists are available for study in this category and thus, survival models are presented for the likelihood of political change and the direction of that change in the aftermath of terrorist assassinations which target journalists. The attacks on *Charlie Hebdo* in France and a systematic campaign against journalists in Algeria in what is often referred to as the Black Decade (1992–2002) serve as interesting case studies for this category.

Chapter 9 deviates slightly from the other case study chapters, in that two main categories are combined into one chapter. The categories of military and religious leaders possess similar characteristics—either no subtype of target exists or no significant number of attacks on a subtype exists. The same quantitative approach applies to this chapter and the categories of military and religious leaders are tested to determine the likelihood of directional shifts toward or away from democracy in the aftermath of assassinations of these targets. The case study approach is wholly different and rather than present an in-depth case study of one particular assassination or assassination campaign, multiple examples of assassinations of military and religious leaders are provided with the intent of painting an overall picture of the nature of terrorist assassinations of military and religious leaders.

Finally, chapter 10 aims to summarize the findings from this project, suggest a framework for better understanding of terrorist assassinations, and discuss potential avenues for further research. This book offers what is hopefully the beginning of advanced research into differences across those categories of targets selected for assassination in terror campaigns. Much can be gained from insight into these terrorist target choices—security for potential terrorist targets can be improved, governments will be better equipped to devise policy that addresses expected political changes after these events, and scholars can gain a better understanding of the overall impact of terrorist assassinations.

Chapter 2

Characterizing Contemporary Assassination

Since the end of the nineteenth century, assassinations have occurred as one tactic of many in broader campaigns of violence. Anarchist terror spread from Europe to the United States in the late 1800s in a campaign that included bombings and assassinations of government leaders. The assassin of King Umberto I of Italy in 1900 was at the very least inspired by the anarchist movement, if not an active anarchist himself. King George I of Greece was assassinated in 1913 by an anarchist and there is some question as to the inspiration for U.S. president William McKinley's assassination in 1901 by Leon Czolgosz (possible anarchist motivations).[1] Nevertheless, these assassinations and others occurred during a long terror campaign conducted by an international anarchist movement. However, it wasn't until the mid-1970s that assassination again became a popular tactic of terrorism.

Assassinations occur with considerable frequency in today's terror campaigns. The nature and the frequency of these events should therefore distinguish terrorist assassinations from that of assassinations of state leaders, which occur outside sustained campaigns of violence, or state-sponsored assassinations ordered by governmental leaders in efforts to eliminate perceived security threats. Yet, what *is* an assassination? In order to properly establish an argument for categories of any act, that act must first be defined.

ASSASSINATION DEFINED

In one of the first scholarly examinations of political assassination, Havens, Leiden, and Schmitt define assassination as ". . . killings or murders, usually directed against individuals in public life, motivated by political rather than by personal relationships."[2] In another study, assassination is defined by

Crotty as "the murder of an individual, whether of public prominence or not, in an effort to achieve political gain."[3] Cooper defines assassination as "the willful killing of a human being in order to alter the normal course of events in a particular public sphere in which the victim has been influential,"[4] and Katchadourian defines assassination as follows:

> Killing a private person or public figure mainly or wholly for political reasons or motives . . . [and] . . . political assassination is, by definition, essentially directed toward the victim insofar as he or she occupies or is believed to occupy a position of political influence in a particular country or in the world as a whole.[5]

While the *political* nature of assassination is a consistent component of these definitions, there is some contradiction in the public versus private position of the target. Two of the four definitions suggest that the target of the assassin does not necessarily have to be a public figure in order for the killing to be a political assassination. Two definitions emphasize the victim's public influence as an important component, while tow emphasize mainly the perceived political gain for the assassin.

Reflection on the evolution of assassination, particularly since the 1970s, begs the larger question of how to categorize these events for empirical analyses. Havens, et al. argue that the question of motivation for the assassin necessitates development of an assassinations classification system—yet, motivations are often ambiguous and vary significantly. The authors posit that understanding of assassination is woefully inadequate in the political violence literature. It is striking that more than four decades after the studies of Havens, et al., Crotty, and Katchadourian that this inadequacy still exists—scholars have yet to develop a consensus on how to categorize or study the differences across assassination events.

However, improvements are occurring within the literature, such as work by Iqbal and Zorn. Iqbal and Zorn utilize Katchadourian's definition and provide two robust studies of leader assassinations, finding that assassinations of heads of state lead to political unrest, such as protests, but the degree of unrest is mitigated when the government has stable, regulated means of succession (essentially, stronger political institutions diminish the effects of leader assassinations). The authors also discover positive relationships between unrest and instability and the likelihood of assassination. Iqbal and Zorn examine the role of repression in regime type and the assassination risks to heads of state, determining that weak, repressive leaders face the greatest risk of assassination and weak, non-repressive leaders face the lowest risk of assassination.[6]

Another important advancement in the study of assassination is that of Perliger, in which he offers a detailed definition of political assassination comprised of three key elements and suggests a typology of assassination. The first element in Perliger's definition requires that the target holds a leadership role in a group that is promoting a certain ideology or certain policies as part of the political process. The second element requires that the goal behind the assassination be political in nature, and the third component requires that the act lead to the death of the intended target.[7]

Perliger argues for the need to classify or categorize assassinations, similar to the argument made in this project. His work suggests five types of assassination, which include tyrannicide (the killing of a tyrannical ruler), elite substitution (the killing of a top political leader), anomic (the killing of a leader for private, rather than public reasons), propaganda by deed (the killing of a leader motivated by a single policy issue), and terrorist assassination, which he defines as "the mass and indiscriminate killing of political figures, usually as part of a revolutionary dynamic."[8]

I concur with Perliger's (and others) assessment of the need for categorization as well as his definition of terrorist assassination but argue that motivations (as would be necessary for some of Perliger's categories) vary widely. As an example, Cooper highlights motivations from several assassinations including that of Egyptian president Anwar Sadat in 1981, the Dominican Republic dictator Rafael Trujillo in 1961, and president-elect Bashir Gemayel of Lebanon in 1982. Cooper argues that Sadat was targeted and killed in an effort to alter public policy, Trujillo was killed in order to end his regime, and Gemayel was killed in order to prevent him from taking office.[9]

Thus, it may be more effective to focus on broader categories of assassination, such as the three discussed in this project. For example, tyrannicide and the killing of leaders by assassins with mental health issues may be better suited as a subset of the larger category of leader assassinations (termed by Perliger as elite substitution). Regardless, the desire for political change and the role, or perceived role, of the target in the political sphere are important components in these definitions. Therefore, I argue that scholarly consensus in defining assassination exists to the following extent: *an assassination is a killing that occurs when there is a political component to the act and the target is selected due to the influence, or perception of influence, the individual holds in public life.*

Assassination is defined in this project as the targeting and killing of an individual for reasons that are distinctly political in nature, based on the individual's influence and/or role in public life. If an individual is targeted based on their influential role and/or standing in the political system and killed in a non-hostage situation, then the killing qualifies as an assassination. Deaths that occur during a hostage situation, while tragic, may be political in nature but introduce a different variable into the equation, which may include ransom or some public or private demand in exchange for the life of the hostage. An assassin neither offers mercy on the lives of their targets nor negotiates.

CONTEMPORARY ASSASSINATION

The death in 2015 of Ruben Alfaro Ventura, a former government official in Peru, at the hands of the Shining Path or the killing in 2016 of Abdul Jabar Mussadiq, a district governor, by the Taliban in Afghanistan are examples of the contemporary trend of the use of assassinations by extremist groups. This trend, first identified by Snitch, began in the 1970s when extremist groups began targeting diplomats and business executives for death.[10] The killings of these individuals brought media attention to the political messages of the groups, and thus assassination proved to be a useful tactic in terrorist campaigns. Premo argues that assassination is intended to "produce a psychological state of fear and uncertainty within the general population"[11] and is therefore inherently terroristic in nature.[12] George argues that assassinations of the twentieth century are "a categorically different kind of political murder"[13] from the classical tyrannicide of Julius Caesar.[14]

To date, much of the scholarly and popular attention given to assassination focuses on attempts on heads of state, such as Yitzak Rabin of Israel or Ronald Reagan of the United States. What is often missed in the discussion of contemporary assassinations is that a target does not have to be a high-ranking official to be assassinated. While status or leadership rank is important in declaring at attack an assassination, it is not as important as the presence, or absence, of the victim's influence in the political environment.

Contemporary assassins do target heads of state and other government officials, but military leaders, law enforcement officials, journalists, politicians, and religious leaders are also in the crosshairs of groups seeking political change. Categorizing these assassinations is dependent upon the context within which they occur. Is there a broader campaign of violence within which these killings occur, with support from an organized group for instance, or does the assassin act alone out of a personal desire to seek policy change? Does the assassination occur during a time of instability and as a tactic in a sustained campaign of violence, or is the assassination a singular event during a time of relative stability and peace? Herein lies the distinction of terrorist assassinations.

DEFINING TERRORISM

In order to develop terrorist assassination as a category of assassination, terrorism in general must be addressed and we must ensure first, when labeling an assassination a *terrorist* assassination, that the event is actually terrorism. Terrorism studies, particularly since the terror attacks of September 11, 2001, on the United States, abound with empirical discussion of the proper definition of terrorism. In an early study of what the author terms revolutionary terror, Price posits that a standard terrorism definition includes political violence with an intention to exert psychological influence.[15] To that end, Enders and Sandler define terrorism in a pre-9/11 study as "the premeditated use or threat of violence by individuals or subnational groups to obtain a political or social objective through intimidation of a large audience beyond that of the immediate victims."[16]

Another pre-9/11 study by Crenshaw defines terrorism as "the systematic inducement of fear and anxiety to control and direct a civilian population."[17] In her examination of the causes of terrorism, she argues that terrorist violence is a select strategy in pursuing goals and theorizes that the attractiveness of terrorist violence is its ability to draw attention to a cause, provoke governments, and/or intimidate anyone who opposes them.

The terrorism literature expanded significantly in the years after the attacks of 9/11 as understandably, both scholars and policymakers sought to develop a better understanding of asymmetrical conflict. In a post-9/11 edition of Hoffman's seminal text, *Inside Terrorism*, he defines terrorism as follows:

> . . . the deliberate creation and exploitation of fear through violence or the threat of violence in the pursuit of political change. All terrorist acts involve violence or the threat of violence. Terrorism is specifically designed to have far-reaching psychological effects beyond the immediate victim(s) or object of the terrorist attack. It is meant to instill fear within, and thereby intimidate, a wider "target audience" that might include a rival ethnic or religious group, an entire country, a national government or political party, or public opinion in general. Terrorism is designed to create power where there is none or to consolidate power where there is very little. Through the publicity generated by that violence, terrorists seek to obtain the leverage, influence, and power they otherwise lack to effect political change on either a local or an international scale.[18]

Terrorism researchers face inherent challenges such as access to reliable quantitative data, access to individuals for qualitative interviews, and endogeneity issues tied to the unstable environments within which these events occur. Despite more than four decades of research, there is much we have yet to understand about terrorism.[19] However, what is clear is that terrorist groups are more deadly in recent years than in the past. Outside the anomaly of September 11, 2001 (with nearly 3,000 deaths on that one day), the lethality of terror attacks is still evident in the years since 2000 and continues with a worldwide death toll of 26,400 people in 2017 alone.[20] Fortunately, there is evidence of a continued four-year trend (through 2018) of decline in the number of attacks and deaths, but terrorist violence continues to be a significant international security concern.

Multiple tactics, such as armed assaults, bombings, hijackings, and kidnappings, are used in terror campaigns. Since 1970, assassination is the third most utilized tactic of terrorism behind bombings and armed assaults, and the Global Terrorism Database (GTD) records 20,283 assassination events across the globe through December 2018.[21] In the following chapter, I will address the assassination count in GTD and argue that by narrowing the definition of terrorist assassination, researchers can gain a more accurate count and an improved understanding of these events. However, even after refining and cleansing the data, which results in fewer numbers of actual terrorist assassinations, the count still indicates that assassination is most assuredly a widely used tactic in contemporary terrorism campaigns with nearly 10,000 terrorist assassinations occurring from 1977 through 2017.

In an examination of the strategies and tactics utilized by terrorists, Kydd and Walter argue that terror groups utilize "strategic logic" in pursing their goals.[22] The authors posit there are five logics at play: attrition, intimidation, provocation, spoiling, and outbidding. The idea is that terrorists use these strategies to achieve their desired goals and the strategies are summarized as follows.

Terrorists aim to show the enemy that they are capable of imposing costs on said enemy if the targeted government does not comply with the group's demands (attrition). Terrorists will use methods designed to show the public that the government cannot stop the terrorists in efforts to frighten and thereby control the public (intimidation). A terror campaign may include methods designed to provoke the enemy government into responding aggressively and harshly, in an attempt to turn the public against its own government and become supportive of the terror group (provocation). Extremist groups may engage in attacks designed to undermine moderates who may be willing to compromise or reach peace settlements (spoiling) and these groups may also devise a strategy aimed at convincing the public and other extremists that their group is the most effective and thus, the one group worthy of support (outbidding).[23]

Terror groups often find that assassinations are useful and may be effective in achieving their terroristic goals. Killing government officials imposes a cost on the government, these attacks may provoke the government into overresponding, may spoil peace processes, and may prove the effectiveness and strength of the terror group. Assassinations of political candidates, for instance, may intimidate other candidates, as well as the public, and discourage others from seeking office. Assassinations of law enforcement officials, military leaders, religious leaders, and journalists may yield similar results.

The terrorism definitions discussed above highlight some common themes in defining terrorism, including indiscriminate violence, the targeting of governments, the targeting of civilians, and the desire to influence the wider population. Political motivations and political goals are an important component in determining whether an act of violence is terrorism, in both scholarly and policymaking circles.[24] Assassination—an act of political violence— serves as a strategic tool in the terrorists' toolbox and is often utilized during campaigns of terrorist violence.

PREVIOUS RESEARCH ON TERRORIST ASSASSINATIONS

A body of literature on terrorist assassinations is not well established, but since the 1970s, some scholars have focused their research efforts on assassination by terror groups as a phenomenon of political violence. In Bell's study of the Lehi Gang (also known as the Stern Group), he suggests that the Middle East terrorist group's 1944 targeting and killing of the British minister of state (Lord Moyne) in Cairo served dual purposes.[25] Bell posits that the terror group sought to affect both the British government's policy and world public opinion on the Palestinian issue.[26] He does not go so far as to suggest that terrorist assassinations are a distinct category of assassination types, but he does argue that the scholarly community should examine categories of assassination, the motives of assassination, and assassinations linked to revolutionary movements.

Snitch's study is the first to place assassination into the terrorism literature. He identifies 721 assassinations in 123 states from 1968 through 1980 and finds evidence of a growing trend of assassinations targeting prominent public figures (including government officials) by extremist political groups. He argues that assassination is a powerful tool for terrorists and posits that political assassinations attract media attention. Snitch also suggests that these assassinations may lead to repression when government overreacts to the assassination, thereby alienating citizens from the government. Thus, according to Snitch's argument, assassinations by terror groups achieve at least two terrorism strategies.

Snitch asserts that the chosen targets of assassination are shifting, finding that business executives and diplomats are more likely to be the targets of extremist groups. He also identifies a rise in the frequency of political separatist groups utilizing assassinations (20% of the extremist group perpetrators in his study are identified as separatist groups) and argues that the number of lone assassins (i.e., individuals with no group ties) is increasingly rare.[27] In Price's work referenced earlier, he highlights the use of assassination by

revolutionary groups in an effort to deter government officials from pursuing the group. Price argues that these groups may also assassinate their own
members if they are suspected of betraying the group. Nevertheless, data support the assertion that groups engaging in campaigns of terror utilize political
assassination regularly.[28]

George contributes a qualitative piece, delineating terrorist assassinations
from tyrannicide (the killing of a tyrannical leader for the good of society).
George makes this distinction in several ways and posits that in contemporary politics, it is rare for one person to operate as a tyrant along the lines of
Caesar. He suggests that unlike tyrannicide, terrorist assassinations are ideologically driven and the victim of the assassination is an institutional symbol
rather than a unique victim. The attack, he argues, is meant to convey a message of fear to a broader audience, while tyrannicide targets only the tyrant
with no other audience in mind.

Therefore, George argues, terrorist assassinations have dual targets (the
victim and the broader constituency) and are less "personal" than the assassination of a tyrant. Terrorist assassinations expose bystanders to danger
unnecessarily (bombs are often used, for example) and thus, are indiscriminate in nature. Importantly, George posits that while tyrannicide is an isolated
event, terrorist assassinations are part of a sustained, broader campaign of
violence.[29]

George also addresses the purpose behind assassination events and argues
that in order to conceptualize assassination type, the purpose is paramount to
the argument. He suggests that acts of tyrannicide exhibit a level of moral-
ity—intending to protect oppressed citizens from the tyrant. Terrorist assassinations, George argues, hold no such moral equivalence and is in fact, an
effort by the terrorists to impose their will upon citizens. This vital distinction
makes tyrannicide and terrorist assassination not only categorically different
but also antithetical. In George's view, terrorism is an attempt at tyranny and
is a contemporary, ideologically driven phenomenon very different from the
classical conduct of politics in earlier centuries.[30]

Pinfari builds upon George's work and suggests the concept of terrorist
assassination is growing in policy circles. He cites instances in 2006 of then
U.S. ambassador to the United Nations John Bolton and then secretary-general of the Arab League Amr Moussa referring to the assassination in Beirut,
Lebanon, of Industry Minister Pierre Gemayel as a "terrorist assassination."
Pinfari also notes that members of the media refer to the 2007 killing of former Pakistani prime minister Benazir Bhutto as a terrorist assassination. He
agrees with George's assertion of terrorist assassinations having dual targets
(both the victim and a wider audience) but suggests that while the dual target
criteria is a necessary component, it is not sufficient as a stand-alone component for classifying an assassination as terrorism.[31]

Pinfari asserts that when the assassination target is not random (and by definition, an assassination is not random), it is meant as a warning to the wider public. If the attack results in disproportionate violence and civilian casualties, Pinfari argues that the assassination is meant to "spread a political message"[32] and does indeed qualify as a terrorist assassination. He posits that terrorist assassinations must be both politically motivated and indiscriminate to constitute a terrorist assassination.

Both of Pinfari's points are in line with George's argument that the assassination must be ideologically driven and that an act of tyrannicide is distinctly different from a terrorist assassination (due to the indiscriminate nature of the terrorist act). Pinfari adds nuance to the indiscriminate component of the terrorist assassination argument, positing that the nature of the attack (potentially maiming or killing bystanders) provides insight into the terrorists' intended audience. Essentially, if the perpetrator has no qualms about collateral damage of an assassination (the innocent bystanders), then the terrorism definition is met with both the "political message" and "instilling fear in the wider public" components. If an assassination is discriminate in some way (i.e., aimed at preventing collateral damage), Pinfari seems to argue that it serves more as a warning to the public rather than an actual attempt to instill fear in the public at large. Regardless, both George and Pinfari contribute to the conceptualization of terrorist assassination and both appear to agree that it is, in fact, a unique category of political assassinations.

Outside of the sociopolitical studies of assassination and political science studies of terrorist assassination, criminologists have recently began studying terrorist assassinations. In a comparative study of terrorist assassinations and suicide attacks, Mandala[33] finds that certain contextual conditions were associated with the use of either assassination or suicide attacks. Typically, states with higher levels of religious diversity experienced fewer assassinations but states that experienced high levels of political violence, generally, experienced more assassinations.

In efforts to determine the explanation for why some assassination attempts are successful and others are not, Mandala and Freilich[34] discover that the likelihood of success (death of the target) is greater when assassins use firearms rather than explosives and attempts on targets who are in vehicles are less likely to be successful. Additionally, the study finds that assassination attempts are less likely to be successful if the attempt occurs indoors rather than outdoors, and surprisingly, the presence of security guards or a security detail did not decrease the likelihood of a successful assassination. However, if the security personnel realized that an attack was imminent or underway and were able to engage, the likelihood of success did decrease. This recent foray by criminologists into terrorism studies bodes well for the advanced of the body of terrorism literature, but especially for the advancement of the literature on terrorist assassinations.

Lastly, the work of Perliger (discussed earlier) further builds the terrorist assassination literature and as a reminder, he defines terrorist assassination as "the mass and indiscriminate killing of political figures, usually as part of a revolutionary dynamic."[35] He identifies the ideology of the perpetrators in his study with ethnic/separatist movements constituting 29 percent, left-wing groups constituting 23 percent, and religious groups constituting 17 percent of the assassination perpetrators in his dataset.[36] While Perliger's analyses do not delineate differences across types of assassinations, his study nonetheless advances the assassination and specifically, the terrorist assassination literature.

Based on the work of these scholars and in consideration of the contemporary context, terrorist assassinations are defined in this project as *the targeting and killing of specific individuals as a tactic in a broader campaign of violence. Those targeted for assassination are selected based on their role in public life and influence in the political system.*[37]

THE RELEVANCE OF TERRORIST ASSASSINATIONS

Why do terrorists conduct assassinations and why do tactics matter? If one of the aims of terrorists is to instill fear in the public at large, as is the consensus in the scholarly community, then why use vital resources (time and weaponry) with the extra planning and strategizing necessary in order to target specific individuals? Attacking any random market or street corner filled with pedestrians would suffice, and in fact, this does happen frequently. Yet, the killing of people who serve a political role in society or exert political influence is a tactic frequently utilized by terrorist groups, as discussed earlier. Despite decades of robust terrorism studies, we have yet to rigorously address the proverbial five W's of investigation—the "who, what, when, where, and why" questions—of one of the most frequently used tactics of terrorism.

As with all tactics of terrorism (and terrorism generally), answering most, if not all, of these questions is an ambitious task. One noteworthy attempt at addressing why assassination is chosen as a tactic of terrorism is an examination of the psychological underpinnings in terrorist decision-making. Wilson, Scholes, and Brocklehurst seek to determine the reasoning behind terrorists' decisions for carrying out bomb attacks versus assassinations.[38] The authors use data from 1980 through 2007 from descriptive accounts of the Euskadi ta Askatasuna (ETA) terrorist organization (a Basque organization) in Spain. The authors identify 275 assassinations and 1,073 bombings from 1980 through 2007 and based on the analysis of the assassinations, they find a positive relationship between the proximity of the victim and bystanders. Thus, the authors argue that the number of potential casualties that may result from an assassination plays a role in terrorists' decision-making. Delineating assassinations from bombings is problematic since many contemporary assassinations are bombings, however, this study contributes to our understanding of the use of assassination by terror groups and certainly advances the literature on terrorist assassination.

This book aims to establish a baseline understanding of the differences in political outcomes across terrorist assassination events, delineating outcomes according to the type of target. The intention is to examine who is targeted and the political changes, if any, after these terrorist assassinations. In doing so, this project provides insight into the type of political changes experienced after assassinations of various target types. The chapters that follow will examine who is most often targeted in these attacks and explore the repercussions of these events on political institutions.

Lower-level government officials, such as police chiefs, local politicians, and army generals, are more likely to be targeted by terrorist organizations than, for instance, heads of state. The assassination of a local political leader of the Baloch National Movement in Pakistan in 2010 and the killing of a British military attaché in Athens, Greece, in 2000 by the November Revolutionary Organization (17N) are examples of this contemporary trend of terrorist assassinations.

In line with the literature on terrorism, many assassination events occur because of the desire for change, be it a change in state policy, a change in leadership, a change in territory, or any array of desired political agendas held by the terrorist group. However, many of these contemporary attacks also occur in order to *prevent* change to the system such as hindering democratic progress or preventing a particular candidate from winning an election. Dual purposes are achieved in many of these events by eliminating a prominent individual while simultaneously striking fear and uncertainty in the heart of the population at large, creating doubt over the future.

As defined and counted in the GTD, terrorist assassinations have consistently constituted the third most utilized tactic of worldwide terrorism. Only as recently as 2017 has another tactic begun to match the number of assassination events per year—kidnappings. Bombings are consistently the most often used terrorism tactic with armed assaults the second most utilized terrorism tactic. The analyses in the following chapters focus on forty years of data from 1977 through 2017 and table 2.1 provides the GTD event count of all terrorism tactics during this forty-year period.

By comparison, data on what I term "leader assassinations" (killings of government officials outside of any indiscriminate, sustained campaign of violence targeting the state) indicates that leader assassinations are

Table 2.1   Worldwide Terrorism Events by Attack Type, 1977–2017

Attack Type	Frequency	Percent
Bombing/Explosion	85,348	48.9
Armed Assault	41,239	23.6
Assassination	17,842	10.2
Hostage Taking/Kidnapping	10,828	6.2
Facility/Infrastructure Attack	9,641	5.5
Unarmed Assault	894	0.5
Hostage Taking/Barricade Incident	946	0.5
Hijacking	611	0.4
Unknown	7,205	4.1
TOTAL	**174,554**	**100**

Source: Global Terrorism Database, 1977–2017.

increasingly rare and table 2.2 highlights the stark differences in event counts between leader assassinations and terrorist assassinations across available datasets. Assassination definitions and approaches to counting assassinations differ across datasets, but this information offers support to the argument that terrorist assassinations constitute a different type of assassination and should be examined and analyzed separately. The table also provides support for the assertion that leader assassinations are increasingly rare.[39]

The databases listed in table 2.2 measure political assassination differently. *Archigos* measures the length of time a state leader remains in office and records the manner of entry into and exit out of office—whether the exit is by assassination, natural death, or coup. Therefore, this dataset only counts assassinations of heads of state and as the table indicates, even with the most generous count of *potential* assassinations (23 leader exits are coded as

Table 2.2   Leader Assassinations and Terrorist Assassinations Datasets

Type of Assassination	Database	Count	Dates
Leader	*Archigos*	23	1875–2014
Leader	Cross-National Time Series Database (CNTS)	1,994	1919–2018
Leader	The Social, Political, and Economic Event Database Project (SPEED)—The Cline Center	1,040	1946–2005
Terrorist	Database of Worldwide Terrorism Incidents—RAND (RDWTI)	2,846	1968–2009
Terrorist	Global Terrorism Database (GTD)— START Consortium/Univ. of Maryland	20,283	1970–2018
Terrorist (international)	International Terrorism: Attributes of Terrorist Events (ITERATE)	1,268	1968–2018

assassination, 13 as irregular/other, and 147 as unknown), there are relatively few instances of leader assassination in modern history.[40]

The Cline Center (University of Illinois) for Democracy's Social, Political, and Economic Event Database Project (SPEED) dataset includes assassination in its "extraordinary event" count of what is considered a politically disruptive event. It is unclear how well the target types are delineated in this dataset, but the definition of assassination is "targeted murders of public figures."[41] This dataset appears to include targets deemed as leaders and only when news reports label the killing as an assassination. Under these parameters, the dataset counts 1,040 assassinations in the years 1946 through 2005.

When assessing terrorist assassinations the event count is significantly higher. The RAND Database of Worldwide Terrorism Incidents (RDWTI) does, unlike *Archigos* and SPEED, count terrorist assassinations. From 1968 through 2009, an online search in the RDWTI database finds 2,846 assassination events but the true count is likely higher. The RAND data provides excellent case information on each event, but if there are multiple events linked to one so-called trigger event, all events are counted as one in RDWTI. For instance, in the 1970s the Black September terror group mailed letter bombs to officials around the world and each campaign of letter bombs (sometimes as many as fifty were mailed) is counted as one event in the database. Thus, under closer inspection, it is likely that there are more terrorist assassinations in the RDWTI than is reflected in the number above.

The University of Maryland's National Consortium for the Study of Terrorism and Responses to Terrorism (START) in 2005 completed digitizing terrorism data previously collected by the private security firm, Pinkerton Global Intelligence Service (PGIS). Upon completion, START continued the data collection and since 2005, continues to update and improve the data while making it publicly available as the GTD. The event counts are gathered and coded based on media sources and are further refined by the GTD research team, according to the terrorism criteria developed by START.

The challenge for researchers is to delineate types of terrorism (domestic versus international)[42] and the accuracy of the events, targets, and so on. However, I believe most agree that GTD is currently the most comprehensive, most reliable, publicly available source of data on terrorism events in existence. The GTD covers the years from 1970 through 2018 and counts an astonishing 20,283 assassination events.

As will be discussed in the next chapter, the GTD assassination count decreases once these events are reviewed to match a more specific definition of terrorist assassination. By "cleansing" the GTD assassination counts, a more accurate picture of the frequency of terrorist assassinations is possible and the details are discussed in the following chapters. For now, the datasets discussed above and listed in table 2.2 highlight the need for clarification of assassination types (leader versus terrorist versus state-sponsored). Database comparison also indicates the extent to which assassinations occur and the extent to which these events are tactics of terrorism—relevant to the field of terrorism studies and to the study of political violence in general.

WHY THE TARGETS MATTER

The individual targeted for death is at the heart of the assassination definition—the victim, or rather the public role of the victim, determines whether a killing qualifies as a political assassination. Shoppers killed in a mall bombing are victims of terrorism, but not necessarily assassination victims. The victims in this scenario are, sadly and unfortunately, innocent civilians who happened to be in the proverbial wrong place at the wrong time. However, if a candidate for political office is targeted while shopping at that same mall and evidence shows that the candidate was the target of the attack (not random civilians), then the attack is an assassination (likely with innocent bystanders as collateral damage) as opposed to a terrorist bombing. Thus, the target type is a crucial component in determining if a terror attack is in fact a terrorist assassination.

Previous work on assassinations focuses largely on the killings of elite targets such as prime ministers and presidents, and yet over time, improved security measures ensure that heads of state are harder targets for assassins, resulting in fewer assassinations of top leaders. In an examination of terrorists' targets, Brandt and Sandler provide evidence of transnational terrorists shifting their chosen targets in response to improving security measures, finding that over time as certain targets are hardened (due to improved security), terrorists' shift to softer, more accessible targets such as private individuals or entities.[43]

With increased security around heads of state and top leaders, it is reasonable to posit that softer political targets are now the focus of terrorist assassination attempts. In fact, the GTD indicates that lower-level government officials, police officers, politicians, military personnel, and journalists are frequently targeted as part of terrorist campaigns. These individuals serve as symbols of a formal (such as the judicial system) or informal state institution (such as the media) and are targeted due to their public positions. Table 2.3 breaks down the targets of terror assassinations for the forty-year period from 1977 through 2017. These categories are further refined and information on the sub-target types (such as judges, mayors, etc.) is provided and discussed in the following chapters.

Table 2.3   Top Ten Worldwide Terrorist Assassination Target Types, 1977–2017

Target Type	Frequency	Percentage
Government Officials	5,858	32.8
Private Citizens	3,583	20.0
Police	2,723	15.2
Military	1,347	7.5
Business	900	5.0
Journalists & Media	737	4.1
Violent Political Party	619	3.5
Terrorists/Non-State Militia	599	3.4
Religious Figures	441	2.5
Educational Institution	350	2.0
TOTAL	**17,157**	**96**

Global Terrorism Database, 1977–2017.

These target types vary significantly and thus any repercussions from these events may also vary significantly. Killing a religious leader should result in different political outcomes than killing a mayor or legislative member, for instance. Lacking empirical insight into political repercussions across target types, however, it is impossible to know the extent of these differences. Popular literature abounds with studies of leader assassinations arguing either for or against the proverbial assertion that assassinations alter the course of history. The killings of lower-level governmental leaders and political candidates do not receive the same attention either in popular or scholarly literature as heads of state assassinations, despite the evidence that lower-level officials are the most likely targets of assassination today. One intent of this book is to spur increased scholarly (and even popular) attention to today's targets of assassination—from mayors to journalists and all those in between.

CONCLUSION

As the third most utilized method of terrorism in recent decades, it is imperative that theoretical and scholarly advancements occur in the study of assassinations. This chapter sets the stage for the remainder of this text by explaining the challenges in the defining and categorizing of political murder, as well as the challenges of defining terrorism. The killing of Franz Ferdinand of Austria did not occur in a similar context as that of John F. Kennedy of the United States. The attempted assassination of U.S. president Ronald Reagan is wholly different from the killing of Israeli prime minister Yitzhak Rabin, despite the fact that these two (and the others) were all top leaders at the time of the attacks.

The most likely assassinations today are those carried out as part of broad campaigns of violence—terrorist assassinations. The murder of a human rights activist in Iraq[44] or the murders of approximately twenty-seven clerics in Yemen since early 2016[45] are prime examples of the types of assassinations occurring today. In Mexico, estimates are that at least thirty-six candidates in local elections have been killed since September 2017 (as of November 2018)[46] and the Committee to Protect Journalists (CPJ) estimates that fifty-three journalists were killed in 2018.[47] Therefore, it behooves scholars and policymakers alike to seek an improved understanding of the relevance, the repercussions, and importance of terrorist assassinations.

Chapter 3

The Data and the Targets

Empirically analyzing terrorist assassinations is an incredibly challenging endeavor, as is the case with most forms of political violence. Data reliability and endogeneity, for instance, are common challenges for researchers when studying conflict situations and events. Conflict situations and campaigns of violence are complex, and more often than not are ambiguous situations with a mixture of personal and political grievances. Multiple types of violence with differing motivations may occur during one civil war and sometimes even in one location. Sexual violence, state repression, ethnic rivalries, and personal vendettas may all comingle in one conflictual situation and/or location.[1]

In the study of political assassinations, challenges abound. For instance, whether a death was an actual assassination as opposed to a natural death may not be clear. Controversy surrounding the death of Palestinian leader Yasser Arafat (originally believed to have died from natural causes) arose over whether the leader may have been poisoned and lead to the exhumation of his body for testing.[2] If assassinations are covert (as suggested in the Arafat case), it is difficult to properly count or study these events. This is both a qualitative and quantitative challenge. If researchers do not know the true universe of events, it is difficult to measure outcomes, conduct rigorous case studies, and/or obtain accurate event counts.

To this end, this chapter is dedicated to explaining the data and the data cleansing processes undertaken for this project—the clarifying and then culling, when necessary, of the existing count of terrorist assassinations in the GTD. An explanation of the use and application of other datasets used in this project is provided as well. Finally, descriptive statistics regarding where terrorist assassinations occur, the types of weapons used in these attacks, the groups most often perpetrating these attacks, and other interesting data points are discussed.

THE GTD

As introduced in the previous chapter, the GTD tracks domestic and transnational terrorist attacks occurring worldwide since 1970. The data compilation began with a private security agency—none other than the famed agency formerly known as the Pinkerton National Detective Agency. The roots of the agency can be traced back to the 1850s when Scottish immigrant Allan Pinkerton left the Chicago police department to form his own detective agency. In its early days, the Pinkerton agency gathered intelligence for the Union during the U.S. Civil War, provided protection for the railroads after the war, and pursued outlaws like Jesse James and Butch Cassidy.

Before the war, Allan Pinkerton was tasked with aspects of protecting President-Elect Lincoln as he traveled from Illinois to Washington, D.C. for his inauguration in 1861. Pinkerton and his undercover operatives reportedly uncovered a plot to assassinate Lincoln during a scheduled stop in Baltimore (referred to as the Baltimore Plot) on the way to the inauguration. While there is some dispute over the credibility of Pinkerton's intelligence, Lincoln's original plans for the stop in Baltimore were revised because of the intelligence, and Lincoln arrived safely in Washington.[3]

The Pinkerton organization established offices nationwide from the late 1800s into the 1900s, and still exists today as the PGIS. In 1970, PGIS began gathering information on terror attacks across the globe, gleaning data from government reports and media services, and by 1997 had a substantial trove of written records on terrorism. The University of Maryland began updating and digitizing Pinkerton's records, completing the conversion in 2005. The National Consortium for the START was formed in 2005 and, working in conjunction first with the Center for Terrorism and Intelligence Studies (CETIS) and then the Institute for the Study of Violent Groups (ISVG), continued collecting data on global terrorist events.

In recent decades, the data have been refined and the entire database updated to reflect revisions and improvements. Any new variables added to the database are coded retroactively when possible, but the original PGIS data (1970 through 1997) do not contain information on all the variables being tracked today. Improved methodologies, such as natural language processing and machine learning, allow for robust data collection from global media sources.[4] The GTD makes sustained efforts to consider the quality of the global media source from which data is taken and higher quality sources are prioritized over less reliable sources. In fact, for an incident to be included in the GTD at least one of the higher quality sources must report on the event. Thus, the GTD updates variables and codes retroactively whenever possible and notes this for its users in the database when it is not possible.

As of May 2020, the GTD contains information on 191,464 terror incidents from 1970 through 2018 and identifies 8 tactics of terrorism, including assassination, armed assault, bombing/explosion, hijacking, two categories of hostage taking (barricade and kidnapping), facility/infrastructure attack, and unarmed assaults. The database also provides an *unknown* category for coding when adequate information on the event is lacking. It should be noted that terror incidents from January through December of 1993 are not included in the database. During an office relocation, boxes containing the records for 1993 were misplaced and despite attempts to recreate the data, validity and reliability concerns have prevented START researchers from including these twelve months of data in the GTD.

For inclusion in the GTD, the first determination is whether an attack meets the GTD definition of terrorism, which is "the threatened or actual use of illegal force and violence by a non-state actor to attain a political, economic, religious, or social goal through fear, coercion, or intimidation."[5] Additionally, any attack counted in the GTD must be intentional, must involve violence, or the immediate threat of violence. Note that the database does not include incidents of state repression—this dataset compiles only incidents perpetrated by non-state actors. This of course does not preclude the possibility that state actors may be behind attacks by non-state actors, such as the assassination of former Lebanese prime minister Rafik Hariri in 2005. For over a decade, most believed that Hezbollah with the support of Syria was behind Hariri's death. However, an international tribunal found no evidence of direct ties to Hezbollah or Syria in this attack, making this announcement in August 2020.[6]

That said, once these requirements are met, attacks must meet two of three predetermined terrorism criteria. The motivation of the attack must be political, social, religious, or economic; the intent of the attack must be to intimidate or coerce a wider audience than the target; and/or the attack must be outside the context of legitimate war activities. Should circumstances of an event (or lack of information) provide doubt regarding these terrorism criteria, the event is flagged (coded 1 in the *doubtterr* variable), providing a qualifier for researchers.

The GTD counts both domestic and international (or transnational) terrorism and provides four categorical variables regarding the international nature of an attack. The *international-logistical* variable is coded 1 if it is determined that the perpetrator group's nationality is different from the location of the attack and thus, coded 0 if the attack is determined to be perpetrated by actors of the same nationality as the location of the attack. If by chance, the perpetrators are a multinational group and any of the nationalities of the group are the same as the location of the attack, then it is considered a domestic attack.

The second of these variables is *international-ideological* and examines the perpetrator group nationality and the nationality of the target. If these nationalities are different, then the attack is considered ideologically international and coded 1. As with the previous variable, a code of 0 identifies the attack as ideologically domestic in nature. The third is the *international-miscellaneous* variable, which compares the location of the attack and the nationality of the target. This variable is coded 1 when the location of the attack is different from the nationality of the target and is used when information on the nationality of the target group is not available. Thus, any attack coded 1 in this category also fits into either *international-logistical* or *international-ideological*, but it is unclear which. The same domestic coding as explained above is used for this variable.

Lastly, the *international-any* variable is used when the attack is considered international on any of the variables discussed above. If so, this variable is coded 1 and if the attack is domestic on all of the above variables, it is coded as 0. For all of these international variables, if information is unknown on any relevant dimension, it is assigned -9 for unknown.

The majority of assassinations in the database are database are unknown as it relates to the domestic/international dimension. For example, the *international-any* variable indicates that of all the assassinations counted in the GTD from 1970 through 2017, 52.8 percent are unknown. Approximately 28 percent are domestic in nature and slightly more than 19 percent have some international dimension. In the assassination count for this project (discussed in detail later), 50.7 percent are unknown, 32.6 percent are domestic, and just under 16.7 percent are international. With the majority of terrorist assassinations considered unknown, it is impossible to draw a definitive conclusion on whether the majority of these events are driven by domestic or international factors. However, nearly half *are* known and in both the full GTD data and the cleansed data used in this project, domestic assassinations are more prevalent than those with an international dimension. For comparison, 33.3 percent of all attacks (assassinations, bombings, assaults, etc.) in the GTD database from 1977 through 2017 are coded as international with nearly 19.7 percent coded as domestic.[7] The rest are unknown.

ASSASSINATION IN THE GTD

The previous chapter provides the number of events for each attack type in the GTD from 1977 through 2017 (see table 2.1). As the table indicates, assassination is the third most utilized tactic of terrorism in that forty-year period. The raw numbers of assassination—17,842—may surprise readers. This is certainly a substantial number of assassination events, but as will be explained later, a deeper examination demonstrates that the actual number of terrorist assassinations is much lower. By this researcher's count, the true number is still significant but slightly less than 10,000 during these forty years.

The GTD defines assassination as follows:

> An act whose primary objective is to kill one or more specific, prominent individuals. Usually carried out on persons of some note, such as high-ranking military officers, government officials, celebrities, etc. Not to include attacks on non-specific members of a targeted group. The killing of a police officer would be an armed assault unless there is reason to believe the attackers singled out a particularly prominent officer for assassination.[8]

A major challenge for GTD coders, as well as all conflict researchers, is the unpacking of tactics and methods. The bombing of a souk in the Middle East by a terrorist group is obviously a bombing, but if there is an intended target—if, for instance, the local mayor is shopping in the souk that day—then the bombing may also be an assassination. A simple reading of the GTD assassination definition portends some of the challenges. Without adequate information on the target of an attack, it is often difficult to determine if the attack is a terrorist bombing, an armed assault, or an assassination.

Even when information *is* available, if neither credit is claimed nor a perpetrator is apprehended, intended targets may still be hard to ascertain. For instance, in May 2015 a bomb exploded at a coffee shop in Ceel Waaq, Somalia, injuring seven people. District Commissioner Ibrahim Kajiko was at the coffee shop at the time of the explosion and thus, he may have been the target. No group claimed responsibility for the attack, but this event is coded in the GTD as an assassination attempt.[9] Is this an example of an attempted terrorist assassination or simply a case of the district commissioner being in the wrong place at the wrong time?

That said, the GTD does an excellent job of identifying victims and targets in attacks, including 22 target types in the dataset and as many as 111 target subtypes (discussed in more detail later). This information is particularly important in the study of assassination. The target is a critical piece of information needed to determine if an attack, particularly during wide-reaching campaigns of violence, is an assassination.

TERRORIST ASSASSINATION TARGET CATEGORIES

The GTD codes for twenty-two target types and includes target categories such as *business*, *government (general)*, *police*, *military*, *abortion related*, *airports and aircraft*, *food and water supply*, *maritime*, and *religious figures/ institutions*.[10] Chapter 2 presents information on the target distribution of assassinations based on these target type categories. Within each of these twenty-two target categories, referred to in the remainder of this project as the first-level target types, are numerous sub-target categories, ranging from *business* subtypes, such as *bank/commerce* or *construction*, to *government (general)* subtypes, such as *royalty* or *head of state*.

Table 3.1 presents the distribution of the top five target subtypes, referred to as second-level target types in the remainder of this project, from 1977 through 2017.[11] These five second-level categories represent over half the assassinations in the dataset and include the targets of *government personnel, military personnel, politician/political party, police security forces,* and *unnamed civilians.* These second-level categories are part of the *general (government), military, police,* and *private citizens* first-level target type categories.

For a terror attack to be included as an assassination in this project, the target must be an individual with the ability to influence politics, public policy, and/or society. The individual target must have a public persona. Thus, the murder of an abortion clinic doctor is unlikely to be an assassination, but the killing of a pro-life activist likely is an assassination because that individual has crossed from private life into the public sphere via their attempts to influence public policy. The doctor who works in the abortion clinic is a private professional with no influence on policy—unless that doctor enters the public sphere by engaging in pro-choice advocacy, for example.

A businessperson murdered in a terrorist attack because of their nationality is a victim of a terrorist attack, but not necessarily a victim of terrorist assassination. Truly private citizens—be they businesspersons, students, or farmers—are not able to influence politics or public policy in any meaningful way. The deaths of these individuals at the hands of terrorists are a tragic part of most political violence campaigns, but do not meet the criteria of assassination. The difficulty in delineating terrorist assassinations from other terror attacks becomes clear when reviewing the details of specific events. What degree of influence in politics or society must a victim possess in order to be assassinated rather than simply murdered? How heavily should past

Table 3.1   Top Five Worldwide Terrorist Assassination Target Subtypes, 1977–2017

Target Type	Frequency	Percentage
Politician/Political Party Movement	2,647	15.47
Police Security Forces/Officers	2,504	14.63
Government Personnel	2,307	13.48
Military Personnel	1,148	6.71
Unnamed Civilian/Unspecified	916	5.35
TOTAL	*9,522*	*55.64*

Source: Global Terrorism Database, 1977–2017.

political influence or political involvement of the victim be weighed when determining whether to count an attack as a terrorist assassination?

In the GTD first-level target category of *business*, some of the victims are private citizens in the business sector, but who were formerly involved in public policy or politics. For instance, in May 2013 near Tacuati, Paraguay, Luis Lindstron was shot and killed allegedly by the Paraguayan People's Army (EPP). At the time of his death, Lindstron was a rancher, but had previously served as mayor and as president of a logging company.[12] Another event in this target category is the killing of a Colombian lawyer, Rigoberto Gil Gonzalez, in October 2014. Gonzalez reportedly had ties to Senator Dilian Francisca Toro and sources attributed the killing to the Revolutionary Armed Forces of Colombia (FARC).[13] Yet another event in the *business* target category is the shooting and killing in April 1997 of the head of the ice hockey Sports Federation in Dmitrov, Russia, by unknown perpetrators.[14]

These three events showcase the variation of assassination events in the GTD—in this case the first-level *business* target category. Questions arise regarding the amount of public or political influence held by these individuals. Lindstron likely held political ties from his time in office and may have yielded political influence. Gonzales may or may not have held any political influence—it is dependent upon his relationship with the senator—and it is unlikely, barring any unforeseen connections, that the head of the Sports Federation in Russia yielded significant political influence. As it happens, in the investigation of Lindstron's death, multiple perpetrators with possible motives were identified—from drug-traffickers to the state to the EPP.[15]

The *government (general)* category is less opaque in determining whether the victim holds the ability to influence public policy and thus, whether the attack is appropriately labeled an assassination. Victims in this target category include judges, politicians, heads of state, intelligence personnel, and other various local government officials such as mayors. All of these target types are persons with political and/or public influence by virtue of their positions. The killing of Santa Rosa mayor Leon Arcillas in the Philippines in May 2005, allegedly at the hands of the New People's Army, is an example of an assassination in this target type category.[16]

The *military* target category is complicated and more ambiguous, resembling the *business* category in this respect. Second-level categories in the *military* category include *military unit/patrol/convoy*, *military checkpoint*, and *military personnel (soldiers, troops, officers, forces)*. Chapter 9 is devoted, in part, to military targets and thus only minimal discussion is provided here. What is important is that it is difficult to assign public policy influence to military members who have not achieved some degree of rank or status and thus, many of the assassinations of military targets counted by the GTD are not included in this project. For now, the killing of Lieutenant

Colonel Antonio Munoz Carinanos in Seville, Spain, in October 2004 serves as an example of an assassination in the *military* category that is counted here. Members of the ETA (English translation of Basque Fatherland and Freedom) shot and killed the military doctor as one in a series of assassinations in Spain.[17] In fact, 288 of the assassinations counted in this project are attributed to ETA—the third most attributed to any group after the Sendero Luminoso in Peru (English translation of Shining Path) with 643 and the Taliban in Afghanistan with 304 (see table 3.2).

However, in the same *military* first-level category a 2014 attack on a Somali National Army base outside Mogadishu is less of an assassination and more of an armed assault, although it is counted as an assassination in the GTD. Five soldiers were killed when Al-Shabaab militants attacked the base on October 17 of that year. Al-Shabaab claimed credit for the attack, but it does not appear that any specific military leader was targeted.[18] Thus, some of the first-level and second-level target categories are more complex than others when counting terrorist assassinations. These cases highlight the need for closer examination of target categories in the GTD as well as the need for case-by-case review when possible, particularly in categories that are more open to mis-inclusion. A case-by-case examination provides a more accurate

Table 3.2   Descriptive Statistics—Terrorist Assassinations, 1977–2017

Top 3 Target Types	Frequency	Percentage
Government Officials	3,733	37.59
Police	1,965	19.78
Private Citizens & Property*	1,361	13.70
Total	7,059	71.07
Top 3 Known Weapon Types Used	Frequency	Percentage
Firearms	7,829	78.83
Explosives	862	8.68
Melee (close contact weapon)	311	3.13
Total	9,002	90.64
*Top 3 Known Perpetrator Groups**	Frequency	Percentage
Shining Path (Peru)	643	6.47
Taliban (Afghanistan)	304	3.05
Basque Fatherland & Freedom (ETA) (Spain)	288	2.90
Total	1,235	12.42
*International Assassinations***	Frequency	Percentage
International	1,660	16.68

Source: Cleansed assassinations data taken from the Global Terrorism Database.
*This category includes politicians, protestors, and others with public roles.
**More than 47 percent of the perpetrators are unknown.
***An assassination is considered "international" in the GTD if the attack involved any dimension of internationality—such as location of the attack, nationality of perpetrators and victims, and/or if any aspect of the attack in some way crossed borders. See GTD Codebook (2017), p. 58–60.

reflection of the universe of terrorist assassinations than the broader, more inclusive count in the GTD.

Here, I have "cleansed" much of the assassination events data by excluding certain second-level categories and conducting case-by-case examination of others. Yet, the data cleanse is still not exhaustive. With such a large dataset, a literal case-by-case cleanse of the entire set was not possible. However, as discussed in more detail later, this project presents a significant review of the assassination count in the GTD. The aim of this work is to first, offer a more accurate picture of the count of terrorist assassinations with the data cleanse and second, to offer insight into the repercussions of terrorist assassinations across certain target types. Following is a further explanation of all the exclusions and inclusions made to the data for these analyses.

CLEANSING THE DATA

To prepare for rigorous analyses, the target categories that do not match the definition of assassination utilized in this project are removed from the final dataset of terrorist assassinations. Excluded are the first-level target categories of *food or water supply*, *tourists*, *unknown*, *transportation*, and *utilities*. Examples of second-level categories excluded from the final count of terrorist assassinations are *airport*, *clinics* (as part of the *abortion related* first-level category), *school/university/educational building*, *other personnel* (as part of the *educational institution* first-level target category), and *unnamed civilians*.[19]

For example, in table 3.1, the *unnamed civilian* second-level category in the GTD represents 5.35 percent of the assassinations, however, it is difficult to determine if these events are assassinations without more information. If the targets are unnamed, it is impossible to determine if these individuals play a politically influential role in society. Thus, the subcategory of *unnamed civilians* is excluded from the final count of terrorist assassinations for this project.

A case-by-case examination of several categories cleanses the data further. For example, in the *airports and aircraft* first-level target category, the killing of the manager of El Al airlines in January 1980 is counted as an assassination in the GTD. The manager, Abraham Elazar, was Israeli and the killing occurred in Istanbul. While Elazar may have been targeted due to his nationality, he held no known influence in politics or society—therefore this is an example of an excluded event and is not counted as a terrorist assassination in this project.

However, in the same GTD target category, the attempt on the life of Yemeni Houthi leader, Deputy Chief Abdullah al-Mutawakel, would be included in the event count for this project if the attack had been successful. In July 2014, a bomb was planted on the vehicle of al-Mutawakel at Sanaa International Airport (he was also an airport official), exploding and injuring al-Mutawakel's son. No credit was claimed for the attack, but none is needed to understand that al-Mutawakel was the intended target, qualifying this attack as an assassination attempt. Several GTD first- and second-level target categories underwent cleansing and refining, particularly for the target categories examined in later chapters. Further discussion of the inclusions and the exclusions is provided in those chapters.

The GTD terror attack designation and the success (or not) of the attack are part of the cleansing process as well. As discussed earlier, the *doubtterr* variable in GTD gives researchers an indication of the certainty of the attack motivation. Is the attack clearly a terrorist attack? This information is only coded consistently in the attacks after 1997, but any assassination event in doubt regarding terrorism is excluded from the assassination count here. While this unfortunately provides a less robust measure of the event count prior to 1997 than for the post-1997 data, applying this exclusion still improves the overall final dataset.

Additionally, while some assassination studies include both assassination attempts and successful assassinations (i.e., attacks that result in the death of the target), this project incorporates only those that are successful. An unsuccessful attempt is unlikely to achieve the desired outcome of the perpetrator—if the target survives, he or she can continue with their influence in the public sphere (as in the attack on al-Mutawakel in Yemen) and may result in an outcome altogether different from a successful assassination. The impact of an unsuccessful attempt likely will still reverberate to a certain extent throughout the political and societal environment, but limiting this study to successful attempts clarifies the analyses.

Terrorist assassinations and suicide bombings may comingle in the terrorists' toolbox and with multiple studies of suicide attacks (such as the work of Mia Bloom and Robert Pape), understanding of this type of attack is more advanced than that of assassination. While these two tactics sometimes merge into one, for the purposes of this study, an assassination is excluded if it is also coded as a suicide attack in the GTD. The *suicide* variable is distinct from attack type variables and when evidence indicates that the perpetrator had no intention of surviving the attack, it is coded as a suicide attack. In total, the GTD codes 6,566 suicide attacks from 1977 through 2017 and of those, 261 are assassinations.[20] Seventy-two assassinations are also coded as kidnappings in the GTD, but the logistics of being taken as a hostage and then killed belie the definition of assassination and are therefore also excluded from the event count herein.

Once the assassination events are cleansed of the above—questionable terrorism, unsuccessful attacks, suicide attacks, targets holding no known political or societal influence, and kidnapping events—the final terrorist assassination count for this project is 9,932. This is a significant decrease from the original count of more than 17,000 and I argue a more accurate reflection of the true event count. Yet, it is still far from a "perfect" count. Some first-level target categories, such as *police*, are so substantial, with 2,721 assassinations, that time constraints prohibit the ability to vet each and every event. However, as discussed, certain target categories are much more likely to be true assassinations and the second-level subtypes allow for some cleansing even in the more substantial first-level categories. While not a perfect depiction of events, this project does provide a more accurate picture of the universe of terrorist assassinations.[21]

Table 3.2 provides descriptive data relating to the 9,932 assassinations counted herein. In the chapters that follow, studies of certain target categories are conducted—government officials, politicians, law enforcement, journalists, military leaders, and religious figures—and an explanation of the inclusions for each category is provided in each chapter.

The quantitative analyses in this book examine the length of time after a terrorist assassination occurs until a state experiences a change in its political institutions—enough change to posit that the state is moving toward or away from one regime type or another. Regime types included are democracies, autocracies, those that are not fully democratic or authoritarian (referred to here as mixed), and those in a state of transition or collapse (referred to here as tumultuous). Additional analyses measuring the relevance of state repression are also a part of this study. A state with democratic institutions, one might assume, would not engage in repression. Unfortunately, this is not the case and in fact, many states that are democratic in nature engage in various forms of repression—from media censorship to detention for political views to civil rights violations. Despite multiple model runs for each target category, the tests for the impact of assassinations on repressive versus non-repressive regimes did not yield any significance in the models. However, as a point of comparison, repression levels in the qualitative case studies are discussed and thus, an explanation of the categorization of regime type *and* repression is necessary before moving into empirical analyses of the data.

REGIME TYPE AND THE *POLITY IV INDEX*

Regime type, for the purposes of this project, is determined by *Polity IV Project* (Polity) scores.[22] The Polity index measures levels of democratic and autocratic institutions for states with populations greater than 500,000 by assigning scores based on, for instance, political competition and the extent to which state executives are constrained in their power. Polity scores are assigned using a 21-point sliding scale with the low-end scale score (-10) indicating a fully autocratic state and the high-end of the scale (10) indicating a consolidated democratic state. Polity also measures failed states and those in transition, identified with specific scores (-88, -77, or -66).

For example, Lebanon was nearing the end of a civil war in 1988 and was assigned a Polity score of -77 for that year, indicating the failed nature of the state. Essentially, this reflects the total collapse of the central government as happened during the lengthy civil war in Lebanon. After the end of the war in 1990, Lebanon's Polity score was -66, indicating instability and occupation by Syrian forces. In April 2005, Syrian troops were forced from the state after the assassination of former prime minister Rafik Hariri in Beirut (see chapter 6 for a detailed discussion of this event) and the Polity score changed to 6. This score indicates the autonomy of the central government and the steps toward democratic governance and institutions of the small Mediterranean state.

Using the Polity scale to differentiate democratic states, authoritarian states, and those in the middle (mixed/hybrid), I test for outcome variation in the aftermath of an assassination event by searching for changes in Polity scores. The Polity scores are calculated using component variables that measure institutional structural changes in political competition, the transfer of power of the executive, the competitiveness of the executive selection process, and others. Any change in Polity scores therefore signals a change in state political institutions.

In this project, states that fall in the Polity score range of 7 to 10 are considered fully democratic states. States that fall in the score range of -6 to 6 are considered mixed/hybrid states, meaning that these states have some mixture of autocratic and democratic characteristics. States with Polity scores of -7 to -10 are considered authoritarian states and states with the alternative rankings of -66, -77, or -88 are labeled as tumultuous regimes.

REPRESSIVE REGIMES AND THE
POLITICAL TERROR SCALE

Another approach to the study of state regime type is the level of repression within a state. Repression is any form of state-led violence or oppression toward citizens, including repression of basic rights such as freedom of speech, freedom of the press, and freedom to form political groups. Repression also includes violent actions such as disappearances of civilians or members of opposition parties by governmental authorities, or the jailing of journalists in attempts to subvert a free press.[23]

Repression may vary significantly from overt to covert actions and occurs in all manner of regimes—democratic, authoritarian, mixed, and tumultuous.

The Political Terror Scale (PTS)[24] project measures human rights violations using a five-point coding scheme. The project began in the 1980s with the intention of measuring human rights violations in states receiving foreign aid monies from the United States. PTS continues with annual updates, measuring state violence such as state-sanctioned killings, disappearances, torture, and political imprisonment.

Information for coding is taken from the human rights reports of the U.S. State Department (SD), and the nongovernmental organizations of Amnesty International (AI) and Human Rights Watch (HRW). Scores are assigned on a scale of 1 to 5 with a score of 5 representing the worst human rights violators. Scores of 1 and/or 2 indicate respect for the rule of law exists, there is little imprisonment for political activity, and state violence (such as torture or murder) is rare. Scores of 3, 4, and/or 5 indicate increasing instances (as one moves up the scale) of political imprisonment, civil and political rights violations, and political murder.[25]

Scores are reported annually by PTS for each state under review with each receiving an AI score, a U.S. SD score, and in recent years, an HRW score. Using PTS allows for categorization of repressive and non-repressive regimes apart from the regime-type designation of democratic, authoritarian, mixed, and tumultuous. Examining repression levels enriches the qualitative analyses in the remainder of this text.

WHERE TERRORIST ASSASSINATIONS OCCUR

Terrorist assassinations are distributed across the globe, however, data indicate that from 1977 through 2017, over half (in fact nearly 59%) of all terrorist assassinations occurred in ten states. These states, in order of frequency, are Colombia, Peru, India, the Philippines, Pakistan, Iraq, Afghanistan, Spain, the UK, and El Salvador. Table 3.3 provides the frequency and percentage of attacks in these states. The states of Algeria, Guatemala, Somalia, Turkey, South Africa, and Yemen all experienced a significant number of assassinations in this time period as well, ranging from as many as 165 to 290 terrorist assassinations. Yet, nearly 84 percent of the states in the dataset (142 of 170 states) experienced at least one successful terrorist assassination between 1977 and 2017.[26]

Improving our understanding of the type of political system under which these assassinations occur is vital. Authoritarian regimes in states such as Syria have experienced terrorist assassinations as have states with transitioning or failing political systems such as Somalia. Democratic states have also experienced terrorist assassinations—such as Canada and the Netherlands. In fact, 51.8 percent of the terrorist assassinations in this dataset occur in consolidated democracies. This is in line with empirical terrorism studies,

Table 3.3   Top Ten States Experiencing Terrorist Assassinations, 1977–2017

State	Frequency	Percentage
Colombia	920	9.24
Peru	761	7.65
India	723	7.26
Philippines	711	7.14
Pakistan	662	6.65
Iraq	581	5.84
Afghanistan	513	5.15
Spain	362	3.64
UK	315	3.17
El Salvador	291	2.92
TOTAL	5,839	58.66

Source: Cleansed assassinations data taken from the Global Terrorism Database

which indicate a trend of terrorist attacks in democracies beginning toward the end of the twentieth century. Mixed regimes, often referred to as anocracies, experience 30 percent of the terrorist assassinations and authoritarian regimes experience slightly more than 5 percent in this study. Regimes in a state of chaos or tumult experience approximately 13 percent of the assassinations.

Much of the terrorism studies literature explores the relationship between terrorism—both domestic and international—and regime type. Democracies are open societies and one argument is that the openness makes these states more vulnerable to terrorist attacks. A counterargument is that democracies provide processes for grievances to be heard and should disincentivize terror activity. Some argue that authoritarian states have such control over society that opportunities for terrorism are more difficult to find and consequences for the perpetrators more severe if captured by authorities. For new democracies, an argument is made that these states are more vulnerable to terrorism due to the perceived weakness of the new government.[27] Understanding and explanations are mixed, but the cleansed assassinations data here indicates that this particular terrorist tactic is utilized most often in democracies and mixed regimes (or anocracies)—a combined 81.8 percent of the 9,932 assassination events.

In examining repression levels within states, 80 percent of terrorist assassinations occur in repressive regimes. Here, repression is measured using the average annual PTS scores and any state with an average combined score of 3.5 or higher is labeled a repressive regime. Of the 5,134 observations of democratic states experiencing an assassination, nearly 71 percent scored 3.5 or higher on the PTS scale qualifying those states as repressive regimes. Applying a narrower interpretation of a repressive regime, labeling regimes with an average score of 4.0 or higher, only reduces repressive democracies by 668 observations. This suggests that even democratic states repress civil liberties and individual freedoms, and those states also experience terrorist assassinations at higher rates.

OTHER DESCRIPTIVE DATA

Table 3.2 provides additional descriptive data, including the most common targets of assassination, the top weapon types, the top perpetrator groups, and the percentage of assassinations that qualify as international attacks. As explained earlier, the GTD assigns various international designations for attacks and if an assassination is considered international in any way by the GTD, I count it as an international attack. All others are obviously domestic attacks and constitute the majority of known events at 32.56 percent of the assassinations. However, slightly more than half (50.75%) are unknown.

As for the timing of these attacks, the one year with greatest number in this dataset is 1989, constituting 5.89 percent and an event count of 585 assassinations. In fact, the end of the Cold War witnessed the highest annual percentages of assassinations in the dataset. In 1988, 518 assassinations occurred and in 1990, which I consider a transition year, 512 occurred. These three years (1988–1990) constitute 16.27 percent of all the successful assassinations in the dataset. Generally, terrorist assassinations were less frequent from 1998 through 2009, but began a steady increase in 2010, with the most significant increases beginning in 2012 and then dipping slightly in 2016 and 2017. From 2012 through 2017, 2,363 terrorist assassinations occurred, accounting for 23.8 percent of all the assassinations in the dataset and an average of 393.8 per year. This trend and trajectory correlates with the aggregated terrorist attacks during this time frame.

Regarding the lethality or collateral damage of these events, the data suggests that these attacks are precise. In 74 percent of the assassinations only one individual is killed, slightly more than 12 percent result in the death of two people, and nearly 4.3 percent result in the death of three people. Thus, significant collateral damage in terrorist assassinations is seemingly rare. While attacks do occur that kill significant numbers of people, assassinations with a death count of four or more individuals make up only 5.05 percent of the dataset with increasing rarity after a death count of five.

CONCLUSION

This chapter seeks to explain to the reader the data selection and the logic behind the cleansing of the data. The GTD is the absolute best public source of data on terrorist assassinations. An advantage of this dataset, however, also serves as a disadvantage—the inclusiveness of questionable events. Yet, an important benefit of this database is that variables and notifications are available to the researcher for narrowing, or cleansing, the data to suit rigorous analyses and various researcher needs. The researcher has the ability to decide for herself whether to include certain events in her study.

While the cleansing process is essential, it may also be complicated to those unfamiliar with the GTD. The intent of this chapter is to provide an introductory explanation of the GTD, an adequate detail of the cleansing process undertaken, and the methods utilized for categorization of regime type and repression levels. The event count and data utilized here is in no way a perfect reflection of terrorist assassinations occurring from 1977 through 2017. However, I believe this to be a more accurate reflection of the true universe of terrorist assassinations than is available in previous studies, and therefore the analyses in this book also provide a more accurate reflection of the repercussions of these events.

Chapter 4

Target Selection and Political Institutional Changes

This chapter replicates, to an extent, earlier work in which political institutional changes are examined in the aftermath of terrorist assassinations, across target types from 1970 through 2012. The original research note identifies varying post-assassination outcomes across target categories, finding that the impact of terrorist assassinations on political institutions varies by regime type and across target type. For instance, if a terrorist assassinates a religious figure in a state which qualifies as a mixed regime, the original analysis indicates a hazard ratio of 3.47 for that mixed regime type. However, if in the same mixed regime, a terrorist assassinates a government official, the hazard ratio increases to 3.73. The "hazard" here refers to some change in political institutions, measured using Polity scores. Essentially, a mixed regime is more likely to experience a political institutional change after the terrorist assassination of a government official than after the assassination of a religious leader. The models in this chapter replicate five of the analyses in the original research, using the newly cleansed dataset for the years from 1977 through 2017, with one new model added, and an enhanced literature review on target selection from the original article.[1]

As a reminder, assassination is the targeting and killing of an individual for reasons that are distinctly political in nature, based on the individual's influence and role in public life. If an individual is targeted based on their role or influence in the political system and killed in a non-hostage situation, then the killing qualifies as an assassination. A terrorist assassination is an assassination that occurs as part of a broad campaign of violence. As discussed in the preceding chapters, a range of individuals is targeted in contemporary terrorist assassinations—including government officials, politicians, law enforcement officials, military officers, journalists, and religious leaders. These assassinations are a tactic utilized in wider campaigns of violence which target lower-level officials, such as police security forces. For instance, in Afghanistan, from 1977 through 2017, 116 members of police security forces were assassinated.

Assassinations typically are a shock to political institutions, disrupting both formal and informal political processes, and often leaving citizens to question the stability of their state institutions. These events also create a window of opportunity for actors with grievances against the government to generate upheaval and instability within society. Malign actors may take advantage of the sudden societal and political shock created by the killing(s) to sow seeds of division and violence. After the 1951 assassination of King Abdullah I bin al-Hussein of Jordan in Jerusalem, the city experienced an outbreak of riots and looting. During the approximately three days of unrest, violence erupted between Palestinians and Arab Legion soldiers and resulted in several deaths with injuries to many.

The window of instability created by this assassination generated sovereignty concerns for Jordan. Interference in Jordan's affairs by other states—particularly Syria and Saudi Arabia—was a concern. Many in Jordan believed regional neighbors might take advantage of the situation and attempt to destabilize the state. Yitzhak[2] argues that Iraq did, in fact, intend to annex Jordan during this crisis, and it is only because of the actions of Britain and Israel that the annexation attempt was averted. Yitzhak concludes that Jordan was not seriously threatened after the assassination, but one can argue that the outcome (and seriousness of the threat) may have been different had the Palestinians been better organized or had allies not thwarted Iraq's plans. Regardless of the threat level to the country after the assassination of King Abdullah, it is significant that it was, in fact, the assassination that created the opportunity for the threat to surface.

Scholars have examined the repercussions for political institutions after leader assassinations as well as the economic repercussions of Israel's state-sponsored assassinations of terrorists.[3] Iqbal and Zorn find that leader assassinations have no effect on political institutions in consolidated democracies while Zussman and Zussman[4] find evidence that the Israeli stock market declines after the targeting of senior political leaders of Hamas. This study also finds that the stock market in Israel increases after the assassination of Hamas' senior military leaders, with no impact on the stock market when lower-level Hamas officials are assassinated.

Building upon these and other studies discussed further, this chapter examines post-terrorist assassination political outcomes and the chapters that follow will examine the same in specific target and sub-target type (i.e., second-level) categories. The focus here is the likelihood of political institutional changes across regime type (detailed later) after terrorist assassinations. As discussed in the previous chapter, the GTD includes twenty-two categories of target types in the data, ranging from business individuals to government officials to religious figures. This chapter analyzes the aggregated data (all assassinations regardless of target) in order to provide comparative points, along with select first-level target categories. Each chapter that follows is devoted to one target group, described in detail in each chapter.

Additionally, certain second-level targets have been reassigned (from the GTD categories) to the most appropriate first-level categories and/or have been granted a category of their own (again, relative to GTD grouping). In the GTD, politicians are included in the *government (general)* target category—here, politicians are a stand-alone category. *Judges/attorneys/courts* are also included in the *government (general)* GTD target category, but it has been moved to the law enforcement category for this project. Diplomatic targets are granted their own category in the GTD, but this project moves diplomats to the government official group.

The remainder of this chapter includes a review of the literature on target selection, a description of the data and methodology, presentation of models and hypothesis results. The likelihood of political institutional change by target type across regime type in the aftermath of a terrorist assassination event is the focus. This chapter concludes with a discussion of the results and the challenges of empirically evaluating political assassination targets and post-assassination outcomes.

TARGET SELECTION LITERATURE

Snitch[5] is the first to situate political assassinations in the terrorism literature and one of only a few scholars in the contemporary literature to address the differing assassination targets. He identifies an increasing trend of political assassinations and finds that the assassins' target selection is shifting toward business individuals and diplomats, noting that the highest absolute frequency of successful assassinations target business and foreign government officials. He argues that these individuals are softer targets with less protection and yet are symbols of what the terrorists oppose, such as Western countries or capitalism. Here, I take issue with the inclusion of the killing of businesspersons as an assassination. As stated in chapter 2, to constitute an assassination the target must be an individual with a public, not private, role in society. Those engaged in business abroad may be symbols of their home country, but outside of their nationality, these individuals hold no other motivation for terrorist targeting under normal circumstances.

Over time, national leaders such as presidents and prime ministers have become increasingly harder targets with improved security measures and technologies, but in order for terrorists to achieve one of their main goals (gaining media attention) it is not necessary to kill a head of state. Thus, terror organizations can instead assassinate softer targets such as diplomats or local electoral candidates who are much more accessible. This may achieve other terrorist goals as well, such as preventing democratic processes/elections, or exhibiting the strength and abilities of the group. Snitch notes the kidnapping in 1981 of U.S. army general James Dozier in Italy by the Red Brigades group as anecdotal evidence of extremist groups seeking out easier targets.

In line with Snitch, Brandt and Sandler[6] show evidence of transnational terrorists' shifting their targets in response to several factors—improved security measures, decreased state sponsorship of terrorism, and an increase in the number of fundamentalist terror groups. The authors find that as certain targets harden, terror groups shift all types of attacks (not just assassinations) to softer, more accessible targets such as private parties, which supports Snitch's identification of a trend of increasing assassinations of lower-level government officials and businesspersons. Brandt and Sandler examine four types of targets (business, government officials, the military, and private parties) and find that governments are increasingly better at preventing all attacks on public officials and military targets, which leads to the targeting of private individuals.

In an earlier study, Drake[7] examines the role of ideology in target selection and argues that a group's ideology shapes the worldview of the group members. This, in turn, shapes the strategic and tactical decisions of the group on who is a legitimate target. Asal, et al.[8] build on this study and examine, among other things, the role of ideology in target selection of soft targets. The authors posit that civilians are typically unaware of their risk, or at least not as aware as those in the public eye such as government officials, and thus are the easiest of targets. At least two major goals of terrorism are achieved in targeting civilians—sending political messages and instilling fear in the public at large. Interestingly, in this study of soft targets, the media, religious groups, and nongovernmental organizations are included in the soft target category along with civilians and educational institutions. Their findings indicate that religious ideology plays a role in target selection and that any terror group with religion in its ideology should be watched closely by counterterrorism officials as they may be more likely to attack soft targets.

In a study of tactic choice by terror groups, Ahmed[9] seeks to determine if different types of terror groups choose different tactics. Left-wing, right-wing, nationalist/separatist, religious, and environmental groups are all examined and, especially relevant to this project, Ahmed finds that right-wing groups are more likely than the other groups to use assassination as a tactic in their terror campaigns. The premise is that right-wing groups are seeking to destabilize the state and by perpetrating assassinations, they aim to create chaos and instability.

Studying the targets of state-sponsored killings, Zussman and Zussman[10] examine Israeli stock market data following assassination attempts by Israel of Palestinian terrorist leaders. The article examines the immediate aftermath of an assassination (albeit a state-sponsored assassination) and delineates target type. While this work examines a different category of assassination than is addressed in this book, the study is relevant due to its delineation of Palestinian senior and junior level leadership targets, as well as the delineation of military and political leader within the organization.

The authors find that the Israeli stock market does not react when junior level targets are killed but does react to the assassinations of senior level targets. Specifically, when the target is a senior political leader, a decline of 1.1 percent occurs and when the target is a senior military leader, an increase of 0.6 percent occurs. Findings indicate that the 1.1 percent decline weakens somewhat over the following two weeks, but it did not reverse course. The 0.6 percent increase after the assassination of a senior military leader actually strengthens over the following two weeks. Thus, this study offers evidence that post-assassination economic outcomes, vary according to the type of target.

Finally, Marchment and Gill[11] proffer a theoretical framework for analyzing and understanding the target selection of terrorists, building upon the prior work of Clarke and Newman.[12] Marchment and Gill suggest five factors that terrorists consider when selecting targets. These factors are based on the premise that terrorists are rational actors who seek to minimize efforts and maximize rewards. These five factors are referred to as *tolerable* (T), *relevant* (R), *accessible* (A), *close* (C), and/or *known* (K).

Tolerable refers to the ability of the perpetrator to reach the attack point and the level of detection risk. *Relevancy* speaks to whether the victim is suitable according to the ideology of the group: Is the target a legitimate one in the eyes of the group? *Accessibility* refers to the ease of reaching the target, *close* refers to the physical proximity of the possible target to the terrorist: Does the terrorist have to travel a long distance to reach the target? Lastly, *known* refers to how familiar the perpetrator is to the space being considered for the attack: Does the terrorist know the area well, the streets, the alleys, and all other routes of egress and ingress? This is a recent contribution to the target literature and while its viability is yet to be established, it may prove to be a useful tool in advancing understanding of terrorists' target selection.

METHODOLOGY

The central purpose of this chapter is to lay the foundation for the theory that repercussions of terrorist assassinations vary dependent upon the target. Political institutional changes in authoritarian, mixed, and tumultuous regimes are compared against democratic regimes (utilizing Polity score changes as the indicator of institutional change). Determining the extent to which the type of target may or may not be linked to political institutional change provides a first-cut analysis of post-terrorist assassination institutional outcomes.

By examining institutional changes in the aftermath of terrorist assassinations, baseline insight into terrorist assassinations is achieved and this book, in its entirety, presents an opportunity for comparative discussion of the repercussions for political institutions after terrorist assassinations. Changes in political institutions are measured here using Polity index scores from the *Polity IV Project*.[13] Discussed in detail in chapter 3, the Polity index measures levels of democratic and autocratic institutions within states, such as political competition and the extent of executive constraint, for states with populations greater than 500,000.

Using Polity scores to differentiate democratic states, authoritarian states, and those in the middle (mixed) allows for testing of outcome variations in the aftermath of an assassination event. Polity also provides a measure of failed states and those in transition with specific scores, making it possible to test for transitioning (or tumultuous) regimes as well. Shifts in Polity scores signal a change in the political institutions of the state and thus provide insight into governmental and political changes after terrorist assassinations. This chapter presents results of hypothesis testing regarding the occurrence of Polity score change across regimes (e.g., authoritarian, mixed), after terrorist assassinations generally, and then examines these same changes after the assassination of certain first-level target types.

The quantitative method utilized here and throughout the book is survival analysis (also known as event history modeling) with a discrete dependent variable based on the occurrence of a Polity score change (or not) and numerous control variables included. Box-Steffensmeier and Jones[14] argue that discrete data are perfectly suitable in event history studies and this method is well suited for examining the institutional changes in regimes after an assassination. The event of interest is whether a change in Polity score is observed and grouping by state provides insight into the likelihood of Polity changes in the aftermath of assassinations for each state.

Originating from the medical and biostatistics field, survival analysis is essentially the longitudinal study of events. In medicine, the length of time a patient survives after receiving an experimental treatment, for instance, is of vital importance and it is therefore easy to understand the use of survival analysis in that field. Over time, social scientists began applying survival analysis to their research, such as recidivism rates of criminal offenders or time from first marriage to divorce.[15] Box-Steffensmeier and Jones posit that social science, and particularly political science, can benefit from survival analysis in questions related to the duration of events—such as militarized disputes or peace between rival states. Survival analysis models are an appropriate method for determining the impact of assassinations on survival of the institutional status quo of the state. The larger question here, in essence, is how long does a regime survive (i.e., last) after a terrorist assassination before experiencing some change to its political institutions?

Survival analyses measure the time span in which the observed subject is in danger of experiencing a failure event (this is referred to as the time at risk). In biostatistics, the failure might be the death of the patient and in political analyses, the failure might be the end of the regime or the end of a conflict. The subjects are measured from entry time (which is the onset of risk) to the time of failure, with multiple model types available to fit various data structures. Failure and risk are fundamental components of survival analysis and for the analyses here, states are at risk of failure once a terrorist assassination has occurred. Survival curves and hazard rates can be estimated from continuous data survival models and provide insight into the likelihood of subject survival (i.e., time to failure). Survival analysis allows for data on multiple observations and variables over time, unlike a traditional time-series model that provides for examination of a single unit. The flexibility in survival analyses makes this methodology a solid choice for examining the time from event (assassination) to failure (any Polity change) and estimating survival likelihoods across states.

Terrorist assassination events are delineated by first-level target type in this chapter. For instance, analyses are conducted for assassination targets such as general government officials, journalists, and religious figures. The event of interest is whether a change in Polity score is observed—thereby using this score as a proxy for political change. Grouping by state (via a shared frailty model) provides insight into the likelihood of Polity changes in the aftermath of assassination events for each state. The analysis seeks only to determine a change in Polity score, not the directional shift or the severity of the score change (this is a component in later chapters). Thus, the hypothesis is as follows:

H1: The target type of a terrorist assassination affects post-terrorist assassination political institutional stability.

SURVIVAL ANALYSIS: REGIME CHANGES AND TARGET TYPES

A Cox proportional hazards (PH) model examines the span of time from risk onset (here, the assassination event) to failure (Polity score change). Cox models are widely accepted as the preferred survival PH model and this semi-parametric approach to the Polity and terrorist assassinations data fits—no assumptions are required concerning the baseline hazard. The Cox model utilizes partial likelihood estimation and can be adjusted for tied events, which are events occurring on the same time measurement. The maximum partial likelihood assumes that the time intervals between event occurrences provide no information on the hazard rate and that the key source of information is the ordered failure times. In survival analysis, ordered failure time data does not include multiple types of failures; rather the same type of failure occurs, and each failure indicates an end to that particular span of time.

The most appropriate model is a shared frailty model in which the observations are clustered by state in order to account for the unobserved heterogeneity created by the differing "frailties" between the states. Essentially, a shared frailty model accounts for the shared likelihood, or shared risk hazard, in the observations—Canada, for instance, has a different risk level for political instability than Lebanon. The Cox shared frailty model determines the risk of failure for each state after experiencing an assassination of a particular target type, assumes a gamma frailty with unknown variance, and examines the risk of failure by regime type measured against democracies.

For comparative purposes, this chapter presents an initial model of political institutional changes in the aftermath of terrorist assassinations—all terrorist assassination regardless of target type. Next, models of political institutional changes across select first-level target categories are presented to highlight the differing outcomes and lay the foundation for the chapters that follow.

To clarify, the hazard ratios and survival curves indicate the length of time (in days) after the occurrence of a terrorist assassination until a change in Polity score across authoritarian, mixed, and tumultuous regimes (measured against democratic ones). A major concern in these models is a violation of PH. The PH assumption speaks to the idea that the time dependence is the same across the model, making it safe to assume that none of the predictor variables are biased.

In this first set of models, I intentionally err on the side of the fewest possible PH violations and thus only a few predictor variables are included—population of the state (logged), infant mortality rate (logged), an interaction of population (logged), and the date of the assassination (also logged). The Cox models in table 4.1 indicate no evidence of significant PH violations in any of the regime types (authoritarian, mixed, or tumultuous) and few indications of PH violations in the remaining variables. The only potential PH violations across these models are found in the log of infant mortality rate and the interaction of state population (logged) and event date (logged). That said, in most of the models the PH test results were close to or exceeded .05, which is the desired starting point for good PH models.

Table 4.1 Cox Shared Frailty Models—Regime Type, 1977–2017

Shared Frailty Models—Political Institutional Changes
Gamma Frailty/Efron Method

	All Assassinations/Law Enforcement			Government Officials			Military/Politicians/Journalists			Religious		
	Coefficient (SE)	Hazard Ratio (SE)	p values	Coefficient (SE)	Hazard Ratio (SE)	p values	Coefficient (SE)	Hazard Ratio (SE)	p values	Coefficient (SE)	Hazard Ratio (SE)	p values
Authoritarian	3.02 (.20)	20.43 (4.18)	.001	3.02 (.20)	20.37 (4.17)	.001	2.99 (.21)	19.82 (4.07)	.001	3.00 (.21)	20.12 (4.16)	.001
Mixed	3.26 (.15)	26.17 (3.83)	.001	3.26 (.15)	26.00 (3.80)	.001	3.25 (.15)	25.86 (3.78)	.001	3.25 (.15)	25.66 (3.76)	.001
Tumultuous	5.42 (.23)	226.65 (51.05)	.001	5.41 (.22)	222.52 (50.06)	.001	5.34 (.23)	209.12 (47.26)	.001	5.28 (.23)	197.19 (45.17)	.001
Population (log)	3.29 (1.01)	25.24 (25.56)	.001	3.25 (1.01)	25.73 (26.21)	.001	3.04 (1.03)	20.91 (21.60)	.003	2.77 (1.05)	15.98 (16.84)	.009
Population (log) x Day (log)	-.38 (.11)	.68 (.07)	.001	-.38 (.11)	.68 (.07)	.001	-.36 (.11)	.70 (.08)	.001	-.33 (.11)	.72 (.08)	.003
Infant Mortality Rate (log)	-.18 (.04)	.84 (.03)	.001	-.18 (.04)	.83 (.03)	.001	-.18 (.04)	.83 (.03)	.001	-.18 (.04)	.83 (.03)	.001
Day	.01 (.01)	1.00 (.01)	.001	.01 (.01)	1.00 (.01)	.001	.01 (.01)	1.00 (.01)	.001	.01 (.01)	1.00 (.01)	.005
Theta	3.04 (.38)			3.05 (.39)			3.11 (.40)			3.14 (.40)		
N Failures	607			607			604			599		
N Observations	158,124			158,083			157,651			156,914		
N Groups	136			136			136			136		

Source: Polity, GTD & Penn, 1977–2017.

In survival models, hazard ratios less than one signal a decreasing hazard or risk of experiencing the failure event and hazard ratios greater than one signal an increasing hazard or risk. Hazard ratios close to one indicate a constant rate and thus, the coefficient has no effect on the hazard or risk of experiencing a failure. A Cox shared frailty model is utilized in this analysis and a separate model is produced for each target type category—government officials, journalists, law enforcement, military, politicians, and religious officials.

For initial comparative purposes, a model of all terrorist assassination events suggests that authoritarian states have a hazard ratio of 1,943 times greater than democracies after an assassination. Thus, after a terrorist assassination, an authoritarian state is 1,943 more likely than a democratic state to experience a Polity change. A mixed regime (one with both autocratic and democratic structures of governance) is 2,517 times more likely than a democracy to experience a Polity change. A tumultuous regime is 22,565 times more likely than a democratic regime to experience a Polity score change. All of these have strong p values and are statistically significant at the .001 level. Negatively signed coefficients indicate a decreasing hazard risk per unit change and thus, the results for infant mortality rate (as a proxy for development) and the interaction of population and event date suggest a decreasing risk with each positive change. For instance, as infant mortality decreases so too does the risk of Polity change. As shown in table 4.1, this is true across all models.

Examining target categories, evidence indicates support for the hypothesis that the target of the assassination matters—killing a government official is likely to have a different impact on political institutions than killing a religious official, for example. While the killing of members of law enforcement result in the same hazard to the regimes as all the assassinations grouped together, the killing of government officials is slightly less hazardous across all regime types than that of law enforcement or all assassinations. The assassination of military officials, politicians, and journalists result in equal hazards, but all three are less likely to lead to Polity score changes in any of the regimes than the assassinations of law enforcement or government officials.

In fact, the killing of military officials, politicians, and journalists are the least likely of the target groups to result in a Polity score change in authoritarian states. The killing of religious officials is the least likely to lead to Polity score changes in mixed and tumultuous regimes. All of the variables in these models are statistically significant and while the standard errors are high, this is an example of some of the efficiency that is sacrificed in Cox PH models. That said, while the differences across these models are slight, the null hypothesis is rejected. There are variations across target types in these survival models.

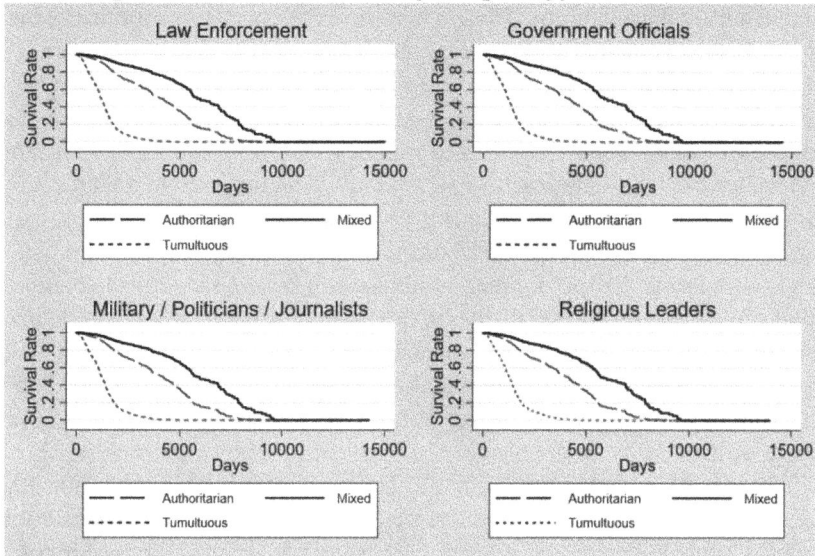

Figure 4.1 Survival Curves—Regimes, and Target Types, 1977–2017.

To illustrate this point further, figure 4.1 presents the survival curves for the models. The curves present the time to Polity score change in days for each regime type across targets. The curves indicate in all models that tumultuous regimes are the most likely to experience a Polity score change (i.e., a failure) after a terrorist assassination. The failure of tumultuous regimes by the 5,000-day mark is virtually assured at 100 percent in all the models. Immediately after an assassination, whether it is the killing of a law enforcement officer, a government official, a politician, or a religious leader, the curves indicate only an approximate 80 percent survival rate within a few hundred days of a terrorist assassination.

By the 5,000-day mark, the curves indicate that authoritarian regimes have a higher likelihood of failing compared to mixed regimes (all in comparison to democracies). After the assassination of a law enforcement officer or a government official in an authoritarian state, the probability of no Polity score change is only 39 percent while in the same regime type, after the killing of a politician, military officer, or journalist, the probability is around 38 percent. The model for religious leaders appears to show a probability of no Polity score change of around 36 percent.

For mixed regimes, after a terrorist assassination of a law enforcement official the survival probability is around 70 percent, after a government official, politician, military officer, or journalist is killed the probability is around 68 percent. After the killing of a religious leader, mixed regimes have about a 65 percent survival probability. Thus, while the differences are not drastic, there are differences nonetheless across target types in the survival probabilities of regimes.

A point of note in comparing the hazard ratios to the survival curves is that the hazard ratios suggest that mixed regimes may have higher hazard ratios than authoritarian regimes (across all models). This fits with an understanding that authoritarian regimes may generally be more stable and less likely to experience any government institutional changes due to the control exercised by an authoritarian state. Mixed regimes are those with both democratic and authoritarian components and are likely more susceptible to institutional changes. Yet, when the survival curves are calculated, it is the authoritarian states which appear to have lower survival probabilities than mixed regimes. According to the curves, mixed regimes "survive" longer after terrorist assassinations before experiencing a Polity score change. The hazard ratios, however, have wide confidence intervals and are only estimates. The true survival likelihoods lie within the 95 percent confidence intervals calculated in the models and across all the models discussed here, there is overlap in the authoritarian and mixed regimes.

CONCLUSION

The examination of first-level target categories yields interesting results. Evidence shows that post-terrorist assassination institutional outcomes do vary between target types and across regime types. Survival probabilities of regimes vary depending upon the target type of the assassination. Far from conclusive, however, is the *degree* to which assassination targets matter politically. Much work is necessary to delineate expected outcomes in the aftermath of terrorist assassination events and to further explain the results here.

This initial examination provides support for the theory that targets matter to the likelihood of political changes after an assassination event. The aim of this chapter is to provide the groundwork for the remainder of the book and to argue for more empirical studies of terrorist target types, generally, and terrorist assassination targets, specifically, in the literature. By disaggregating the types of targets, the potential exists for improving understanding of political violence at the national level when national leaders are killed and at the local level when local officials fall victim to terrorist assassinations. Internationally, an improved understanding of the domestic ramifications of these events will aid in policymaking and planning when institutional changes occur within states. These institutional changes may very well impact the stability of the international system and thus it behooves scholars and decision makers to develop a deeper understanding of these events.

Chapter 5

Government Officials

The assassinations, terrorist or otherwise, of government officials are typically some of the most publicized and well-known acts of political violence. These killings sometimes draw worldwide attention, such as the assassinations of Indian prime minister Indira Gandhi in 1984 or Israeli prime minister Yitzak Rabin in 1995. Yet, the data indicate that these higher-profile assassinations of heads of state are more the exception than the norm. Government officials targeted for assassination are typically local officials, such as the 2012 assassination of the Ministry of Water Resources director in Borno State, Nigeria, by Boko Haram, or sometimes diplomats, such as Brigadier Stephen Saunders who was killed in 2000 while serving in Athens, Greece, as the British military attaché.

An estimated 1,836 government officials were assassinated during terror campaigns from 1977 through 2017. The second-level categories are discussed in more detail later, but it is worth noting that government officials constitute roughly 18 percent of all the assassination victims in this project. This chapter includes quantitative analyses of six second-level categories of government officials and a qualitative discussion of two select assassination events. The two cases—one which captured international attention in the 1980s and the other which received much less attention in the 2000s—are important examples of the potential impact from terrorist assassinations.

The first case is that of Indian prime minister Indira Gandhi, who was assassinated on the morning of October 31, 1984 as she passed through her garden on the way to a media interview in her office. The attack on the prime minister was not a shocking event in and of itself. Many feared for her safety in the aftermath of a tragic event from earlier in the year when many innocents were killed during a government crackdown on Sikh separatists at the Golden Temple. What was most shocking was the level of violence carried out with impunity against the Sikh community in the days immediately following Gandhi's death. This event is a dismaying yet intriguing example of the repercussions of an assassination of a head of state and serves here as an appropriate case study.

Yet, heads of state assassinations are anomalies—an example of the more likely type of assassination is that of Brigadier Stephen Saunders, serving as a military attaché in Greece at the British Embassy. Saunders was targeted by a Greek terror group known as 17 November (17N) on his way to work on the morning of June 8, 2000. 17N had operated for decades within Greece, largely unimpeded with no arrests of their members despite carrying out approximately twenty-two assassinations since the 1970s. Outrage over the attack on the British diplomat and concern over the international spotlight about to be shone on Greece for the 2004 Olympics led to arrests and convictions of 17N members for the attack on Saunders. The killing of Saunders may have been the trigger that led to the dismantling of 17N and thus, serves as a worthy case study of an assassination of a lower-level government official.

Following these case studies are multiple models, tested as part of the quantitative analyses in this chapter, successfully highlighting the premise that targets do matter to the outcomes of terrorist assassinations. First, testing for instances of changes in Polity scores finds evidence that institutional changes may happen faster in authoritarian regimes, for instance, after the assassination of a member of an international organization or an international peacekeeper. Next, an examination of the direction of Polity changes indicates that political institutional shifts differ in direction after a terrorist assassination across regimes and indicates that the type of target matters here as well.

Lastly, an examination of the likelihood of Polity change after a terrorist assassination in repressive regimes suggests that a binary examination of government repression is not significant to these analyses. However, an explanation of the results of model testing is still reported before concluding the chapter.

SECOND-LEVEL CATEGORIES OF GOVERNMENT OFFICIALS

The GTD includes various second-level categories of officials in the first-level "general government" category—*judges/attorneys/courts*, *politicians*, *royalty*, *head of state*, *government personnel*, *election-related*, *intelligence*, and *government facilities*. For this project, the *judges/attorneys/courts* second-level category was moved from "general government" to "law enforcement" and the "diplomat" first-level category was moved into the "government officials" category. Thus, for the analyses of government targets in this chapter, the second-level target types included are diplomatic personnel, election-related officials, embassy/consulate personnel, government personnel, government facilities, heads of state, intelligence personnel, and royalty.

By far, government personnel constitute the greatest percentage with nearly 78.8 percent of terrorist assassinations targeting various types of government officials. Local leaders, such as municipal representatives, village officials, and government administrators (such as telecommunication department heads and water ministers), are included in the government personnel category.

Examples in this category include advisers to local and regional leaders—such as the attacks on an adviser of Yasser Arafat in Gaza in 2004 and on the secretary-general for the mayor of Djougani, Mali, in 2017.[1] In both of these attacks, the perpetrators shot and killed the targets, there were no claims of responsibility, and no arrests were made. In the case of Arafat's adviser, Khalil al-Zaben, the killing came at a time of dissent within the Palestinian community over leadership control. Al-Zaben, who reportedly had been a loyal adviser to Arafat since the 1960s,[2] was hit multiple times by gunshots as he left his office in the neighborhood of Sabra. This case is a particularly good example of the ambiguity of many of these events—without the apprehension or identification of the perpetrator, accompanied by a stated motive, the details are often murky and leave room for debate over the exact type of assassination event. Another layer of ambiguity here is the label one wishes to ascribe to Yarafat's organization and those who served as his advisers during volatile times in the contemporary Middle East. Still, the examination of these events holds the potential for improving our understanding of not only terrorist assassinations but political violence in general and the targets of said violence.

Diplomatic personnel constitute slightly more than 7 percent of targeted government officials and intelligence personnel make up approximately 6.3 percent of the targets in this category. Given the public nature of diplomatic work, it may be surprising that diplomats are not targeted more often. Typically, security is soft for diplomats even though they are the public face of their home country in many locales around the world.

For instance, Antanios Hanna was a Syrian diplomat stationed in Brussels, Belgium, when he was shot and killed outside his home in October 1987. Perpetrators were not arrested, but anonymous calls to local news outlets claimed that the killing was perpetrated by Syrian Mujahideen and/or the People's Mujahideen and that Hanna was a secret agent of the Syrian government.[3] Despite the ease of targeting diplomats, terror groups tend to focus on government personnel within domestic borders rather than diplomats who typically live and work outside of their home country. Interestingly, between 1977 and 2017, attacks on diplomats were most common in the early 1980s, dipping in the mid-to-late 1980s, only to increase again in the early 1990s. These attacks ebbed in 1999 with no successful assassinations of diplomats recorded. Since then, the years with the most assassinations of diplomats are 2005 and 2012 with four successful attacks carried out on diplomats, but not reaching the high of 1982 when nineteen successful attacks were carried out.

Intelligence officials, similar to diplomatic officials, constitute only a small percentage of the assassinations of government officials, however, it is still important to note that over 6 percent of successful attacks are aimed at intelligence officers. These officers may be senior officers in national security divisions of a state, such as the 2012 killing of a senior officer in the National Directorate for Security in Herat, Afghanistan, or they may be military officers involved in intelligence, such as the 2017 assassination of Lieutenant Colonel Ammar Mahdi in Kirkuk, Iraq. Interestingly, the majority of the assassinations of intelligence officials, slightly less than 76 percent, occur in four states—Yemen, Afghanistan, Somalia, and Iraq.[4]

Election-related personnel are 2.3 percent of the targets, while heads of state constitute 2.1 percent of the targets. The remaining attacks are aimed at embassy personnel, personnel at government facilities, and royalty. These attacks are rare with all three of these sub-target categories accounting for only 3.5 percent of all successful assassinations of government officials. Thus, the argument can be made that election officials and heads of state are at low risk of falling prey to a terrorist assassin, with embassy personnel and members of royalty at an even lower risk.

Yet, attacks on these government officials still occur and can be deadly. In national midterm elections in May 2007, three poll workers were wounded and a candidate for local office was killed in the Philippines during a chaotic day of violence. Multiple attacks occurred at polling locations in the Abra province with reports of the perpetrators attempting to disrupt the election by stealing ballots in addition to the shootings. One polling station in Sumisip was set ablaze and burned down. Election inspectors were attacked in one location and in total, at least sixteen people were wounded and four killed on this day of electoral violence.[5]

Heads of state certainly have vastly improved security measures, particularly since the 1963 assassination of U.S. president John F. Kennedy. These individuals are harder targets, surrounded by security details and with every precaution taken to ensure their safety, and so it is logical that only 2.1 percent of assassinated government officials are sitting heads of state. Included in this count are the killings of Lebanese prime minister Rashid Karami in Tripoli in June 1987 and Lebanese president Rene Mouawad in

Beirut in November 1989. Karami was killed when the helicopter he was riding in exploded and Mouawad was killed when a remote-controlled bomb was trigged as his motorcade passed by shops in Beirut after leaving Independence Day celebrations.[6]

In October 1999, gunmen stormed into parliament in Yerevan, Armenia, killing Prime Minister Vazgen Sarkisian before taking some fifty people hostage. Other government leaders were killed, including Parliament Speaker Karen Demirchian and Deputy Speaker Yuri Bakhshian. This incident is an anomaly and security measures for heads of state are typically such that it is extremely difficult for terrorists to target these individuals. Precarious environments, such as the Lebanese civil war, make these types of assassinations more possible and in fact, Lebanon accounts for over 10 percent of the heads of state assassinations in this dataset with a total of four. Otherwise, these killings are distributed across states such as Afghanistan, El Salvador, India, and Rwanda, among many others. Possibly one of the least surprising, but most evocative, attacks on a sitting head of state was the assassination of Indian prime minister Indira Gandhi in 1984.

INDIA—PRIME MINISTER INDIRA GANDHI

On October 31, 1984, Prime Minister Indira Gandhi started her day as many people do—catching up on the news of the day and sitting down to breakfast with family members. Within hours, her life would come to an end. Scheduled for an interview on the lawn outside her residential office, Gandhi exited her residence, escorted by staffers, on a pathway through her garden. Gandhi was shot multiple times by two of her bodyguards, who were standing watch in the garden. The assassins were Beant Singh and Satwant Singh, Sikh members of Gandhi's security detail. Neither tried to escape and once the gunfire stopped, both men stood, hands raised, and Beant Singh reportedly stated, "We have done what we set out to do. Now you can do whatever you want to do."[7]

Indira Gandhi, it seems, was destined for politics. As the daughter of Jawaharlal Nehru, India's first prime minister, she was exposed to the political world from birth. In fact, it is reported that Gandhi attended her first Congress Party meeting at the age of three and spent much of her youth surrounded by foreign dignitaries, while also experiencing the pain of her parent's political imprisonments.[8] As she entered adulthood, Gandhi became involved in her father's party and was elected as president of the Congress Party in 1959. She also served as the Minister of Information and Broadcasting and after her father's death, and the subsequent unexpected death of Prime Minister Lal Bahadur Shastri in 1966, Gandhi was nominated to lead the country. She was sworn in as India's first female prime minister in January 1966, serving three consecutive terms through 1977, and then was elected to her fourth and final term in 1980.

Events in India prior to the assassination help to explain not only the killing of the prime minister but the violence that occurred afterward. A movement in the Punjab region in the Sikh community calling for more autonomy had been an ongoing issue since Indian independence in 1947. As a minority population, Sikhs experienced social, economic, and political discrimination in India, which led to the desire for more autonomy. This desire grew into a more radical movement that called for a fully independent state for the Sikhs, referred to as Khalistan. Gandhi worked to address this discrimination during her time as prime minister, appointing a member of the Sikh community to her cabinet and nominating Zail Singh as the first Sikh president of India.

However, the more radical elements in the Sikh community remained unsatisfied and throughout the early 1980s, tensions increased. This culminated in the occupying of the Golden Temple, one of the holiest shrines for Sikhs, by armed extremists and presented a difficult situation for Gandhi's administration. Gandhi gave the order to the military to take back the Golden Temple, leading to an armed confrontation of tanks and troops that lasted for four days. Operation Blue Star, as it was called, led to the deaths of approximately 100 troops and hundreds of civilians. The Golden Temple was damaged during the siege and with many innocent people injured and killed, even moderates in the Sikh community expressed resentment and anger.

Prime Minister Gandhi received much criticism for the authoritarian-style crackdown at the temple and along with the emergency order she issued a few years prior, public support was not what it once was. Many, including Gandhi's own advisers, feared for her safety and for retaliatory actions against her, suggesting that she remove Sikhs from her protective detail. Gandhi refused, arguing that their presence did not pose a safety risk. Unfortunately, Gandhi was proven wrong by the events of the morning of October 31.[9]

After the shooting in the garden, aides along with Gandhi's daughter-in-law rushed her to the hospital. Lifesaving measures were taken, and doctors worked feverously to save the prime minister, but her body had taken too many bullets and she was pronounced dead at 2:30 that afternoon. Once the news of the assassination spread, a crowd gathered outside the hospital.

According to witnesses, the crowd was initially peaceful and traffic in the area continued on as normal. Without explanation, a group of young men left the crowd and ran to a traffic island nearby. Journalist Dev Dutt recalls that a scooter was parked on the traffic island and the group of men proceeded to set it ablaze. The fire caused traffic in the area to slow and then the men went to some buses that had slowed and "began to pull Sikhs out of buses. They started to pull off their turbans and beat them relentlessly."[10] Police were not in the area and the violence went on for about twenty minutes before another group of men chased the mob away. This was the first instance of violence in the hours after Gandhi's death, and unarguably one of the lesser violent attacks of all that would transpire in the days that followed.

By the evening of October 31, mobs led in many cases by identified leaders of Gandhi's Congress Party pillaged and ransacked Sikh neighborhoods and homes throughout Delhi. Buses of men arrived in neighborhoods and some were reported to have lists containing the names of Sikh families to be targeted. Houses were burned and businesses were looted. Sikh men were taken into the streets by the mobs, many suffering brutal deaths. The men were beaten, some were burned alive, and some dismembered. Sikh women were forced to remove their clothes in some cases and were often raped. Young Sikh boys were sometimes castrated. The violence spread from Delhi into the states of Uttar Pradesh with over 1,000 Sikhs killed in the cities of Kanpur, Lucknow, and Ghaziabad. In most cases, the police were complicit with the violence—simply refused to intervene and sometimes even participated. A political science professor from Jawaharlal Nehru University, Ashwini Ray, reported that he witnessed police drinking tea and reading newspapers while looting and arson occurred around them.[11]

Journalist M. R. Narayan Swamy recounts being told by a police officer that he and his colleagues should go to the morgue if they wanted real insight into what was happening. The journalists did so and found bodes lined up in rows and in one particular room, witnessed stacks of bodies of both men and women, some clothed and some not, covered in blood. Swamy himself estimates that he counted approximately 172 bodies placed in rows, not counting the additional stacks of bodies. There was, in those days after Gandhi's assassination, a "festival of death"[12] in the streets of Delhi.

Those left in charge after Gandhi's death exhibited questionable leadership. The home minister, P. V. Narasimha Rao, was criticized for being too slow to act—it was two days before he imposed a curfew and it took another three days to quell the violence. In the five days after the death of the prime minister, it is estimated that around 3,000 Sikhs were murdered and property damage was likely more than $250 million. Gandhi's son, Rajiv, who became prime minister after his mother's death is quoted as saying, "When a big tree falls, the earth shakes,"[13] which left many feeling that Gandhi was dismissive of the deaths and the violence against the Sikh community in the wake of his mother's death. In the end, it was the army that was able to stop the violence and restore some semblance of order late on November 2, 1984.

In 1991, Rajiv Gandhi would also die at the hands of assassin, and in a now declassified Central Intelligence Agency (CIA) report, analysts believed there was at best a 50/50 likelihood that Rajiv Gandhi would suffer an assassination attempt. In 1987, analyses of the Sikh extremists in India suggested that even though security forces had reduced the violence and had arrested or killed approximately one-third of the extremists, the threat still lingered. Because of continued support and an active number of around 200 extremists in the Punjab region, the CIA did not believe the Indian government would be able to eliminate the terrorist threat.

According to the analysis, the Sikh extremists received financial support from temples, remittances from outside the country, and also profited from drug trafficking. Thus, the extremists were likely to remain a threat and a particular threat to the life of Rajiv Gandhi and others. In fact, the CIA concluded that assassination would likely be the extremists' "principal tactic"[14] in their violent campaign.

Despite the violence and unrest, India did not see a significant change in political institutions in the years after Indira or Rajiv Gandhi's assassinations. In fact, India was able to maintain a stable democracy and a score of 8 on the Polity index until 1995 when the democratic institutions in India improved and the Polity score increased one point.

However, repression levels within India did not fare as well as the democratic institutions. The average score on the PTS[15] worsened in the years after Indira Gandhi's assassination from an average of 3 in 1984 to an average of 3.5 in 1985. By 1987, the PTS average score increased to 4, indicating increasing levels of government repression in the years following the assassination and the post-assassination violence. In fact, during Indira Gandhi's last term as prime minister, repression increased as measured by PTS—from an average score of 2.5 in 1979 to 3 by 1984. Thus, it appears that government repression was increasing prior to Indira Gandhi's assassination and continued in the years thereafter.

Gandhi's assassination in 1984 was a significant event and resulted in immediate and violent repercussions for the Sikh community in India. Assassinations of other, lower-level government officials typically hold less violent consequences and do not lead to reprisals against an entire community. But this does not mean that other assassinations are inconsequential and in fact, killings of lower-level officials can lead to significant changes, be they political or societal changes. Some of these assassinations are an element in environments that can lead to significant change. The assassination of Brigadier Stephen Saunders as he drove to his job at the British Embassy in Greece one morning in June 2000 is one such example.

GREECE—BRITISH MILITARY ATTACHÉ BRIGADIER STEPHEN SAUNDERS

Much more likely to fall prey to an assassin's bullet are lower-level government officials, such as the attack on British military attaché Stephen Saunders who was killed in Athens, Greece. Driving to work on the morning of June 8, 2000, Brigadier Saunders was shot and killed by two men on a motorcycle. The group responsible was the anti-American 17N group, which issued a statement after the shooting claiming that Saunders was targeted due to his involvement in the NATO bombing of Serbia. Yet, the British Defense Ministry refuted the claims and stated that Saunders was based in Kuwait at the time of the Serbia bombing.[16]

17N formed after a student uprising against the ruling junta in Greece was brutally repressed on that date in 1973. Dozens were killed during the revolt and it triggered the beginning of the end of the junta, which fell the following year in 1974. Believing that the United States, via the CIA, supported the junta the 17N group formed and carried out numerous attacks, assassinating the CIA Chief of Station in Athens in 1975 and killing approximately twenty-two others before the group's demise in 2003.

Despite public statements by the group after the killings, no arrests were made in over twenty years of the group's terrorist campaign across the country, until two years after Saunders's assassination. International outrage over Saunders's death and the upcoming 2004 Olympic Games, which would shine a light on all of Greece, in part prompted the government and the authorities to make moves against 17N. Throughout much of its existence, the group garnered quiet support from much of the Greek public who seemed to believe that many of the group's actions were justified. The United States was one of several states that called out Greece for its inability to control 17N.

After Saunders's assassination and the 2001 terror attacks on the United States, family members of some of the Greek victims of 17N formed a group, Os Edo, to publicly speak out against the group. These events seemed to be the perfect storm for turning the public tide against the group and the Greek government in 2002 passed an anti-terrorism law that now made membership in a terror organization against the law. The new law also arranged for protection of witnesses, and allowed for trial by judges rather than jurors—none of which was possible prior to the passage of the new law.

After an attempted bombing went awry in July 2002 (the bomb detonated early), the Greek authorities, with the help of tips from the public, made the first arrest of a 17N member. This arrest proved to be a tipping point, leading to the arrest of fourteen additional members of the group. Dimitris Koufodinas was convicted of killing Brigadier Saunders, and for twelve other assassinations, in 2003 and sentenced to 1,300 years in prison. The Greek legal system approved a forty-eight-hour leave from prison in 2017 for Koufondinas and unlike one of his fellow terrorists who received a similar furlough, Koufondinas did report back to prison at the conclusion of his two-day reprieve.

Understandably, the two-day leave sparked international backlash and Saunders's widow, Heather Saunders, issued a public statement that she was "appalled" at the two-day furlough and that no member of 17N had ever apologized or shown any remorse for the killing of her husband.[17] In all, Koufondinas and his group were responsible for the deaths of four U.S. government officials, two Turkish diplomats, and several Greek businessmen and politicians in addition to Brigadier Saunders. Saunders was the last of the assassinations before the arrests, subsequent trials, and convictions of most of the 17N members.

From 1997 until 2000, Greece did not experience any changes in Polity score or in the average PTS score. Greece retained its firm grip on democracy with Polity score of 10 and an average PTS score of 2, indicating a fully consolidated democracy and little state repression. In 2000, the PTS average score changed slightly based on the interpretations of U.S. State Department's Human Rights report resulting in an upgrade of Greece's score from 2 to 1. The following year, Greece's score based on the State Department report was again 2 (the year after Saunders's assassination). Greece's democracy remains firmly intact and consistently holds the Polity score of 10 through 2017.

SURVIVAL ANALYSIS MODELS—
TARGETS AND POLITICAL CHANGE

Thus, anecdotally these cases provide evidence of assassinations as a trigger for societal violence and new anti-terrorism policies albeit as one event in much larger environments. But do these particular assassinations lead to significant change, or any change at all, in political institutions? To address this question, a series of survival models are tested here across the second-level targets discussed earlier. The theory is that the type of government official matters to the likelihood of institutional change after an assassination and the hypothesis is as follows:

H2: The likelihood of political institutional change after a terrorist assassination will vary across subtypes of government officials.

Cox shared frailty models, discussed in previous chapters, are utilized here in order to account for the unobserved heterogeneity created by the differing "frailties" between states. For example, states such as Haiti or Mali are more likely than the United States or Denmark to experience a change in Polity score. A shared frailty model accounts for this shared risk hazard in the observations. These models determine the risk of failure for each state after experiencing an assassination event, assume a gamma frailty with unknown variance, and examine the risk of failure by regime type. The authoritarian, mixed, and tumultuous regime types are measured against democracies.

Several explanatory variables are included in the models, including population, employment rate, and infant mortality rate. These variables are logged with population and employment often performing best when interacted with the time variable (day). The key diagnostic of a Cox shared frailty model is the PH violation test. The PH assumption is premised on the notion that covariates have an effect that is both proportional and constant across the timing of covariate changes.[18] Some violation of the PH is expected—the aim is to find the model with the least amount of PH violation that is also theoretically sound. The models presented in this chapter show little to no PH violations and all are theoretically strong.

In survival models, hazard ratios less than 1 signal a decreasing hazard or risk of experiencing the failure event (with each unit change in the coefficient) and hazard ratios greater than 1 signal an increasing hazard or risk. Hazard ratios close to 1 indicate a constant rate and thus, the coefficient has no effect on the hazard or risk of experiencing a failure. In table 5.1, the results of the Cox shared frailty models for the second-level target categories of government officials are reported. Evidence exists to support the hypothesis that the likelihood of political institutional change (measured via Polity scores) varies according to the type of government official targeted. Thus, the null hypothesis is rejected.

Hazard ratios are different in each category, but there are obvious trends. Across all six models, tumultuous regimes are at the highest risk of experiencing a Polity change after an assassination. This is to be expected—tumultuous regimes are in a state of chaos or flux and are not expected to remain in those situations for long periods of time. The most significant finding here is that the hazard ratio (i.e., likelihood of experiencing a Polity change) is much lower when a member of an international organization or international peacekeeper is assassinated compared to other government targets. Granted, the likelihood of change for a tumultuous regime is still extremely large at 8,703 percent but when compared to targeting of intelligence officials, for instance, the difference is stark. When intelligence officials are assassinated in a tumultuous regime, the likelihood of Polity score change is 18,343 percent—tumultuous regimes are over 18,000 times more likely to experience a Polity score change than when a democracy experiences the assassination of an intelligence official. Further analyzing the results, the assassination of government personnel present the greatest hazard to tumultuous regimes, keeping in mind that the hazard represents a Polity score change of any kind. The change here, may in fact, be a positive one. This examination is seeking only to determine the risk of change—an altering of the status quo—after terrorist assassinations across target types.

Table 5.1   Government Officials by Regime Type, 1977–2017

Shared Frailty Models—Political Institutional Changes
Gamma Frailty/Efron Method

	Government Personnel			Diplomats			International Organizations/ Peacekeepers			Intelligence Officials		
	Coefficient (SE)	Hazard Ratio (SE)	p Values	Coefficient (SE)	Hazard Ratio (SE)	p Values	Coefficient (SE)	Hazard Ratio (SE)	p Values	Coefficient (SE)	Hazard Ratio (SE)	p Values
Authoritarian	2.90 (.21)	18.19 (3.84)	.001	2.86 (.21)	17.45 (3.69)	.001	3.20 (.27)	24.44 (6.65)	.001	2.88 (.21)	17.81 (3.79)	.001
Mixed	3.21 (.15)	24.89 (3.67)	.001	3.19 (.15)	24.31 (3.57)	.001	2.80 (.15)	16.38 (2.44)	.001	3.20 (.15)	24.56 (3.62)	.001
Tumultuous	5.33 (.23)	207.04 (47.17)	.001	5.24 (.23)	189.11 (43.08)	.001	4.48 (.24)	88.03 (21.37)	.001	5.21 (.23)	184.43 (42.41)	.001
Population (log)	-1.56 (.80)	.21 (.17)	.050	-1.42 (.81)	.24 (.20)	.080	-.48 (.21)	.62 (.13)	.025	-1.35 (.81)	.26 (.21)	.097
Employment (log)	1.41 (.76)	4.09 (3.12)	.066	1.24 (.78)	3.47 (2.69)	.108				1.19 (.78)	3.28 (2.56)	.128
Infant Mortality Rate (log)	-.17 (.04)	.84 (.03)	.001	-.18 (.04)	.84 (.03)	.001	-.22 (.05)	.81 (.04)	.001	-.17 (.04)	.84 (.04)	.001
Event Date (log)	1.22 (.69)	3.39 (2.36)	.079	1.46 (.71)	4.30 (3.04)	.039	-.76 (.47)	.47 (.22)	.107	1.43 (.71)	4.19 (2.99)	.045
Population (log) x Day	-.001 (.01)	.99 (.01)	.171	-.01 (.01)	.99 (.01)	.091	3.82 (.01)	1.00 (.01)	.736	-.01 (.01)	.99 (.01)	.098
Employment (log) x Day	.001 (.01)	1.00 (.01)	.382	.01 (.01)	1.00 (.01)	.222				.01 (.01)	1.00 (.01)	.240
Theta	3.13 (.38)			3.17 (.40)			3.97 (.51)			3.16 (.40)		
N Failures	597			596			512			592		
N Observations	157,520			157,103			139,024			156,993		
N Groups	136			136			136			136		

Shared Frailty Models—Political Institutional Changes
Gamma Frailty/Efron Method

	Election-Related			Heads of State		
	Coefficient (SE)	Hazard Ratio (SE)	p Values	Coefficient (SE)	Hazard Ratio (SE)	p Values
Authoritarian	3.05 (.23)	21.26 (4.80)	.001	2.90 (.21)	18.09 (3.86)	.001
Mixed	3.08 (.15)	21.85 (3.22)	.001	3.20 (.15)	24.46 (3.60)	.001
Tumultuous	5.02 (.24)	152.50 (35.92)	.001	5.23 (.23)	186.69 (43.15)	.001
Population (log)	-.11 (.19)	.90 (.17)	.559	-1.25 (.82)	.29 (.23)	.127
Employment (log)				1.08 (.78)	2.93 (2.30)	.170
Infant Mortality Rate (log)	-.15 (.04)	.86 (.04)	.001	-.17 (.04)	.84 (.04)	.001
Event Date	.47 (.38)	1.60 (.61)	.215	1.48 (.72)	4.40 (3.17)	.040
Population (log) x Day	-.01 (9.70)	.99 (9.70)	.048	-.01 (.01)	.99 (.01)	.090
Employment (log) x Day				.07 (.01)	1.00 (.01)	.213
Theta	3.04 (.43)			3.16 (.40)		
N Failures	560			590		
N Observations	149,610			156,659		
N Groups	136			136		

Source: Polity, GTD & Penn, 1977–2017.

As discussed earlier, the least risk to tumultuous regimes of the second-level targets is that of international organizations/peacekeepers with election-related attacks as the next less risky. The assassinations of diplomats, intelligence officials, and heads of state all present different, but similar, risks to tumultuous regimes with hazard rates ranging from 18,811 percent to 18,343 percent.

That said, this partial likelihood methodology accepts some loss of efficiency, as evidenced in the large standard errors. More important than the staggering percentages presented here is the fact that across all six models there are variations in outcomes. Thus, the target type *does* matter when considering the likelihood of changes in political institutions after terrorist assassinations occur in a state. This is true for tumultuous regimes, but is also true for mixed and authoritarian regimes when compared to democratic regimes.

Mixed regimes experience hazard rates ranging from 1,538 percent (international organizations/peacekeepers) to 2,389 percent (government personnel). Again, the assassinations of members of international organizations create less hazard for mixed regimes compared to the other target types. For this regime type, the assassinations of intelligence officials, diplomats, heads of state, and government personnel all pose similar risks to the regime with only slight variation, but variation nonetheless. Keeping with the trend from the analyses of tumultuous regimes, election-related assassinations are the next least risky for mixed regimes at 2,085 percent after the killings of international organization members.

An interesting finding is that unlike the other five models, the test of election-related assassinations provides extremely similar hazard ratios for mixed and authoritarian regimes. In all models, the 95 percent confidence intervals show some overlap and the hazard ratios are indeed simply point estimates. When examining the survival curves for the models discussed here, the mixed regimes do consistently survive longer before experiencing a Polity change than the authoritarian regimes across all six models. Examples of these survival curves are presented in figure 5.1. Yet, in the election-related model, the authoritarian regime hazard is 2,025 percent (compared to 2,085% for mixed regimes) and thus only 60 points separate the two. In none of the other models, were the estimated hazard ratios this close for the two regimes.

Another interesting departure from the model trends is that for authoritarian regimes, the assassinations of international organization members pose the *greatest* risk for Polity change at 2,344 percent. The election-related assassinations pose the next greatest risk at 2,025 percent (another departure). The killings of government personnel, diplomats, heads of state, and intelligence officials all pose risks to authoritarian regimes with hazards ranging from 1,719 percent (government personnel) to 1,645 percent (diplomats).

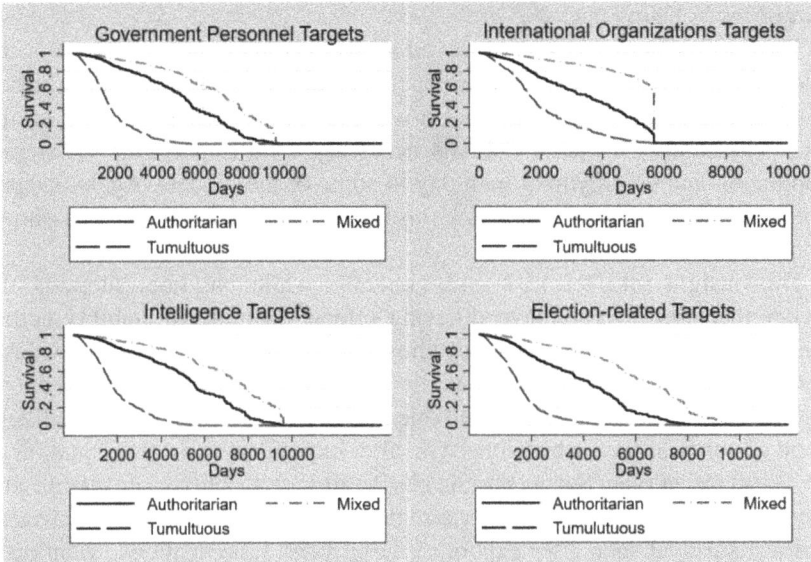

Regime Survival Curves -- Select Government Official Targets, 1977-2017

Figure 5.1   Survival Curves—Regimes and Government Officials, 1977–2017.

Based on these findings when compared to democratic regimes, when government officials are assassinated, a Polity score change is most likely to occur in an authoritarian regime after the terrorist assassination of a member/employee of an international organization and least likely after the assassination of a diplomat. For mixed regimes, the risk is highest after the assassination of government personnel and the lowest after the killing of an international organization employee or peacekeeper. For tumultuous regimes, the risk is highest after the assassination of government personnel and lowest after the assassination of members of international organizations. It is important to stress that these risks are all in comparison to democracies. By far, democracies are the least likely (i.e., at the least risk) of all regime types to experience a Polity score change after the terrorist assassination of any government official.

The explanatory variables in the models help to control for differing contexts across states. The log of population is statistically significant in at least a two-tailed test in all the models except that of the election-related assassinations. The negatively signed coefficient for this variable and hazard ratios of less than 1 indicates a decreasing hazard risk per unit change, which is consistent across all six models. As population increases, it is expected that the hazard of experiencing a Polity change will decrease. The measure of infant mortality rate, which is a proxy measure of development, also indicates a decreasing hazard for Polity change with negatively signed coefficients and hazard ratios below one.

The employment variable improved all models, with the exceptions of the international organizations/peacekeeper and election-related models, albeit with large standard errors and not always as statistically significant as the other explanatory variables. It was necessary for PH purposes to interact population and employment with day in some of the models. Again, despite not being significant in each model, this interaction improved the PH assumptions in said models.

This insight into terrorist assassinations, while baseline, supports the theory that these events have differing effects on political stability across regimes and is dependent upon the chosen target type. Figure 5.1 provides a comparison of four select survival curves from the models discussed above (all model results are displayed in table 5.1). These curves suggest the likelihood of survival for each regime type after experiencing an assassination of the select target type. Survival indicates the time to a Polity score change and the curves indicate that tumultuous regimes, across all the models, have the shortest survival span after experiencing terrorist assassinations. Mentioned previously, the hazard ratios are point estimates and the confidence intervals in all models have overlap between mixed and authoritarian regimes. The survival curves indicate across the models that authoritarian states actually have shorter survival times than mixed regimes—and all have shorter survival times than democracies.

In figure 5.1, the table of graphs shows differing survival curves across select target types. While trends are similar with tumultuous regimes, for instance, having the shortest survival curve in all models, tumultuous regimes experience changes in Polity scores sooner after the assassination of election-related targets than after the assassination of a member of an international organization worker or peacekeeper. For election-related targets, at the 2,000-day mark the survival rate for a tumultuous regime is .2 while in the international organizations model, the survival rate is approximately .4 at the 2,000-day mark. The survival rates for authoritarian and mixed regimes are closest to one another in the government personnel and intelligence targets models. At the 6,000-day mark, the survival rate for authoritarian regimes is lowest in the election-related targets model at slightly less than .2. In these survival curves, mixed regimes fare the best after assassinations of international organizations targets (i.e., the decline is slower). The international organizations model runs out of data much earlier than the other models (indicated by the drop-off of the curves prior to the 6,000-day mark), but the results are still instructive and indicate that deeper examination of the impact of violence against these target types is warranted.

The results here fit with the theory that the targets of terrorist assassinations make a difference in the likelihood of political instability, but additional work is needed to develop meaningful insight into the repercussions of assassination events. The possibility of omitted variable bias or endogeneity with other forms of political violence must be eliminated. On its face, it may seem that understanding links between assassination events and Polity score change provides little insight, yet Polity scores change for a reason. Something within the political institutions of that state have changed, calling for an adjustment in the Polity score. In order to better understand the repercussions of assassinations on institutional changes, next I examine the directional shifts in Polity scores—whether regimes experience positive or negative moves along the Polity scale after terrorist assassinations.

Expectations are that the targeting and killing of government officials, across all types, will result in negative Polity score shifts in authoritarian regimes. These regimes will respond in aggressive ways after "one of their own" is targeted and engage in harsher repression tactics, creating civil strife and instability, which results in lower Polity scores and thus the likelihood of a negative shift toward deeper autocracy as opposed to a positive shift toward democracy.

Mixed regimes, with elements of both authoritarian and democratic characteristics will be more likely to experience positive shifts, signaling more democratic moves in the wake of the assassination of government officials. This is premised on the idea that mixed regimes will encounter the "rally-around-the-flag" effect wherein citizens rally around their leaders and their institutions in the fight against terrorism. With enhanced public support, institutions make democratic moves because it strengthens the regime in the "us against them" mentality. Therefore, the hypotheses for directional Polity shifts are as follows:

H3: Negative political institutional changes are more likely in authoritarian regimes than in mixed or democratic regimes in the aftermath of terrorist assassinations of government officials.

H4: Positive political institutional changes are more likely in mixed regimes than in authoritarian regimes in the aftermath of terrorist assassinations of government officials.

For this part of the analysis, Polity shifts are coded either as negative or positive shifts. When a Polity score changes, if the new score is a move toward authoritarianism or deeper into authoritarianism, then it is coded as a negative shift. For example, if a state's previous score was -1 and the new score is -3 it is coded 1 for a negative shift. However, if the shift is a move toward democracy, then the change is recorded as a positive shift. Thus, if a state's previous Polity score was -7 and the new Polity score is -5, this is coded as a positive shift (i.e., it is a move "up" the scale). If the state's previous score was 2 and the new score is 4, it is coded as a positive shift. If the state's previous score was 7 and the new score is 6, it is coded as a negative shift, and so on.

Tumultuous scores are generally left out of this analysis. The three tumultuous category scores in Polity (-66, -77, and -88) complicate the nature of determining negative versus positive. A Polity score of -66 indicates an interruption to government processes (something akin to a civil war situation) and -88 indicates some type of foreign intervention or occupation. A score of -77 indicates the collapse of state authorities. This last score is more clearly a negative shift—it is difficult to argue that the collapse of any state is positive—and thus all state collapses (-77 scores) are coded here as negative shifts. Scores of -66 and/or -88 receive no coding one way or the other. This coding scheme results in 189 negative Polity shifts and 389 positive Polity shifts in this dataset.

Negative Institutional Shifts

Table 5.2 provides the results of testing for negative Polity shifts. Evidence supports the hypothesis that authoritarian regimes are more likely to experience a negative Polity shift after a terrorist assassination, when compared to democratic and mixed regimes. This is supported in all six models of target types with the international organizations/peacekeepers model indicating the greatest hazard/risk of experiencing a negative shift at 21,662 percent compared to a democratic regime. A mixed regime is only 3,308 percent more likely in this model to experience a negative Polity shift, compared to a democracy. The model indicating the lowest risk of experiencing a negative shift is the one for diplomats, with a risk of 11,217 percent compared to a democracy but with risk for a mixed regime at 4,520 percent. This mixed regime risk is actually the highest risk for mixed regimes in the negative shifts analysis. That said, authoritarian regimes range from a risk of 11,217 percent (diplomats) to 11,367 percent (intelligence officials) to 21,662 percent (international organizations).

Across all six models, the regime categorical variables are statistically significant. Population is statistically significant in most of the models (election-related and international organization models being the exceptions) and infant mortality rate is statistically significant across all models. The coefficients for these two explanatory variables are negative, again across all models, and the hazard ratios are less than one, indicating decreasing likelihood for a negative Polity shift. For instance, the risk for negative Polity shifts decreases anywhere from 20 to 23 percent with each unit improvement in infant mortality rate.

Figure 5.2 presents survival curves from four of the six models of negative Polity shifts. The lowest risk model (diplomats) and the highest risk model

Table 5.2 Government Officials—Negative Polity Shifts by Regime Type, 1977–2017

Shared Frailty Models—Negative Polity Directional Shifts
Gamma Frailty/Efron Method

	Government Personnel			Diplomats			International Organizations/ Peacekeepers			Intelligence Officials		
	Coefficient (SE)	Hazard Ratio (SE)	p Values	Coefficient (SE)	Hazard Ratio (SE)	p Values	Coefficient (SE)	Hazard Ratio (SE)	p Values	Coefficient (SE)	Hazard Ratio (SE)	p Values
Authoritarian	4.73 (.40)	113.40 (45.50)	.001	4.73 (.40)	113.17 (45.46)	.001	5.38 (.54)	217.62 (116.77)	.001	4.74 (.40)	114.67 (46.37)	.001
Mixed	3.83 (.34)	46.07 (15.59)	.001	3.83 (.34)	46.20 (15.69)	.001	3.53 (.37)	34.08 (12.70)	.001	3.83 (.34)	45.93 (15.63)	.001
Tumultuous	6.02 (.46)	410.34 (188.14)	.001	6.01 (.46)	407.75 (187.48)	.001	5.42 (.51)	224.92 (113.56)	.001	5.95 (.46)	383.52 (178.17)	.001
Population (log)	-.39 (.23)	.67 (.16)	.090	-.40 (.23)	.67 (.16)	.085	-.38 (.35)	.68 (.24)	.278	-.42 (.23)	.66 (.15)	.076
Infant Mortality Rate (log)	-.26 (.07)	.77 (.05)	.001	-.25 (.07)	.78 (.05)	.001	-.24 (.09)	.79 (.07)	.005	-.26 (.07)	.77 (.05)	.001
Event Date (log)	.61 (.59)	1.84 (1.09)	.303	.55 (.59)	1.72 (1.03)	.358	.88 (.94)	2.40 (2.26)	.354	.54 (.60)	1.72 (1.03)	.366
Population (log) x Day	-6.60 (.01)	.99 (.01)	.660	-6.15 (.01)	.99 (.01)	.682	-8.69 (.01)	.99 (.01)	.690	-5.12 (.01)	.99 (.01)	.735
Theta	2.42 (.42)			2.40 (.42)			3.10 (.61)			2.42 (.42)		
N Failures	162			162			132			161		
N Observations	158,083			157,651			139,024			157,248		
N Groups	136			136			136			136		

(Continued)

Table 5.2 Government Officials—Negative Polity Shifts by Regime Type, 1977–2017 (Continued)

Shared Frailty Models—Negative Polity Directional Shifts
Gamma Frailty/Efron Method

	Government Personnel (Election-Related)			Diplomats (Heads of State)			International Organizations/Peacekeepers			Intelligence Officials		
	Coefficient (SE)	Hazard Ratio (SE)	p Values	Coefficient (SE)	Hazard Ratio (SE)	p Values	Coefficient (SE)	Hazard Ratio (SE)	p Values	Coefficient (SE)	Hazard Ratio (SE)	p Values
Authoritarian	4.82 (.43)	124.18 (53.92)	.001	4.77 (.41)	118.18 (48.16)	.001						
Mixed	3.64 (.35)	38.17 (13.17)	.001	3.81 (.34)	45.19 (15.42)	.001						
Tumultuous	5.74 (.48)	309.60 (147.24)	.001	6.08 (.47)	438.62 (205.37)	.001						
Population (log)	-.31 (.28)	.73 (.20)	.263	-.41 (.47)	.67 (.16)	.086						
Infant Mortality Rate (log)	-.22 (.07)	.80 (.20)	.004	-.26 (.24)	.77 (.05)	.001						
Event Date	.90 (.73)	2.47 (1.79)	.213	.58 (.61)	1.79 (1.09)	.340						
Population (log) x Day	-.01 (.01)	.99 (.01)	.465	-5.28 (.01)	.99 (.01)	.730						
Theta	2.62 (.47)			2.52 (.44)								
N Failures	148			160								
N Observations	149,610			156,914								
N Groups	136			136								

Source: Polity, GTD & Penn, 1977–2017.

Regime Survival Curves - Select Targets, Negative Polity Shifts, 1977-2017

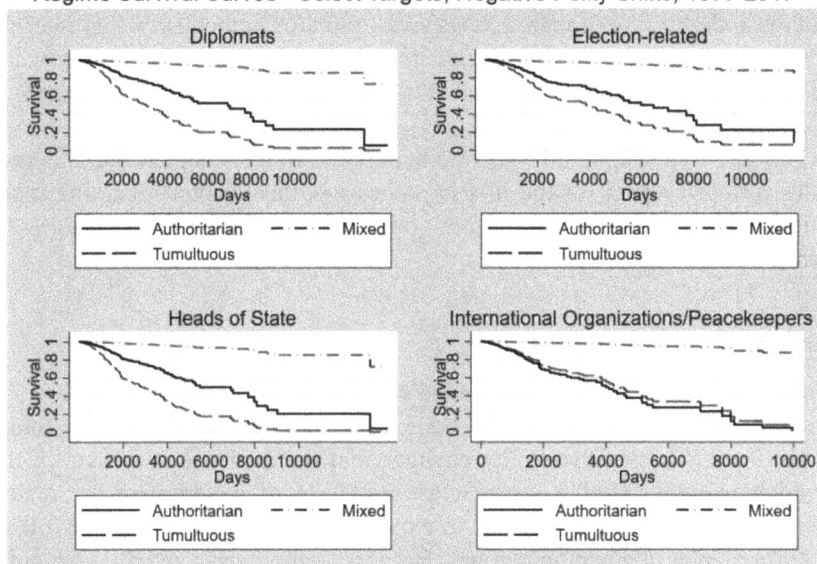

Figure 5.2   Survival Curves—Negative Regime Shifts, 1977–2017.

(international organizations/peacekeepers) are presented along with election-related and heads of state. All four curves clearly indicate that survival for mixed regimes is the most stable (survival here is quantified as not experiencing a negative Polity score shift). Authoritarian regimes are slower to experience a negative shift after the assassinations of diplomats compared to all the other models—with a .8 survival rate at around the 3,000-day mark and a .6 survival rate at around the 5,000-day mark.

After the assassination of election-related personnel, authoritarian regimes experience survival rates of .8 (i.e., experiencing a negative shift) just after the 2,000-day mark, but then appear close to the diplomats with .6 survival rates around the 5,000-day mark. By the 8,000-day mark in this model, survival rates are only around .3. Similar to the election-related model, the heads of state model indicates survival rates of .8 just after the 2,000-day mark and around .3 at the 8,000-day mark but reach the .6 survival rate faster—just after the 4,000-day mark.

As stated previously, this analysis and the coding do not speak to tumultuous regimes directly and in the models discussed thus far, the survival rate in tumultuous has declined faster than either mixed or authoritarian. However, the model for international organizations/peacekeepers is interesting because it not only indicates the most risk in the hazard ratios but the survival curve suggests that authoritarian regimes in this model have lower survival rates than even tumultuous regimes. By the 2,000-day mark, authoritarian regimes have just slightly more than a .6 survival rate after a member of an international organization has been assassinated. By the 4,000-day mark, survival is only .4 and by the 8,000-day mark there is only approximately a .1 survival rate.

This analysis supports the second hypothesis in this chapter, but also provides further support for the first hypothesis in this chapter regarding institutional change as well as the overall position taken in this work—targets of terrorist assassinations matter.

Positive Institutional Shifts

Support for the hypothesis that mixed regimes are more likely to experience positive moves along the Polity scale than authoritarian regimes is found in the models of positive Polity changes, but the evidence is weaker in the positive models. After a terrorist assassination of government personnel, mixed regimes are at greater risk of experiencing a positive Polity shift than authoritarian or democratic regimes. Both the authoritarian and mixed regime variables are statistically significant and results indicate that mixed regimes are 2,240 percent more likely than democratic regimes to have a positive Polity shift, while authoritarian regimes are 670 percent more likely than democratic regimes to experience a positive Polity shift. The killings of government personnel place mixed regimes at the greatest risk of positive shifts, compared to other targets.

For example, the diplomats model suggests that the risk for mixed regimes is 2,236 percent while the intelligence officials and heads of state models suggest that risk is slightly more than 2,220 percent for a positive Polity change. The least risk for mixed regimes in experiencing a positive shift is in the international organizations/peacekeepers model with a risk of 1,560 percent. This model also presents the lowest risk for authoritarian regimes experiencing a positive shift at 485 percent. Over the six models, mixed regimes are more likely to experience a positive Polity shift than authoritarian or democratic regimes after these assassinations. There are differences across targets and even if these difference are slight (with only 3% point differences in some cases), there are still differences across target types and therefore, all three models presented herein support the original hypothesis that institutional outcomes vary across target type. Evidence presented in table 5.3 supports the third hypothesis of this chapter regarding positive shifts in mixed regimes and as with the other models, further supports the thesis of this work that target type matters.

One of the explanatory variables responds differently in the positive model than in the negative model. The population variable is not significant in any

Table 5.3 Government Officials—Positive Polity Shifts by Regime Type, 1977–2017

Shared Frailty Models—Positive Polity Directional Shifts
Gamma Frailty/Efron Method

	Government Personnel			Diplomats			International Organizations/ Peacekeepers			Intelligence Officials		
	Coefficient (SE)	Hazard Ratio (SE)	p Values	Coefficient (SE)	Hazard Ratio (SE)	p Values	Coefficient (SE)	Hazard Ratio (SE)	p Values	Coefficient (SE)	Hazard Ratio (SE)	p Values
Authoritarian	2.04 (.29)	7.70 (2.27)	.001	2.04 (.29)	7.67 (2.26)	.001	1.77 (.38)	5.85 (2.21)	.001	2.03 (.29)	7.58 (2.23)	.001
Mixed	3.15 (.18)	23.40 (4.11)	.001	3.15 (.18)	23.36 (4.10)	.001	2.81 (.18)	16.60 (3.01)	.001	3.15 (.18)	23.22 (4.08)	.001
Tumultuous	-.23 (1.15)	.79 (.92)	.842	-.24 (1.15)	.79 (.91)	.837	-.45 (1.13)	.64 (.73)	.695	-.25 (1.15)	.78 (.90)	.828
Population (log)	.17 (.20)	1.18 (.24)	.408	.16 (.21)	1.18 (.24)	.423	-.18 (.07)	.83 (.22)	.485	.16 (.21)	1.17 (.24)	.440
Infant Mortality Rate (log)	-.15 (.06)	.86 (.05)	.007	-.15 (.06)	.86 (.05)	.008	-.16 (.07)	.85 (.06)	.014	-.15 (.06)	.86 (.05)	.008
Event Date (log)	1.88 (.42)	6.58 (2.76)	.001	1.83 (.42)	6.22 (2.62)	.001	.90 (.60)	1.10 (.67)	.870	1.77 (.42)	5.87 (2.48)	.001
Population (log) x Day	-.001 (.01)	.99 (.01)	.171	-.01 (.01)	.99 (.01)	.091	-.001 (.01)	.99 (.01)	.131	-.001 (.01)	.99 (.01)	.001
Theta	3.26 (.46)			3.27 (.46)			3.77 (.54)			3.28 (.47)		
N Failures	331			331			293			331		
N Observations	158,083			157,651			139,024			157,248		
N Groups	136			136			136			136		

(Continued)

Table 5.3 Government Officials—Positive Polity Shifts by Regime Type, 1977–2017 (Continued)

Shared Frailty Models—Positive Polity Directional Shifts
Gamma Frailty/Efron Method

	Government Personnel			Diplomats			International Organizations/ Peacekeepers			Intelligence Officials		
	Coefficient (SE)	Hazard Ratio (SE)	p Values	Coefficient (SE)	Hazard Ratio (SE)	p Values	Coefficient (SE)	Hazard Ratio (SE)	p Values	Coefficient (SE)	Hazard Ratio (SE)	p Values
	Election-Related			*Heads of State*								
Authoritarian	1.89 (.32)	6.59 (2.13)	.001	2.03 (.29)	7.59 (2.23)	.001						
Mixed	33.04 (.17)	20.88 (3.68)	.001	3.14 (.18)	23.17 (4.07)	.001						
Tumultuous	-.23 (1.14)	.80 (.91)	.841	-.26 (1.15)	.77 (.89)	.823						
Population (log)	.18 (.23)	1.19 (.28)	.446	.16 (.21)	1.17 (.24)	.448						
Infant Mortality Rate (log)	-.12 (.06)	.88 (.06)	.048	-.15 (.06)	.86 (.05)	.007						
Event Date	1.51 (.50)	4.51 (2.26)	.003	1.74 (.42)	5.72 (2.43)	.001						
Population (log) x Day	-.01 (.01)	.99 (.01)	.001	-.01 (.01)	.99 (.01)	.001						
Theta	3.69 (.52)			3.28 (.47)								
N Failures	312			331								
N Observations	149,610			156,914								
N Groups	136			136								

Source: Polity, GTD & Penn, 1977–2017.

model, but the infant mortality rate variable is significant across all six positive models and performs much as it did in the negative models. All coefficients are negative and all hazard ratios are below one—signifying a 12 to 14 percent decrease in the likelihood of a positive Polity change with each unit improvement in the rate of infant mortality.

Figure 5.3 presents survival curves of four of the positive shift target models. While these curves are not as instructive as the curves in the negative shifts model and are not as supportive of the positive Polity shifts hypothesis, we do see differences across target types. The survival rates for authoritarian and mixed regimes track very closely, in fact almost identical, across the models. Mixed regimes do exhibit slightly longer survival rates (i.e., time to a positive Polity shift) and thus, while the hazard ratios fully support the hypothesis here that mixed regimes will be more likely to experience positive shifts, the survival curves are not as clear. Target differences are easier to identify in, for instance, the heads of state model with a survival rate of .7 at the 6,000-day mark, while at the same time mark, the survival rate is closer to .8 in the international organizations model. At the 8,000-day mark, the government personnel model survival rate is .4 while it is slightly above .4 in the heads of state model. Across all the positive shift models, tumultuous regimes experience the lowest hazard rates and the longest survival rates.

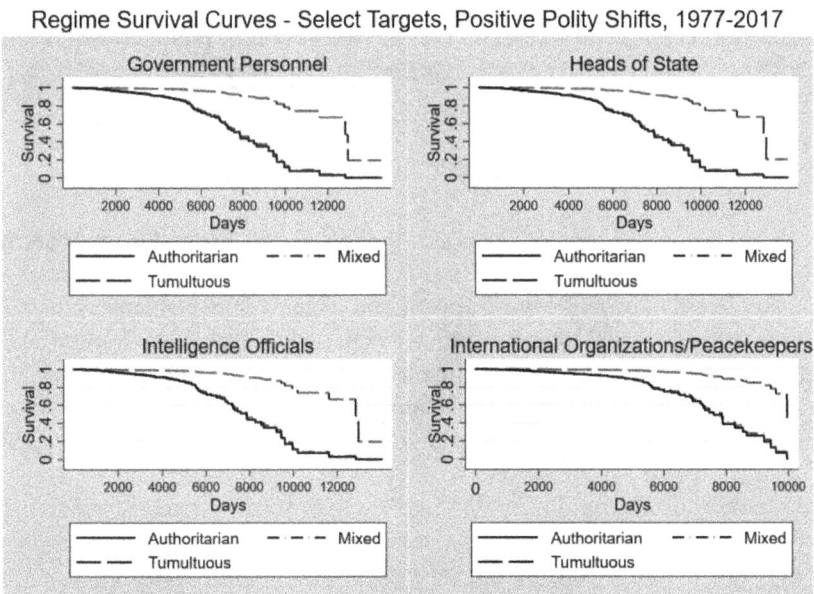

Figure 5.3   Survival Curves—Positive Regime Shifts, 1977–2017.

SURVIVAL ANALYSIS MODELS—TARGETS
AND REPRESSIVE REGIMES

Another approach in examining the effect of terrorist assassinations is utilizing data from the PTS to investigate political stability within states that commit physical integrity abuses against citizens. Are repressive regimes more or less likely to experience a Polity score change after a terrorist assassination? Does the result vary according to the type of target chosen by the terrorists?

In an earlier study, research indicates that after a terrorist assassination, regardless of target, the most repressive regimes are the ones most likely to experience a change in Polity score.[19] Essentially, the more repressive a regime the more likely the state is to experience a change in political institutions. Here, the intention is to determine if categorically, repressive states are more or less likely to have changes in Polity scores after terrorist assassinations across target types.

States that scored an average PTS score of 3.5 or higher are considered a repressive regime for the purposes of this study. An initial Cox shared frailty model for each of the six second-level target categories suggests that, in general, repressive states are only slightly more likely to experience a Polity score change after an assassination. However, in none of the six models was the repressive state variable statistically significant—in fact, the repressive versus non-repressive categorization did not approach significance in any of the models. Thus, the binary categorization of whether a regime is repressive appears to have little to no bearing on the likelihood of political institutional change in the aftermath of a terrorist assassination of government officials.

CONCLUSION

Evidence presented here indicates that in the wake of terrorist assassinations, the likelihood of Polity change for a regime is affected by the chosen target and the likelihood of the direction of the change is dependent upon both regime type and target selection. An authoritarian regime is much more likely than a democracy or a mixed regime to experience a negative Polity change in the aftermath of any terrorist assassination. A mixed regime is more likely than either a democracy or authoritarian regime to see a positive Polity shift after any terrorist assassination.

However, a positive Polity shift is less likely in a mixed regime if the target of the assassination is an international peacekeeper and a negative Polity shift is more likely in the same regime if the target is a diplomat. In an authoritarian regime, a positive shift is more likely if the target is part of the government personnel category and a negative Polity shift is more likely if the target is a member of an international organization or a peacekeeper. Thus, nuanced outcomes exist across targets even if the method of violence is the same.

This chapter contains much information across six different quantitative models of terrorist assassination target types and the effect of this violent tactic on political institutions. It is clear that there are outcome variations across target types and the qualitative discussion provides some insight into the human side of terrorism. Quantitative statistics advance our knowledge and at times assist in developing public policy. However, it is the qualitative study that helps us to understand the human toll of these events. Brigadier Saunders had loved ones who were greatly impacted by his death. 17N was responsible for taking the lives of many others—who also had loved ones. Prime Minister Gandhi not only had loved ones but her position as ruler of India led to an anti-Sikh uprising after her death. Women were raped, boys were castrated, and thousands of Sikhs lost their lives in the days following her death. Scholars and policymakers must develop in-depth understanding of these events and to do so requires both quantitative and qualitative examination.

Chapter 6

The Politically Active

Nearly 2,100 politicians and influential members of political parties were targeted and killed in terror campaigns from 1977 through 2017. Political party members constitute slightly more than 16 percent of this number with politicians accounting for the remainder. Some of these politicians—such as Rafik Hariri of Lebanon and Benazir Bhutto of Pakistan—were former government officials and like these two, many of the victims were candidates for office at the time of their deaths. Local candidates are often targeted, such as Maria Elias de Huapaya who was a city council candidate in Peru at the time of her death in 1989.[1] In fact, her killing was one of many carried out by Sendero Luminoso (Shining Path) in October of that year in Peru, referred to by some as "Red October" when mayors and local political candidates were assassinated at the rate of "three to four a day across the country.[2]"

Politicians and government officials obviously influence politics, but so do those who are active within political parties and who exhibit leadership capabilities. These individuals, working to promote his or her party and/or cause, may be the face of the party at the local level. Thus, party members, such as Senzangakhona Comelius Nkosi of the Inkatha Freedom Party in South Africa, are perceived as viable targets in terror campaigns. Nkosi, a branch chairman in the party, and his wife were shot and hacked to death in their home in Lothair in January 1999. No group claimed responsibility for the attack.

This chapter follows the format of the previous one, but analyzes only two second-level categories as opposed to the six second-level groups of government officials. However, the analyses are similar in that an initial model examining the likelihood of Polity change across regimes is presented, as well as models examining the negative and positive Polity shifts across regimes for the two second-level categories here—politicians and political party members. A qualitative case study for each category is conducted as well, one of which focuses on a single individual—Rafik Hariri, a former Lebanese prime minister—and another which focuses on a series of killings in Peru in 1989, rather than the assassination of a sole target.

SECOND-LEVEL CATEGORIES OF THE POLITICALLY ACTIVE—POLITICIANS AND POLITICAL PARTY MEMBERS

The GTD includes politicians and political party members only as second-level categories within the first-level categories of *government (general)* and *private citizens and property* and not as a stand-alone category. For this project, the second-level GTD categories of *political party member/rally* and *politician or political party movement* are combined into one category. One event, listed in the GTD as a *head of state* target, is also moved into the category here—the assassination of former Lebanese prime minister Hariri.

Thus, there are 2,098 terrorist assassinations of politically active individuals included in the data occurring from 1977 through 2017. Approximately 84 percent of these targets are politicians, such as the assassination of former Yemeni president Ali Abdullah Saleh by the Houthi extremist group Ansar Allah in December 2017. Political party members constitute 342, or 16 percent, of the 2,098 killings in this category, such as the killing of four Pakistan People's Party activists, along with a police constable, in Karachi, Pakistan, in February 1995.

Other examples of terrorist assassinations of politicians include the 2007 killing of former Pakistani prime minister Benazir Bhutto in Rawalpindi and the 1997 killing of Pablo Antonio Hernandez, a mayoral candidate in Saravena, Colombia.[3] Political party members, while not targeted as often as politicians, in many cases are still influential within society and draw the attention of terrorists. In April 2014, a council chairperson and a youth leader of the All Progressives Congress in Nigeria were shot and killed while riding in a vehicle with other party members in Borno State, Nigeria. Sources attributed the attack to Boko Haram though the group did not claim credit.[4] In Burundi, on September 29, 2015, the district head of the Movement for Solidarity and Development, Jean Baptiste Nsengiyumva, was killed when unknown perpetrators opened fire as he walked home that Tuesday evening.[5] Overall, politicians and political party members comprise the second largest target category (the politically active) of all the terrorist assassinations in this project from 1977 through 2017, second only to law enforcement with 2,246. Possibly one of the most impactful assassinations from this category is that of Rafik Hariri, which occurred in Lebanon in 2005.

FORMER LEBANESE PRIME MINISTER RAFIK HARIRI

February 14, 2005 began as any typical Monday in Beirut, Lebanon, for most Lebanese and especially for Rafik Hariri. The former prime minister began the day at home, his wife in Paris, reading the morning news while enjoying an espresso and a light breakfast.[6] Hariri was a self-made billionaire and likely the most prominent political figure in Lebanon, credited as the force behind rebuilding much of Beirut after the brutal civil war that stretched from 1975 until 1990. Hariri had served as prime minister for ten of the nearly fourteen post–civil war years, but resigned in 2004 in protest after Lebanon's legislative body approved a constitutional amendment allowing the Syrian-backed president of Lebanon, Emile Lahoud, to remain in his post for another three years.[7]

Despite the civil war divisions of religious and ethnic cleavages that still existed in Lebanon (and still exist today), politics in the post–civil war era became drawn over anti-Syrian and pro-Syrian lines. Syria was seen by many as a natural partner in all things Lebanese or by some as *the* rightful power broker within the country. Others, however, came to resent not only the Syrian military troop and security forces presence in Lebanon but the interference and at times outright directing of Lebanese affairs. Some were practical in the early years after the civil war—Lebanon was devastated in every possible way and needed funding, resources, and a stabilizing hand so that the rebuilding could begin—and accepted Syrian influence. Over time, however, many such as Rafik Hariri grew weary of Syrian influence and began to demand respect for Lebanese sovereignty.

A person of Hariri's prominence had to be careful; assassinations in Lebanon were common. During the brutal war years, lessons were learned on how to kill and maim and for fourteen years violence was more the norm than the exception. Precautions were necessary for those involved in politics and each day Hariri's security team conducted bomb sweeps and vehicles in his protective motorcade were equipped with electronic signal jammers—only two of many security measures taken to protect Hariri and his family.[8] However, these security measures, including keeping Hariri's meeting schedule and destinations confidential even from lead members of his security detail until the last possible minute, did not save Hariri from the detonation of a massive bomb as his motorcade drove past the St. Georges Hotel in downtown Beirut just before 1:00 p.m. that day.

Despite no longer being in office, Hariri attended a parliament meeting that morning and had no intentions of leaving politics—in fact, the morning of his death, he spoke to reporters at the Café de l'Etoile about the changes he was making to his parliamentary bloc list in the upcoming elections. Hariri had already aligned with the anti-Syrian opposition in Lebanon and was taking it a step further by dropping several pro-Syrian parliamentary members from his list.[9] His electoral chances and likelihood of becoming prime minister again after the next elections were strong and in fact, electoral changes were the topic of the parliamentary meeting scheduled for noon that day.

Hariri's motorcade included not only his private security but also four members of the state's Internal Security Forces occupying the lead vehicle. The motorcade was comprised of a Toyota Land Cruiser (the lead vehicle), Hariri's Mercedes (which he drove himself), and three other Mercedes filled with bodyguards. At the back of the motorcade was Hariri's medical team in what was essentially a private ambulance designed to be ready should Hariri ever come under attack.[10] On this day, the ambulance and medical teams' presence would prove fruitless as even the ambulance was impacted by the blast.

As the motorcade passed the St. Georges Hotel, a bomb exploded killing Hariri, eight members of his security detail, and injuring at least 226 others. The blast left a massive crater in the ground and reports of shattered glass a mile away. A professor of politics at the American University in Beirut, Farid Khazen, reportedly stated to journalist Nicholas Blanford, "It's the first major peacetime political assassination. This is as far as you can go when you target someone of Hariri's stature. This has broken taboos."[11]

Khazen's statement was prescient—Hariri's assassination led to the creation of the first ever international tribunal established to investigate and try those responsible for an assassination and/or an act of terrorism. Hariri's death also led to what is known as the Cedar Revolution in Lebanon. Within twenty-four hours after the bombing, many Lebanese took to the streets in anger over Hariri's killing with most of those protestors blaming Syria. Syrian workers in southern Lebanon were attacked with five injured before police were on the scene, and fires were set outside Syrian government buildings in Beirut. Syria publicly denied any involvement in the assassination, but few in Lebanon gave any credibility to the denials, particularly those on the anti-Syrian side of the political divide.

Hariri's funeral was held on Wednesday, February 16, with dignitaries from around the world flying into Lebanon to attend and pay their respects. Lebanon's president, Emile Lahoud, however, was advised by Hariri supporters not to attend in light of the widespread belief that Syria was behind the assassination. The pro-Syrian president heeded their advice and did not attend Hariri's funeral. An estimated 200,000 Lebanese took to the streets, following the ambulance that carried Hariri's body to the Mohammed al-Amin Mosque in Beirut where he was laid to rest. Anti-Syrian chants, photos of Hariri, and tears were prevalent among the marchers. The crowd, the largest on the streets of Lebanon since the Mass by Pope John Paul II in 1997, was composed of Sunnis, Shiites, Christians, and Druze—church bells rang loudly as did the calls for Islamic prayers.[12]

Public demands continued for the withdrawal of the 15,000 or so Syrian troops occupying the country, which had been mandated by UN Security Council Resolution 1559 passed in September 2004. The Lebanese government collapsed in the wake of the people's demands that Syrian influence be ousted from Lebanese affairs. This popular movement, also known as the Cedar Revolution, called for the removal of all Syrian troops, the resignation of Lebanese intelligence officials, a new neutral government, and an international investigation into Hariri's killing.

However, popular divisions soon became apparent with the organizing and holding of a rally on March 8 backed by Hezbollah and pro-Syrian factions, during which Hezbollah's leader, Hassan Nasrallah, called for a strengthening of Lebanese-Syrian ties. In response, the anti-Syrian factions, which included Sunni, Druze, and Maronite leaders, organized and held a rally on March 14 in which they reiterated their demands for Syria troop withdrawal, a new government, and an investigation into the assassination. In the decade that followed, Lebanese politics was drawn largely along these lines—the March 8 coalition versus the March 14 coalition—and Hariri's son, Saad, took up the mantle of his father's politics and himself became prime minister of Lebanon in 2009 and again in 2016. The nuances of Lebanese politics are vastly more complicated than one coalition versus another or the role of the son of the martyred Rafik Hariri, but the politics of Lebanon were and may continue to be framed around his assassination and legacy.[13]

Other assassinations followed Hariri's, including a former leader of the Lebanese Communist Party, George Hawi, who was killed by a car bomb in Beirut on June 21, 2005. Pierre Gemayel, Lebanon's industry minister and anti-Syrian Christian politician, was shot and killed in his car on November 21, 2006.[14] Following a United Nations investigation (the International Independent Investigation Commission established by UN Security Council Resolution 1595), the Special Tribunal for Lebanon (STL) was created in 2007 via UN Security Council Resolution 1757 to prosecute those responsible for Hariri's killing and any other related assassinations that occurred in Lebanon through December 2005. Four individuals with links to Hezbollah were tried in absentia by the STL and on August 18, 2020 the STL announced a verdict in the case. Three defendants were found not guilty and one, Salim Jamil Ayyash, was found guilty of the killing of Hariri, as well as guilty in the attempted killing of the 226 people who were injured in the attack. The investigation found evidence of a network of assassins who coordinated in the attack, but did not find conclusive evidence that Hezbollah or the Syrian government had any involvement in Hariri's assassination.[15]

The assassination of Rafik Hariri reverberated across Lebanon for years after his death, had a direct impact on politics within the small Mediterranean state, and potentially leaves a legacy within international law on how to hold terrorist perpetrators accountable. Immediate violence occurred on a micro-level toward Syrians within Lebanon, but none rose to the level of brutality against the Sikh community in India after the assassination of Indira Gandhi discussed in the previous chapter.

Yet, the long-term impact of Hariri's assassination is significant and political violence continues in Lebanon. Saad Hariri resigned as prime minister in October 2019 in response to public protests calling for a new government, but is still an influential figure in Lebanese society. On June 17, 2020, while traveling back to Beirut after a visit to the Bekaa Valley, a missile reportedly landed near his convoy. No injuries were reported and the missile did not strike close enough to pose a threat to Hariri or those accompanying him. As of July 2020, an investigation is underway, but it appears he may have been targeted for assassination.[16]

Since 2005, as many as twelve successful terrorist assassinations have occurred in Lebanon with numerous other bombings and acts of political violence. Despite the upheaval, the Polity index score is consistently 6 for Lebanon (since 2005), and the average PTS score has ranged from 3.0 to 2.5 (since 2005). Prior to 2005, the Polity score was -66, signifying the foreign troop occupation by Syria and the average PTS score ranged from 2 to 4, which includes the civil war years.

Rafik Hariri was an extremely prominent individual, both within Lebanon and internationally. He was perceived by many Western leaders as a moderate who would continue to lead Lebanon toward stability. He was hailed by many inside Lebanon as the one man capable of not only maintaining stability, but continuing to rebuild the country. Hariri's wealth and influence made it possible to rebuild Beirut after the damage from the civil war and he was beloved within the country for doing so. Lebanese politics were and are complicated, and Hariri's growing willingness to oppose Syrian influence in his country placed him in the proverbial crosshairs of the Syrian regime and its supporters. Despite the lack of evidence found by the STL, it is reasonable to assert that Hezbollah and Syrian involvement in Hariri's assassination was likely. Thus, it is also reasonable to question whether the STL's verdict resulted in true accountability for the perpetrators.

That said, Hariri's assassination is not the norm and most politicians who are targeted for assassination are local politicians or local political party leaders—not those with the international profile of Hariri. Targeting local politicians has the potential to influence state politics—whether to prevent elections from happening or to interfere with governmental processes and create chaos—by intimidating candidates, voters, and election officials. The Shining Path carried out such a campaign in Peru in October 1989.

PERU—THE SHINING PATH AND RED OCTOBER

Sendoro Luminoso or Shining Path waged a terror campaign against the Peruvian government for more than twenty years. Founded by a philosophy professor in 1970, the group's ideology was influenced by Maoism, and during its founding decade, the group built resources and slowly increased its membership using the public education and university system to indoctrinate and recruit members. Manuel Ruben Abimael Guzmán Reynosa used his position at the National University of Saint Christopher of Huamanga in Ayacucho to indoctrinate young minds and influence peasants in the area, establishing a stronghold for the Shining Path which lasted for decades.[17]

The campaign of terrorism began when the group declared war on the Peruvian government in April 1980 and carried out an attack on the electoral cycle by burning election ballots the following month.[18] Shining Path's long history of violence neither can be covered in detail here nor is it the intention. Rather, the focus lies solely on one deadly month—October 1989—referred to in some Peruvian newspapers as "Red October" and the first few weeks in November 1989 leading up to the municipal elections.

The Shining Path's terror campaign was brutal and long, stretching out over two decades. There were ebbs and flows to the violence, but October 1989 witnessed the killings of more than 100 local government officials and local candidates as part of an intimidation campaign aimed at interfering in the November elections. Peru was also hosting a meeting of foreign ministers from several Latin American states in early October, in advance of a meeting in Palpa on October 11 of regional leaders, which would include the presidents of Argentina, Brazil, Colombia, Mexico, Uruguay, and Venezuela. Thus, a spotlight shone on Peru in the fall of 1989 due to both its role as host of the regional meetings and its municipal elections.[19]

Local officials were targeted leading up to and during Red October and in fact, Tingo Maria in central Peru lost at least three mayors that year to assassins.[20] The third occurred in early October when Carlos Ojeda Candela was killed. Party affiliation did not seem to matter to the Shining Path with mayors and candidates on both the left and the right targeted. A vice presidential candidate at that time, Eduardo Orrego Villacorta of the Democratic Front Party referred to the spate of killings as a "genocide of mayors."[21] In fact, 1989 was the deadliest year in Peru for successful assassinations with 113 counted in this project. From 1977 through 2017, the GTD data indicates that the Shining Path carried out 643 successful assassinations with, for example, 82 successful assassinations in 1990, 65 in 1991, and 48 in 1992. The year 1990 is the only year that comes close to matching the frequency of the 1989 assassination campaign by the Shining Path.

Many of those targeted were not office holders but rather candidates on the electoral ballot in the upcoming November elections. Often, the perpetrators would break into the homes of political candidates in the middle of the night killing them, and sometimes their spouses, as they slept in their beds. On occasion, massive numbers of Shining Path militants would invade a village—locating anyone of authority from justices of the peace to politicians—and conduct "trials" in the village centers. These "trials" typically ended with the politician or justice of the peace being shot in the head.[22] Many attacks occurred in the Andean highlands, such as an attack on Ananea near the Bolivian border on October 10, in which the group killed the mayor, one other government official, and nine policemen. On this same day in El Agustino near Lima, a local council candidate from the Aprista party was assassinated.[23]

In early October, militants bombed a lunch counter in Lima and shot to death Flavio Llerena, a deputy administrator in Huancayo.[24] On a mid-October day when the third mayor of Tingo Maria was killed, eleven others were killed in the village of Huayllay, and a five-year-old boy was killed when perpetrators tossed a bomb at an election office. Local officials and candidates started to resign at this point and over sixty people had reportedly been killed in the preceding weeks.[25]

By October 24, a state of emergency was declared in Lima for the second time in six months. The Shining Path called for strikes in some areas of the country, which led to clashes between police forces and striking workers. The group intercepted buses and after forcing all the passengers to disembark, set the buses ablaze.[26] Both the Soviet and Chinese embassies were bombed—a car bomb outside the Chinese embassy and some other incendiary device outside the Soviet embassy. A car bomb exploded outside a Peruvian government building in downtown Lima with another found and deactivated near a church in Miraflores.[27]

On Monday, October 30, a police commander with Interpol was shot while driving his daughter to school. Their vehicle was intercepted by militants who tossed a bomb under the car before opening fire. Luckily, his daughter was not hurt, but the commander was killed. A police officer was shot and killed in a separate incident on the same day, and the previous evening, eight dogs were killed and hung from lampposts across Lima with threatening notes attached to the bodies—"Death to Gorbachev and Deng Xiaoping."[28]

By the end of October, an estimated 123 mayors, local officials, candidates, and politicians had been assassinated in 1989 alone, with more than 400 resignations from office or withdrawal from the elections. This project counts twenty-three successful assassinations in Peru for the month of October 1989—slightly more than 20 percent of the total assassinations for that year. For the month of November, the assassination count dropped to nine which is slightly less than 8 percent of the year's total. A survey of the public at the time indicated that terrorism was understandably the greatest concern in Peruvian society and it was believed that the disruptions to the November municipal elections were a precursor to the presidential elections scheduled for April 1990.[29]

Despite another call by the Shining Path for a strike in early November, thousands defied the group and marched through Lima chanting pro-democracy slogans. The group always threatened retaliation if people failed to heed the call for a strike, but on this day an estimated 10,000 people gathered in a march organized by multiple political parties proclaiming "We love Peru," "Terrorism will not pass," and "Say yes to democracy."[30]

However, this did not deter the Shining Path from continuing the violence, and on the days leading up to the municipal elections on November 12, the group engaged in multiple destructive acts, particularly in the Andean highlands. On Thursday evening, November 9, militants broke into the home of Juan Guzman, a former election board president in Ayacucho, shooting and killing both his wife and his sister before setting fire to the home. Guzman was not home at the time. The director of a government development agency was not home either when his home was broken into with the same tragic result—the killing of his wife and the burning of their home.

On Friday, November 10, assassinations of town council candidates occurred in both Huanta and Palca, with an election board official killed in Palca as well. A total of seven were shot and killed as part of the preelection terror campaign, which included blowing up power lines, attacking civilians and troops in hopes of hindering the vote.[31] The Shining Path militants stopped civilians as they were traveling and confiscated any identification documents required for voting, while also threatening to cut off the fingers of anyone who dared to cast a ballot.[32] In Peru, voting is compulsory and thus voters faced a tough situation when threatened with violence. The usual practice of dipping voter's finger in ink after voting was suspended in the highlands as not to signal to the militants if someone had, in fact, voted.

In Lima, the election saw long lines and authorities held the polls open two additional hours to accommodate the long lines. However, the situation in the rural locations was markedly different. An estimated twenty explosions occurred on election day and among those bombed was a church and a school in Huancayo.[33] In the Shining Path stronghold of Ayacucho, slightly more than 68 percent of the ballots cast were blank and in an estimated 80 municipalities, there were no candidates listed on the ballot. In Azangaro, a mayoral candidate was shot and killed and the morning after the elections, the homes of several polling station workers in Ayacucho were broken into—the workers were shot and killed. In the central highlands, some forty-one electrical towers were bombed leaving many, including polling stations, without power.[34]

By the end of 1989, the GTD estimates that the Shining Path carried out over 500 acts of terrorism from assassinations to bombings to armed assaults. This group was responsible for the majority, by far, of all terrorist attacks in Peru that year but other groups were also active, particularly the Tupac Amaru Revolutionary Movement—responsible for an estimated forty-eight attacks during 1989. The presidential elections in April 1990 were marred by violence with four congressional candidates assassinated and bombings of multiple locations, such as political party offices, banks, government offices, and hotels. The results of the election ushered in the era of Alberto Fujimori, an independent politician who formed a new party and is now known for his conviction on corruption charges and human rights abuses. Fujimori went on to win in 1990, surprising many by soundly defeating Mario Vargas Llosa of the Democratic Front Party in a runoff election.[35]

In the decade that followed, the violence resulted in approximately 69,000 deaths and likely more than 7,000 disappearances, according to a report by Peru's Truth and Reconciliation Commission. The Shining Path is attributed, officially, with over half of the death and violence. The Shining Path's founder was eventually captured in 1992 and the conflict ended in 2000. Although the group continues to exist under new leadership, it cannot match the influence it yielded in the 1980s and 1990s. The conflict in Peru wreaked havoc in many parts of the country, highlighting existing racial as well as economic divisions. The violence seemingly touched all corners of society, leaving many wounds in need of healing. Luckily, the sort of violence perpetrated by both the Shining Path and governmental forces (attributed with 37% of the violence) in the 1980s and 1990s is no longer prevalent.

With hopes for reconciliation within society and the healing of old wounds from decades of death and destruction, 2018 was declared the Year of National Dialogue and Reconciliation in Peru. Other efforts have been made, such as a museum in Lima which opened in 2015 dedicated to victims of the conflict. Yet, visits to the museum are reportedly low and many in Peru simply wish to forget those violent decades.[36] Forgetting may prove easier with the improved economic and political conditions in the country—poverty rates have declined and government repression has declined from high PTS scores in the 1980s and early 1990s of 5 to an average score as low as 2 by 2017. Significant improvements in democratic institutions have occurred as well with a Polity score swing from 1 in the 1990s to 9 in 2017. Overall, societal and political stability in Peru has improved dramatically since the twenty years of the Shining Path's reign of terror.

SURVIVAL ANALYSIS MODELS—
TARGETS AND POLITICAL CHANGE

Anecdotally these cases provide evidence of assassinations as one influential component in wider campaigns of violence. The Hariri assassination in Lebanon was followed by the Cedar Revolution and additional assassinations while Red October in Peru was followed by additional assassinations, continued violence, and a serious disruption to the municipal elections in the rural areas of the country. The question here is the same as posed in the previous chapter: Do these particular assassinations lead to significant change, or any change at all, in political institutions? The theory is the same as well in that the victim type matters to the likelihood of institutional change after an assassination. The hypothesis is as follows:

H5: The likelihood of political institutional change after a terrorist assassination will vary across subtypes of politically active individuals.

Cox shared frailty models are utilized to test for the likelihood of Polity score change in the aftermath of a successful assassination of either a politician or a political party member. As a reminder, these models determine the risk of failure for each state after experiencing an assassination event, assume a gamma frailty with unknown variance, and examine the risk of failure by regime type. The authoritarian, mixed, and tumultuous regime types are measured against democracies (see table 6.1).

For the politically active category models, the explanatory variables included are population, employment rate, and infant mortality rate. These variables are logged with population performing best when interacted with the time variable (day). One difference here is that the employment rate variable improved the political party member model but not the politicians' model. The PH violations were less robust for the logged variables of population and employment in the political party member model, but the other variables performed well and nearly all were significant in the model.

Hazard ratios are different in each category, but there are obvious trends. Across the two models, tumultuous regimes exhibit the greatest hazard ratios and authoritarian regimes have the lowest hazard ratios of the three regime types, compared to democracies. In the politicians' model, the authoritarian regime hazard ratio is greater than in the political party members model, and the same is true for both mixed and tumultuous regimes. Thus, these models suggest that the assassination of a politician presents a greater hazard

Table 6.1   Politically Active by Regime Type, 1977–2017

	Shared Frailty Models—Political Institutional Changes *Gamma Frailty/Efron Method*					
	Politicians			**Political Party Members**		
	Coefficient *(SE)*	*Hazard* *Ratio* *(SE)*	*p Values*	*Coefficient* *(SE)*	*Hazard* *Ratio* *(SE)*	*p* *Values*
Authoritarian	3.10 (.21)	21.52 (4.50)	.001	2.95 (.22)	19.06 (4.10)	.001
Mixed	3.26 (.15)	26.08 (3.85)	.001	3.22 (.15)	25.02 (3.70)	.001
Tumultuous	5.38 (.23)	217.03 (49.53)	.001	5.20 (.23)	180.75 (42.24)	.001
Population (logged)	-.01 (.17)	.99 (.16)	.953	-2.04 (.55)	.13 (.07)	.001
Infant Mortality Rate (logged)	-.18 (.04)	.83 (.03)	.001	-.16 (.04)	.85 (.04)	.001
Employment (logged)				1.90 (.49)	6.70 (3.31)	.001
Event Date (logged)	.89 (.32)	2.44 (.79)	.005	.71 (.36)	2.04 (.74)	.050
Population (logged) x Event Date	-.01 (8.40)	.99 (8.40)	.002	-.01 (9.30)	.99 (9.30)	.006
N Failures	600			585		
N Observations	157,651			156,066		
N Groups	136			136		

Source: Polity, GTD & Penn, 1977–2017.

to all three regime types than the assassination of influential political party members.

The log of population is statistically significant in the political party members' model, but not in the politicians' model. Otherwise, all variable are statistically significant in a two-tailed test in both models. The negatively signed coefficient for the logs of population and infant mortality rate and hazard ratios of less than 1 indicates a decreasing hazard risk per unit change, which is consistent across both models. As population increases, it is expected that the hazard of experiencing a Polity change will decrease, but in the politicians' model the hazard ratio is so close to 1.00 than little change is expected (and this is again, not statistically significant). The measure of infant mortality rate also indicates a decreasing hazard for Polity change with negatively signed coefficients and hazard ratios below one.

In the political party members' model, the employment variable is statistically significant and suggests a remarkable hazard ratio of 6.70 with a positively signed coefficient. Thus, as population increases, it is expected that the likelihood of experiencing a Polity change will also increase.

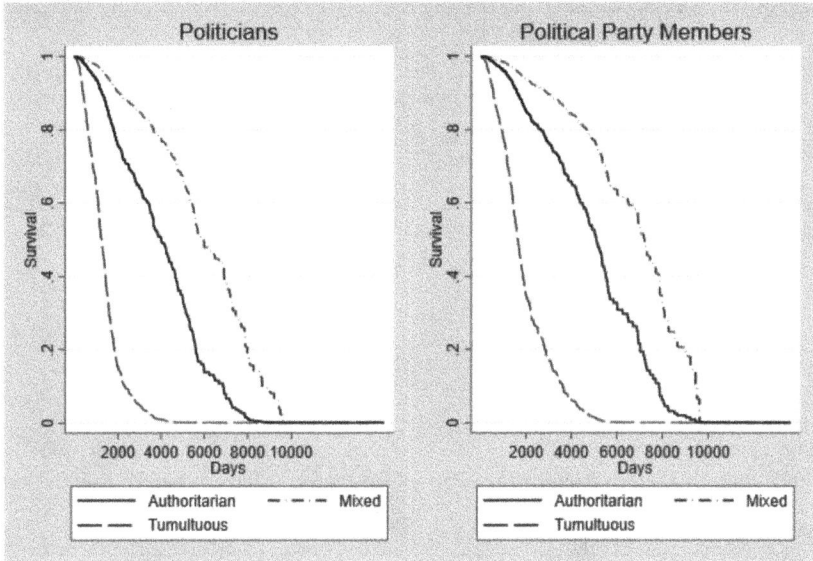

Figure 6.1 Survival Curves—Regimes and the Politically Active, 1977–2017.

These models support the theory that terrorist assassinations of politicians and political party members have differing effects on political stability across regimes. Figure 6.1 provides a comparison of the survival curves from the models discussed above. These curves suggest the likelihood of survival for each regime type after experiencing an assassination of the select target type. Survival indicates the time to a Polity score change and figure 6.1 highlights the difference, however slight, in survival curves for regimes in the aftermath of terrorist assassinations of the politically active. Mixed regimes reach a .8 survival rate around the 4,000-day mark after the killing of a politician, but do not reach .8 after the killing of political party members until closer to the 5,000-day mark. Tumultuous regimes also hit the 0 rate sooner in the politicians' model—on the 4,000-day mark—while in the political party model, tumultuous regimes do not hit 0 until approximately the 5,000-day mark. The same is true for authoritarian regimes, which reach the 0 survival rate at the 8,000-day mark in the politicians' model, but not until around the 9,000-day mark in the political party members' model. Here, the survival curves highlight that hazard ratios are point estimates and thus we see some differentiation between hazard ratios and survival curves. However, the support for the theory that the likelihood of change to political institutions in the aftermath of terrorist assassinations varies according to target type remains solid.

Table 6.2   Politically Active—Negative Polity Shifts by Regime Type, 1977–2017

	Shared Frailty Models—Political Institutional Changes Gamma Frailty/Efron Method					
	Politicians			**Political Party Members**		
	Coefficient (SE)	*Hazard Ratio (SE)*	*p Values*	*Coefficient (SE)*	*Hazard Ratio (SE)*	*p Values*
Authoritarian	4.68	107.40	.001	4.79	120.06	.001
	(.42)	(45.10)		(.43)	(51.91)	
Mixed	3.88	40.47	.001	3.85	46.99	.001
	(.35)	(16.95)		(.35)	(16.57)	
Tumultuous	5.87	354.18	.001	5.98	395.76	.001
	(.47)	(166.26)		(.48)	(190.72)	
Population (logged)	-2.35	.10	.003	-2.22	.11	.006
	(.79)	(.08)		(.81)	(.09)	
Infant Mortality Rate (logged)	-.27	.76	.001	-.25	.78	.001
	(.07)	(.05)		(.07)	(.06)	
Employment (logged)	1.95	7.06	.005	1.91	6.73	.008
	(.70)	(4.94)		(.72)	(4.86)	
Event Date (logged)	.71	2.04	.291	.97	2.63	.173
	(.67)	(1.37)		(.71)	(1.86)	
Population (logged) x Event Date	-.01	.99	.431	-.01	.99	.299
	(.01)	(.01)		(.01)	(.01)	
N Failures	157			154		
N Observations	157,103			156,066		
N Groups	136			136		

Source: Polity, GTD & Penn, 1977–2017.

As in the previous chapter, to further test the overarching theory that targets matter, models for directional Polity shifts after the assassinations of politicians and political party members are presented in tables 6.2 and 6.3. The hypotheses for directional Polity shifts are as follows:

H6: Negative political institutional changes are more likely in authoritarian regimes than in mixed or democratic regimes in the aftermath of terrorist assassinations of politically active individuals.

H7: Positive political institutional changes are more likely in mixed regimes than in authoritarian regimes in the aftermath of terrorist assassinations of politically active individuals.

Negative Institutional Shifts

Table 6.2 provides the results of testing for negative Polity shifts. Evidence supports the hypothesis that authoritarian regimes are at greater risk for a negative Polity change after the assassination of politically active individuals than are mixed regimes. And results indicate that the risk is even greater after

Table 6.3   Politically Active—Positive Polity Shifts by Regime Type, 1977–2017

| | *Shared Frailty Models—Political Institutional Changes Gamma Frailty/Efron Method* | | | | | |
| | **Politicians** | | | **Political Party Members** | | |
	Coefficient (SE)	*Hazard Ratio (SE)*	*p Values*	*Coefficient (SE)*	*Hazard Ratio (SE)*	*p Values*
Authoritarian	2.04 (.29)	7.67 (2.26)	.001	2.01 (.29)	7.49 (2.20)	.001
Mixed	3.15 (.18)	23.36 (4.10)	.001	3.13 (.18)	22.96 (4.03)	.001
Tumultuous	-.24 (1.15)	.79 (.91)	.837	-.28 (1.15)	.75 (.87)	.806
Population (logged)	.16 (.21)	1.18 (.24)	.423	.15 (.21)	1.16 (.24)	.471
Infant Mortality Rate (logged)	-.15 (.06)	.86 (.05)	.008	-.15 (.06)	.86 (.05)	.007
Event Date (logged)	1.83 (.42)	6.22 (2.62)	.001	1.64 (.43)	5.13 (2.20)	.001
Population (logged) x Event Date	-.01 (.01)	.99 (.01)	.01	-.01 (.01)	.99 (.01)	.001
N Failures	331			331		
N Observations	157,651			156,306		
N Groups	136			136		

Source: Polity, GTD & Penn, 1977–2017.

the killing of an influential political party member than after the killing of a politician. The likelihood of a negative Polity shift in an authoritarian regime after a politician is killed is 10,640 percent while the assassination of an influential political party member poses a risk of 11,906 percent. These models, unfortunately, do indicate possible PH violations for the authoritarian variable which weakens this result somewhat. However, the remaining variables do not violate the PH assumption and most of the variables are statistically significant. Importantly, the regime variables are strong with p values of .001.

The explanatory variables perform similarly to the models for likelihood of institutional change and both negative shifts models perform better with the employment variable included. It too performs much as it did in the institutional change model and remains statistically significant across both models.

Figure 6.2 presents survival curves from the negative shifts' models and as with the previous models, there are similarities. The curve for mixed regimes is relatively stable and in neither model does it fall sharply below the .8 survival rate throughout the 12,000 days of the data. Thus, negative Polity shifts after an assassination of either politicians or political party members is less

Regime Survival Curves -- Negative Polity Shifts, 1977-2017

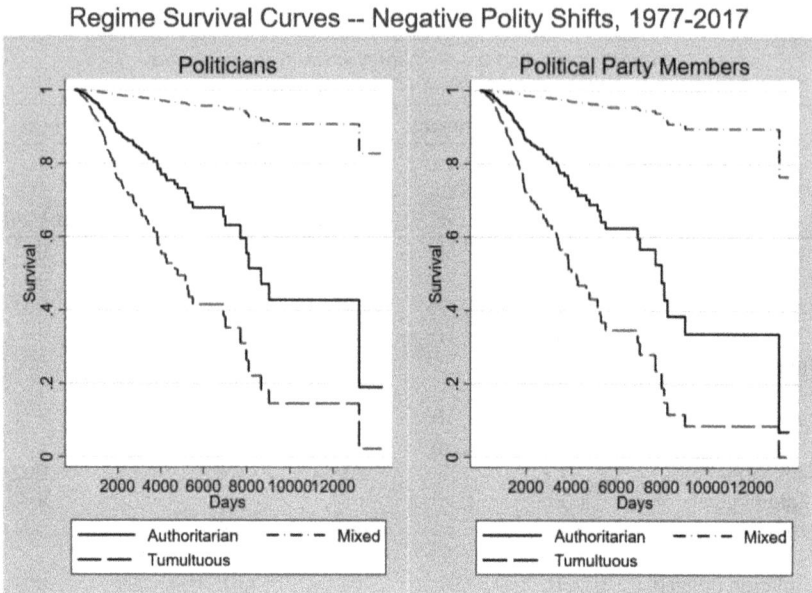

Figure 6.2   Survival Curves—Negative Regime Shifts, 1977–2017.

likely than for authoritarian regimes, but is still more likely than in democratic regimes. The trajectory of the authoritarian survival curve is similar across the two second-level categories, but the decline is slower in the politicians' model than in the political party members' model.

Positive Institutional Shifts

Table 6.3 presents results of testing for the likelihood of positive Polity shifts after the assassinations of politicians and influential political party members. Support is found for the hypothesis that mixed regimes are more likely to experience positive change after these assassinations than are authoritarian regimes. After the assassination of a politician, mixed regimes are 2,236 percent more likely to experience a positive change when compared to a democracy and after the assassination of a political party member, a mixed regime is 2,196 percent more likely to experience a positive Polity shift.

Authoritarian regimes are 757 percent more likely to experience a positive change (compared to a democracy) in the politicians' model and 739 percent more likely in the political party members' model. Neither model exhibits any violations of the PH assumption and the regime variables across both models are statistically significant. As a reminder, few moves were coded for

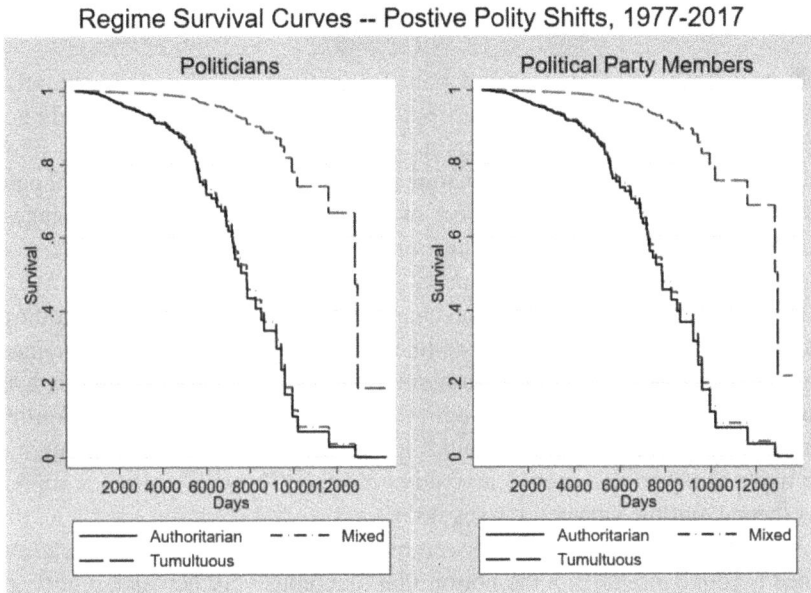

Figure 6.3   Survival Curves—Positive Regime Shifts, 1977–2017.

the tumultuous regimes and thus no extrapolations on tumultuous regimes are considered here. Statistical significance is an issue with the population variable, but the others remain strong, and the model performed better with population included. Employment, however, did not improve model performance and thus is not included here.

Figure 6.3 presents survival curves of the positive Polity shift models and the similarities across the second-level categories are striking. In both the politicians' and political party members' models, the authoritarian and mixed regimes survival curves track one another closely. In these models, the tumultuous regimes have the longer survival curves and although no sound assertions can be made on the directional shifts of tumultuous regimes, the result is nonetheless interesting.[37] Unlike the other models, it does not appear that the second-level target type alters the likelihood of positive Polity change. The political party members' curve is nearly identical to the survival curve in the politicians' model. Thus, despite the notable difference in estimated hazard ratios for mixed and authoritarian regimes in the likelihood of positive institutional change after an assassination of politically active individuals, the survival curves do not reflect a clear difference between the two. Therefore, results in this target category for the hypothesis that mixed regimes are more likely to experience positive Polity changes are mixed.[38]

CONCLUSION

The analyses of the likelihood of political institutional change in the aftermath of the terrorist assassinations of politically active individuals yield interesting results. Across all three regime types, Polity changes are more likely after the killing of politicians than after the killing of influential political party members. The hazard, or likelihood, of some political institutional change is greater across all three regime types after the assassination of a politician as opposed to a prominent political party member.

In the examination of directional change, evidence supports the hypothesis that authoritarian regimes are more likely than mixed regimes to experience a negative Polity shift after an assassination, and a negative change is even more likely for the authoritarian regime if the target of the attack is a political party member. Less support is found for the hypothesis that mixed regimes are more likely to experience a positive change. The risk estimates support this theory, but the survival curves do not.

As with the examination of government officials in chapter 5, clear evidence is found supporting the notion that outcomes vary across target types. The case studies provide insight into the practical repercussions of these terroristic acts. The Hariri assassination had a significant and direct impact on Lebanese politics for at least a decade after his death with the formation of the March 8 and March 14 coalitions, as well as the impact on international law brought about by the formation of the STL. Despite the passage in September 2004 of UN Security Council Resolution 1559 calling for all foreign troops to withdraw, Syrian troops did not leave Lebanon until public outrage over Hariri's death led to the Cedar Revolution.

The Shining Path waged a terrorist campaign for two decades in Peru and its strategic targeting of local government officials and political candidates in late 1989 proved semi-effective. Over 100 individuals were assassinated and estimates are that more than 400 resigned or withdrew from various local council races. Many voters were afraid to vote in the municipal elections in November 1989 resulting in blank ballots and in some cases, there were no candidates on the ballot for which to place a vote. Yet, the Shining Path did not succeed in preventing elections—either in November 1989 or April 1990—from taking place and the uptick in violence caused many citizens to defy the group and take to the streets in support of democracy in Peru.

Both the qualitative and quantitative data presented suggest that target type does matter to post-terrorist assassination outcomes and evidence suggests that after these assassinations, the direction of political institutional change varies by regime type.

Chapter 7

Law Enforcement

It is accepted and understood that members of law enforcement face dangerous situations on a routine basis, especially for those wearing police uniforms and/or working on the streets. Law enforcement personnel with behind-the-scenes roles, such as judges, attorneys, and court personnel, do not typically expect that their lives are at risk simply for doing their jobs. Yet police officers, security forces, judges, and prosecutors are all at risk of assassination if a perpetrator decides that a goal will be achieved or at least furthered by their deaths. From 1977 through 2017, 2,246 law enforcement personnel were assassinated as part of terror campaigns around the world—288 judges, attorneys, or court personnel and 1,900 police security forces, along with 58 police patrol officers.

To be counted as an assassination for this project, police officers killed in bomb attacks or armed assaults were not included unless clear evidence existed that the officer was specifically targeted and/or there are expectations that the targeted officer had the ability to exert influence of some kind beyond that of a rank-and-file police officer. Thus, the killings of 58 police patrol personnel qualify here as assassinations, along with the 1,900 police security officers. Before cleansing the data, the GTD counts 61 police patrol officers and 1,935 police security officers as targets of successful assassination over the forty years under study, as well as 294 judges, attorneys, or court personnel. As a reminder, the definitional criteria for assassination require that the killing be political in nature and that the target is selected due to their role and influence in public life.

An example of an assassination included in this dataset is that of Egyptian prosecutor general Hisham Barakat, who was killed by a car bomb in Cairo in June 2015. The bomb was placed under a parked car, exploding as Baraket left for his office and killing three nearby civilians, shattering windows, and setting fire to trees. Barakat, the most senior figure in Egypt targeted since 2013, was taken to the hospital where he underwent surgery, succumbing to his injuries later.[1]

Interestingly, three claims of credit were made after the assassination—the Popular Resistance Movement (Egypt), the Sinai Province of the Islamic State, and the Muslim Brotherhood all reportedly claimed to have perpetrated the attack (although some reports indicated that the Muslim Brotherhood did not make any public claims). The Sinai Province of the Islamic State, had in fact, called for the targeting of the judiciary in retaliation for the execution by hanging of six militants. After the 2013 ousting of President Mohammad Morsi, Barakat, as the chief public prosecutor, reportedly sentenced hundreds of Islamists to life imprisonment or death as part of the crackdown on Morsi's Muslim Brotherhood party and thus seemed a likely retaliatory target.[2]

In June 2017, thirty individuals were convicted in an Egyptian court of being involved in Barakat's killing with the government officially blaming the Muslim Brotherhood. However, questions arise over the convictions— those who confessed on video later recanted claiming they were tortured and forced to confess. Nine of those convicted were executed in February 2019 and the government continues to blame the Muslim Brotherhood along with Hamas-linked militants for the assassination.[3]

Terror groups are not always forthright about the attacks they perpetrate. Kearns, Conlon, and Young[4] address the question of why groups would falsely claim, blame others, or simply not admit to terror attacks arguing that groups may be less likely to claim credit for attacks when public "credit" is not necessary for goal achievement. When the government or the public is unlikely to retaliate against the terror group for an attack, a group is more likely to claim credit and thus, if, as in the case of Egypt, government backlash is to be expected the perpetrators may be less likely to claim credit and/ or to place false blame on another group. Therefore, despite the convictions and executions, it is difficult to ascertain the true perpetrators of Barakat's assassination.

Police security forces are often targeted, such as the killing of Ghassan Ajaj in Lebanon in January 2015. Ajaj, head of the information branch of the police forces, was shot and killed with no group claiming responsibility.[5] In Mexico, an attempt was made on the life of Mexico City's police chief in June 2020 resulting in the death of two of his bodyguards and an innocent bystander. The chief, Omar Garcia Harfuch, was shot multiple times but survived his injuries. The Jalisco New Generation cartel is believed to be behind the attack, which occurred after the assassination of a federal judge and his wife earlier in June.[6]

Attacks on police security personnel occurred most often in the states of Colombia, Spain, Peru, Iraq, Afghanistan, and Pakistan from 1977 through

2017. The group attributed with the most attacks on security forces in these forty years is the Basque Fatherland and Freedom (ETA) group in Spain (146 successful assassinations) with the Shining Path in Peru attributed with the second-greatest number at 118. The Taliban in Afghanistan is the group attributed with the greatest number of successful assassinations of judges and attorneys with the most attacks, by state, occurring in Colombia, Afghanistan, Iraq, and Peru.

SECOND-LEVEL CATEGORIES OF LAW ENFORCEMENT

This chapter follows the format of the previous ones, analyzing two second-level categories and testing for the likelihood of both institutional shifts (Polity changes) and the direction of said shifts. The two second-level categories are *judges/attorneys/court personnel* and *police security forces*. With only fifty-eight *police personnel* assassinated, the analyses here will focus on the larger categories. Qualitative case studies include the assassinations of judges Aza Gazgireeva and Eduard Chuvashov in Russia and that of Joseba Pagazaurtundua, a police chief in Spain.

RUSSIA—DEPUTY CHIEF JUSTICE AZA GAZGIREEVA AND JUDGE EDUARD CHUVASHOV

As anyone who follows international affairs is aware, the Russian Federation and political murder are not strangers. The deaths of Russian dissident Alexander Litvinenko in London or the journalist Anna Politkovskya made international headlines with most observers positing that elements in the government were responsible for the deaths. However worthy of investigation, those likely government-sponsored killings are of a different nature than the terrorist assassinations examined in this book. Lesser publicized assassinations, such as that of the judges discussed here, occur with some frequency in Russia. In fact, thirty-eight government personnel, thirty-four police security officers, fifteen politicians, and ten religious figures were assassinated in Russia as part of terror campaigns during the years from 1977 through 2017.

In 2009, a string of attacks on law enforcement occurred in the Chechnyan region targeting those involved in prosecuting or arresting militants involved in terror acts. Deputy Chief Justice Aza Gazgireeva of the Ingushetia Supreme Court was the third of six attempted assassinations during the first half of 2009. Gazgireeva was shot and killed in Nazran after dropping her children at school on the morning of June 10, 2009. The van she was riding in was attacked near the kindergarten school—five people were wounded, including a one-year-old girl, and Gazgireeva was rushed to the hospital where she later died. Gazgireeva was an adviser in newly established corruption investigations, but she also oversaw an investigation of an attack on police forces in 2004 carried out by Chechen militants. The widely held belief by Russian investigators was that she was targeted by the militants in retaliation for the investigation and in fact, the Caucasus Emirate group did claim responsibility for her death.[7]

Five days before Gazgireeva's killing, Dagestan's top law enforcement official, Interior Minister Adilgerei Magomedtagirov, was shot and killed while attending a wedding. The violence prompted a surprise visit to Dagestan on June 9 by then-president Dimitry Medvedev who called for order and for ridding the region of terrorists. During his visit, he also noted that low quality of life, including high unemployment and low living standards, were root causes of terrorism and must be addressed.[8]

The presidential visit, somewhat unusual in the more autonomous Chechnyan region, did little to curb the violence. Gazgireeva was killed the following day on June 10 and on June 13, Bashir Aushev was shot and killed outside his home in Nazran. Aushev was a former deputy prime minister in charge of police agencies. On June 22, Regional President Yunus-Bek Yevkurov's convoy was hit by a suicide bomber. Yevkurov was wounded, along with three of his bodyguards, but all survived the attack. Construction Minister Ruslan Amerkhanov was also shot and killed on August 12.[9] Chechnya, however, is not the only Russian region that experiences terrorist assassinations.

In Moscow, Judge Eduard Chuvashov fell prey to an assassin on April 12, 2010 in the stairwell of his apartment building. Chuvashov was shot twice and killed it seemed by a professional killer—reports were that a silencer was used and no shell casings were left behind. Surveillance footage showed a man, around thirty years old, leaving the building shortly after the shooting.[10] Suspects, members of the Combat Organization of Russian Nationalists (aka BORN), would later be arrested in 2012 and 2013. The first two suspects were arrested in June 2012 with another arrested in Serbia in 2013. Serbia extradited Ilya Goryachev to Moscow in November 2013 for trial, who was sentenced to life in prison in 2015 for ordering a total of five killings throughout Russia.[11]

In 2015, Vyacheslav Isayev and Maxim Baklagin were sentenced to life in prison for the killings of Chuvashov, several leaders of anti-fascist movements, and lawyer Stanislav Markelov. Alexei Korshunov, determined to be the actual shooter of Judge Chuvashov, was a former Federal Security Service (FSB) officer who died in 2011 from injuries sustained when a grenade he was carrying exploded.[12] Korshunoy's background explains the characteristics of the assassination—using a silencer and no casings left behind are certainly trademarks of someone with FSB training.

On the day of his death, Judge Chuvashov was scheduled to hear a terrorism case and previously had given long prison sentences to teenage members of a neo-Nazi group known as the White Wolves. Chuvashov's colleagues believed that he was killed in retaliation for the high-profile hate crime cases that came before his court and their suspicions proved accurate. In all, the nationalist BORN group carried out at least ten assassinations of individuals, including Chuvashov, Markelov, a journalist, and three anti-fascist activists.

In the years preceding 2009, Russian political institutions were stable, if not democratic, with a Polity score of 0 dating back to 2001 and remaining 0 in the years after the 2009 and 2010 assassinations discussed above. State repression also remained consistent before and after with an average PTS score of 4. A disadvantage, however, of using national-level scores such as that of Polity and PTS is that it may not adequately reflect happenings in regions of the country, particularly regions with some autonomy such as Chechnya. Though the examination of a state, such as Russia in this case, may not prove as qualitatively fruitful as expected in studying the judge/prosecutor category, valuable insight is gained into motivational differences between the second-level target types. The motivational trend for judge and prosecutor assassinations from Barakat in Egypt to Gazgireeva in Chechnya to Chuvashov in Moscow is retaliation. In these three cases, the killings were motivated by previous prosecutions, long sentences, and/or executions of fellow militants.

In another example, a hostage-taking incident in Istanbul in March 2015 occurred when Devrimici Halk Kurtulus Cephesi took prosecutor Mehmet Selim Kiraz hostage in a courthouse. The group later claimed taking Kiraz hostage, who was killed when security forces breached the building, was in retaliation for Berkin Elvan's death in 2013.[13] Elvan was a fifteen-year-old boy who received a head injury when hit with a tear gas canister fired at close range by police. The boy reportedly was not part of the nearby Gezi Park demonstrations ongoing at the time and had simply left his home to buy a loaf of bread. The boy died after 269 days in a coma and on the day of his funeral, mass demonstrations occurred. Security forces once again used tear gas and water cannons on the crowds and injuries were reported.[14] Thus, while the death of Kiraz in Turkey is not an assassination, it does anecdotally support the theory that the motive of retaliation may play a significant role in the targeting of judges and prosecutors by terrorist organizations.

The motivations for attacks on police are less clear. In March 2017, Andrew Felix Kaweesi of the Ugandan Police Force in Kampala was shot and killed outside his home. Kaweesi was the assistant inspector general, but it is unclear why he was targeted. No group claimed responsibility although some attributed the attack to the Allied Democratic Forces. In Afghanistan on June 5, 2007, a senior investigator with the Afghan Police was shot while driving home from work outside Ghazni City. Ghulam Rasul, the investigator, was killed and although the Taliban claimed responsibility for the attack, the motivation is unclear.

The universe of these events, however, suggests that police forces are often killed in order to prevent investigations from moving forward, to deter government security forces from carrying out their duties, and/or due to the police's lack of support for the terror group's goals. The Basque Homeland and Freedom (ETA) group in Spain is perhaps the best case study for a sustained assassination campaign of police security forces. ETA is attributed with the killings of 146 police security personnel from 1977 through 2017, more than any other group in the database. One assassination in particular resulted in mass protests against the group in Vittoria, Spain: that of Andoain's police chief Joseba Pagazaurtundua, who was killed not in retaliation for any specific act, but rather because he did not support ETA's goals.

SPAIN—POLICE CHIEF JOSEBA PAGAZAURTUNDUA

The Basque region in Spain has long called for and at times fought for its independence. The now-semiautonomous region sits in the north of the country and shares common culture with the Basques in France just across the Pyrenees Mountains. ETA or Basque Homeland and Liberty group carried out a campaign of violence for decades in its plight for independence. ETA's roots can be traced as far back as 1894 to the Basque Nationalist Party. Although banned by Francisco Franco's fascist regime, the party operated underground and/or in exile until the late 1950s when some members lost patience with the party, leaving to form ETA. In the 1960s, the group split over ideology—part of the group still sought autonomy, but another part wanted independence with a Marxist-Leninist approach to governing. Beginning in the late 1960s, ETA began a campaign of terrorist violence with assassination as a key tactic.

ETA is responsible for at least 155 assassinations of law enforcement officials from 1977 through 2017. By far, the second-level category most often targeted was police security forces. Of the 155 assassinations carried out by ETA, 146 were aimed at security forces with 3 attacks on police officers (the remaining 6 were judges/attorneys). One of these successful assassinations occurred in 2003 in the small town of Andaoin in the Basque region.

Around 10:00 a.m. on the morning of February 8, 2003, local police chief Joseba Pagazaurtundua sat in a café enjoying breakfast when a man in a mask fired several shots at Pagazaurtundua before fleeing by car. The chief was taken to the hospital, but was soon declared dead. Blame immediately fell to ETA since Pagazaurtundua was a member of an anti-ETA group known as "Enough is Enough." Angel Acebes, Spain's interior minister, publicly blamed ETA and it was reported that the chief's name had been mentioned as a viable target by ETA and other Basque independence groups in radio transmissions in the past because his views did not comport with ETA's ideology. Thus, ETA seemed the logical perpetrator.[15]

The general public blamed ETA and on the day after Pagazaurtundua's assassination, thousands took to the streets of Andaoin in an anti-ETA protest.[16] However, the mayor and at least three council members did not participate and did not condemn the assassination. The political wing of ETA, known as the Batasuna party, governed Andaoin at the time and thus, Pagazaurtundua's support of the anti-ETA peace movement likely did not sit well with some local officials. Though the victim was a police chief of a small village in the Basque region, his killing garnered national attention and a moment of silence was held throughout Spain in his memory on February 10.[17]

Joseba's younger sister, Maite Pagazaurtundua, became active in politics, speaking out against terrorism and in support of social justice. Her public role made her a target as well, and she lived for thirteen years with constant police protection. She moved with her family out of the Basque region and continued to be active in politics. She became the president of the Victims of Terrorism Foundation in Spain and now serves as a member of Europe's parliament, continuing to work on terrorism-related policies.[18]

When ETA denounced its previous violent ways and announced its intent to disband its militarized structure, a process that seemingly began in 2013, many loved ones of ETA's victims were less than forgiving and less than convinced.[19] Maite Pagazaurtundua, in 2018, was one of the family members of ETA's many victims who spoke out, expressing doubt about ETA's true intentions. Regarding the announcement, she stated, "They have always had violence and lies. They have removed the violence but not the lies."[20]

The killings of police forces in Spain are too numerous for full coverage in this text but suffice to say that ETA's assassination campaign and other terror acts wreaked havoc on daily life in parts of Spain for decades. Assassinations occurred in Barcelona, Bilbao, Madrid, Vitoria, San Sebastian, Durango, and numerous other cities. The attacks were more frequent in the late 1970s and early 1980s in Spain, but began a notable decline into the 1990s. Various cessations of violence were called over the years and the last law enforcement assassination in Spain (at least through 2017) occurred in Arrigorriaga in June 2009. Another police chief was killed when a bomb exploded his car as he left for work that morning. ETA claimed responsibility for the attack.

Despite the violence and the sustained terror campaign, Spain maintains strong democratic institutions and consistently receives a Polity score of 10 (i.e., a fully consolidated democracy). The government engages in only minor repression, scoring 1.5 to 2 on the averaged PTS scale consistently. Thus, the violence brought by ETA and other groups for decades in Spain has not affected its ability to maintain political institutional stability.

SURVIVAL ANALYSIS MODELS—
TARGETS AND POLITICAL CHANGE

The question here is the same as posed in the previous chapters and furthers the intent of this book in addressing the question of whether particular assassinations lead to varying changes, or any change at all, in political institutions. The overarching theory remains the same as well—the type of target matters to the likelihood of institutional change after an assassination. As discussed earlier, this chapter analyzes Polity shifts in the aftermath of the assassination of judges and attorneys in one second-level category and police security forces in another. The hypotheses are as follows:

H8: The likelihood of political institutional change after a terrorist assassination will vary across subtypes of law enforcement personnel.

H9: Negative political institutional changes are more likely in authoritarian regimes than in mixed or democratic regimes in the aftermath of terrorist assassinations of law enforcement personnel.

H10: Positive political institutional changes are more likely in mixed regimes than in authoritarian regimes in the aftermath of terrorist assassinations of law enforcement personnel.

The quantitative examination of second-level target categories of law enforcement personnel yields interesting results. Unlike the categories tested thus far, there are no differences between the subtypes. Across all three models, the likelihoods are the same for Polity changes, for negative shifts, and for positive shifts. Table 7.1 provides the results of all three examinations. It appears that in regard to law enforcement, whether it is a judge or a member of security services targeted and killed, the repercussions for political institutional change are the same.

As a reminder, these models determine the risk of failure for each state after experiencing an assassination event, assume a gamma frailty with unknown variance, and examine the risk of failure by regime type. The authoritarian, mixed, and tumultuous regime types are measured against democracies. Testing for political institutional change, authoritarian regimes are estimated to experience less risk than mixed regimes and mixed regimes are at less risk

Table 7.1 Law Enforcement by Regime Type, 1977–2017

Shared Frailty Models—Judges/Attorneys/Court Officials and Police Security Forces
Gamma Frailty/Efron Method

	Political Institutional Changes			Negative Polity Shifts			Positive Polity Shifts		
	Coefficient (SE)	Hazard Ratio (SE)	p Values	Coefficient (SE)	Hazard Ratio (SE)	p Values	Coefficient (SE)	Hazard Ratio (SE)	p Values
Authoritarian	2.95 (.21)	19.19 (4.07)	.001	4.68 (.42)	107.99 (45.34)	.001	2.04 (.29)	7.70 (2.27)	.001
Mixed	3.25 (.15)	25.71 (3.80)	.001	3.88 (.35)	48.32 (16.80)	.001	3.16 (.18)	23.49 (4.13)	.001
Tumultuous	5.38 (.23)	216.31 (49.59)	.001	5.88 (.47)	356.29 (166.49)	.001	-.23 (1.15)	.80 (.92)	.845
Population (log)	-2.03 (.54)	.13 (.07)	.001	-2.33 (.79)	.10 (.08)	.003	.18 (.20)	1.19 (.24)	.384
Population (log) x Day (log)	-.01 (9.07)	.99 (9.07)	.005	-.01 (.01)	.99 (.01)	.426	-.01 (.01)	.99 (.01)	.001
Infant Mortality Rate (log)	-.17 (.04)	.84 (.04)	.001	-.27 (.07)	.76 (.05)	.001	-.15 (.06)	.86 (.05)	.008
Employment (log)	1.89 (.48)	6.60 (3.20)	.001	1.94 (.70)	6.94 (4.86)	.242			
Day	.74 (.35)	2.10 (.74)	.034	.79 (.67)	2.19 (1.47)	.001	1.93 (.01)	6.89 (2.87)	.001
Theta	3.16 (.40)			2.36 (.42)			3.24 (.46)		
N Failures	595			157			331		
N Observations	157,561			157,561			158,124		
N Groups	136			136			136		

Source: Polity, GTD & Penn, 1977–2017.

than tumultuous ones after an assassination of either a judge or court officer or a member of police security forces.

For both the *judge/attorney/court* model and the *police security forces* model, the explanatory variables included are population, employment rate, and infant mortality rate. These variables are logged with population performing best when interacted with the time variable (day). The PH violations were less robust for the logged variables of population and employment in both models, but the other variables performed well, and all were significant in the model.

Hazard ratios are the same across the two categories. Tumultuous regimes exhibit the greatest hazard ratios and authoritarian regimes have the lowest hazard ratios of the three regime types, compared to democracies. While not presented in this chapter, the survival curves follow trends from the previous chapters with mixed regimes experiencing longer survival times than authoritarian regimes, yet again as in previous models, the point estimates of the hazard ratios suggest lesser risk of Polity score changes in authoritarian regimes.

For the explanatory variables, the log of population is statistically significant as is the log of employment and of infant mortality rate. The negatively signed coefficient for the logs of population and infant mortality rate and hazard ratios of less than 1 indicates a decreasing hazard risk per unit change. As population increases, it is expected that the hazard of experiencing a Polity change will decrease and infant mortality rate also indicates a decreasing hazard for Polity change with negatively signed coefficients and hazard ratios below one.

Nonetheless, despite the differing outcomes across regime type, no evidence is found that the likelihood of political institutional change varies across subtype of law enforcement target. Results are similar regardless of whether a state's top prosecutor is killed or a local police chief. However, first-level category differences do exist in the likelihood of institutional changes after the killing of a law enforcement official versus that of government officials, for instance.

Survival curves for law enforcement second-level categories mirror one another with the survival for mixed regimes being the longest in duration, with a survival rate of approximately .2 around the 9,000-day mark. Authoritarian regimes decline at a faster rate and reach .2 around the 7,500-day mark. Tumultuous regimes decline the fastest reaching a .2 survival rate by the 2,500-day mark.[21]

Negative Institutional Shifts

Differences between the second-level categories of *judges/attorneys/court officials* and *police security forces* regarding the likelihood of a negative institutional shift were not evident, but support is found for the hypothesis that authoritarian regimes are more likely than mixed regimes to experience a negative shift. The hazard ratios suggest that authoritarian regimes are 10,699 percent more likely to experience a negative shift than a democracy, while mixed regimes are only 4,732 percent more likely than a democracy to see a negative institutional shift.

These variables are significant in the model and although some of the explanatory variables are not, population, infant mortality rate, and employment improved the model and are worthy of inclusion. Interacting population with day, while not highly significant, improves the proportional hazard assumption for several variables, including the mixed regime. Proportional hazard violations do exist for the authoritarian variable, as well as the logs of population and employment. Yet, overall, the model presented in table 7.1 is the best negative shifts model for both the *judges/attorneys/court officers* and the *police security forces* categories.

Survival curves for the two second-level categories mirror one another with mixed regime survival rates of .9 around the 12,500-day mark and authoritarian survival rates falling more rapidly. By the 5,000-day mark, authoritarian regimes have a survival rate of just above .6 for both judges/attorneys/court officers and police security forces models, falling to .2 around the 130,000-day mark.

Positive Institutional Shifts

Differences between the second-level categories of law enforcement in the test for positive institutional changes are nonexistent, but support does exist for the hypothesis that mixed regimes are mixed regimes are more likely than authoritarian regimes to experience a positive Polity shift after an assassination of law enforcement personnel regimes. Hazard ratios suggest that mixed regimes are 2,249 percent more likely than democracies to experience a positive institutional shift while authoritarian regimes are 670 percent more likely than democracies to experience a positive shift.

While the statistical significance for the tumultuous and population variables is not strong, the other variables in this model are highly significant and the test for proportional hazard violations is robust. Some efficiency is lost, across most of the models tested in this chapter, with large standard errors, but as stated previously this is expected in semi-parametric models such as these.

As with both the political institutional change and negative shift models, the coefficient for infant mortality rate is negative, which indicates a decreasing risk per unit change in the variable. Employment is not included as an explanatory variable in this model, unlike the previous two. In the positive shifts model, employment did not perform well, and the model was much improved by eliminating it. As with the hazard ratios, the survival curves for positive Polity shifts tracked nearly identically across the second-level categories. Authoritarian and mixed regimes in this model experience very similar survival curves with a survival rate of approximately .8 at the 5,000-day mark and declining to .1 by the 10,000-day mark.

CONCLUSION

The quantitative analyses here support the hypotheses concerning directional shifts across regime types, but no support is found for the hypothesis that differing second-level target types result in differing outcomes and the likelihood of political institutional changes. While differences are detected between law enforcement personnel and government officials or politicians, the *type* of law enforcement target does not seem to matter in regard to political institutional changes. This was a surprising result and not in line with other model testing for this project and in the author's previous work.

Possibly the most interesting aspect in the examination of law enforcement personnel is derived from the qualitative examination. Motivation for assassination is not a focus of this study, but it is impossible to ignore the trend that appears in the cases. More work is needed, but here, the motivations for terror groups in targeting prosecutors and judges appear to be driven by retaliation for trials and sentences handed down to the terrorists' compatriots. Thus, while institutional outcome differences may not exist between judges and police chief assassinations, there are underlying issues worthy of further exploration.

After the killing of law enforcement personnel, evidence suggests that negative Polity shifts are more likely in an authoritarian regime and positive Polity shifts are more likely in mixed regimes. This is in line with the models in the previous chapters and further substantiates the theory that terrorist assassinations bring about different pressures in different regime types.

Chapter 8

Journalists

Experiencing danger in the line of duty is not a new phenomenon for journalists. From political protests to war, wherever and whenever violence breaks out, it is a newsworthy event. Famous journalists and novelists, such as Walter Cronkite, Ernest Hemingway, and Martha Gellhorn, spent time as war correspondents during World War II and some, such as Ernie Pyle, lost their lives while covering the conflict. More recently, Marie Colvin lost her life while covering the civil war in Syria in 2012.

Outside of war, there are other risky endeavors for journalists, such as reporting on organized crime or drug trafficking. In 1989, Todd C. Smith, a reporter from the Tampa Tribune investigating drug trafficking, disappeared while visiting Peru. His body was later found on the side of a highway. Journalists understand the risks when accepting a war zone assignment or some other dangerous investigative assignment into crime or corruption. The risk of being caught in the proverbial crossfire while covering a story is not new. However, what is new is the select targeting and killing of these men and women simply for the jobs they do in reporting global and/or local events.

In recent decades, the character of conflict in many locales has changed with much violence driven by non-state actors, particularly since the September 2001 attacks on the United States. Terror campaigns around the globe in recent years have included journalists as viable targets. In fact, the database for this project indicates that terrorist assassinations of journalists increased in the years since 2013. The year with the greatest number of journalist assassinations is 2015, in which forty-five journalists were killed. The deaths did decline in both 2016 and 2017, with twenty-eight and twenty-three assassinations respectively. However, the years from 1989 through 1997 witnessed an uptick in terrorist assassination of journalists, before ebbing to six assassinations or less in each year from 1998 through 2011.

Other sources of data include the CPJ and The International News Safety Institute (INSI). CPJ tracks imprisonment and deaths of journalists since 1992 and in the twenty-five years from 1992 until 2017, CPJ's data compilation indicates a total of 1,283 journalists were killed—163 of those while on "dangerous assignments," 287 were caught in combat crossfire, and the remaining 824 were murdered.

The INSI tracks violence against journalists as well and lists the states of Afghanistan, Iraq, Mexico, Pakistan, and Paraguay as the most dangerous states for journalists in 2019. This list suggests that states experiencing societal and political instability, terrorist activity, and/or significant crime issues are understandably the most dangerous locales in which journalists can work.

For instance, during the Arab Spring of 2011, journalists were threatened and many assaulted while covering the protests in and around Tahrir Square in Egypt. Reports by several suggest that the attacks came from regime supporters and security forces.[1] Female journalists, such as CBS' Lara Logan and British journalist Natasha Smith, were sexually assaulted while covering the protests in Tahrir Square.[2] Assaults and targeting of journalists certainly happened in the past, but violence directed against journalists was much rarer than it is today. There is a dearth in our understanding and research of this trend, but Cottle, Sambrook, and Mosdell[3] offer the following explanation, in part, for this trend:

> Thirty years ago, journalists were acknowledged as neutral observers, with civilian status. Today, as Lyse Doucet described, they are too often targets. The increasing reach and status of the media and the rise of non-state violence has made journalists useful pawns in the asymmetrical conflicts following the September 2001 terrorist attack on New York and the West's military response in Afghanistan, Iraq and the wider Middle East. This has been accompanied by the changing, and at times increasingly tense, relations between the military and the media. (3)

In fact, one of the more widely known killing of a journalist in recent history is that of Daniel Pearl of the *Wall Street Journal*. Pearl was abducted and then later beheaded while reporting in Pakistan. Pearl vanished from Karachi on January 23, 2002, after leaving for what he believed to be an interview with a prominent member of the Islamic movement in Pakistan.

A group referring to itself as The National Movement for the Restoration of Pakistani Sovereignty sent two e-mails: the first of which showed a photo of Pearl in chains and the second of which demanded the release of Pakistani prisoners from Guantanamo Bay, Cuba, within twenty-four hours or else Pearl would be killed. A video obtained later showed Pearl's death, which happened at some point during the four weeks after his abduction.[4]

Other journalists would share similar fates in the years the followed, such as the abductions and deaths of Steven Sotloff and James Foley at the hands of the Islamic State of Iraq and Syria (ISIS) in 2014. These journalists were kidnapped in foreign locations while covering dangerous stories and murdered for their jobs and their nationalities—seen by their killers as enemies. However, do these killings constitute an assassination?

In line with the definition utilized in this project, the answer is no. As a reminder, the definition of assassination here is the targeting and killing of an individual for reasons that are distinctly political in nature, based on the individual's influence and/or role in public life. If an individual is targeted based on their role and/or standing in the political system and killed in a *non-hostage situation*, then the killing qualifies as an assassination. All journalists have a public role—this is an inherent component of the job. Journalists have the ability via their voice and/or their pen to influence policy by reporting the news to the public. Journalism is often referred to as the "fourth branch" of government because of the important role it plays in an ordered, civil society. Pearl, Sotloff, and Foley were all following stories to then report to the public and were killed, but killed while *hostages* of terror groups. Their deaths, while horrible and tragic, count as kidnappings resulting in death rather than an outright assassination.

What then constitutes a terrorist assassination of a journalist? Any attack on the life of a journalist (not an abduction), of which the journalist is the clear target, during a broader campaign of violence qualifies as a terrorist assassination. A producer for BBC News, Kate Peyton, was shot in Mogadishu, Somalia, in 2005. The shooting occurred outside her hotel and although she was rushed to the hospital and underwent surgery, she later died. Peyton reportedly had arrived in the city just hours earlier to report on the war-torn country and its efforts to create a transitional government.[5]

In Turkey, Naji al-Jarf, editor of the *Hinta Magazine*, was shot and killed on a street in Gaziantep in December 2015 by supporters of the ISIS. Al-Jarf, who was Syrian, edited the opposition magazine and had previously produced a documentary highlighting the violence perpetrated by ISIS.[6] Peyton and al-Jarf are just two of the 478 assassinations of journalists included in this analysis that have occurred during terror campaigns since 1977.

The remainder of this chapter proceeds structurally as the previous chapters. An explanation of the second-level targets is provided, followed by two case studies—the attacks on the *Charlie Hebdo* magazine in Paris, France, in 2015 and what is known as the Black Decade in Algeria in the 1990s when journalists had to take intelligence-like precautions on a daily basis to avoid being killed. Analyses of second-level categories are conducted, examining the likelihood of political institutional change, as well as the direction of said changes. Although survival analysis models were tested for the impact that repressive regimes may have on the outcome, no reportable results in either statistical significance or hazard ratios were found.

SECOND-LEVEL CATEGORIES OF JOURNALISTS

The GTD includes four second-level categories of journalists—*newspaper journalists/staff/facility*, *radio journalist/staff/facility*, *television journalist/ staff/facility*, and an *other* category, which includes online news agencies and bloggers. Bloggers are often targeted, particularly when the blogger advocates for a cause that is antithetical to a terror groups' goals. Yameen Rasheed was stabbed to death in 2017 at his home in Male, Maldives, likely due to his role as a prominent blogger who routinely advocated for human rights. Niladri Chattopadhyay Niloy and Ananta Bijoy Das were bloggers in Bangladesh killed in machete attacks. Das advocated for secularism and was killed in May 2015 while Niloy advocated for minority rights and was killed in August 2015.[7]

For the analyses here, however, the intent is to focus on more traditional journalism and thus, models discussed below will analyze the second-level categories of newspaper journalists, radio journalists, and television journalists. The analyses include the relevant cases discussed above, but also cases such as Roberto Sarasty Obregon, editor and owner of *El Cronista* magazine in Colombia, who was killed in 1989, and film director Mani Ratnam, who was killed in India in 1995. In Algeria in the 1990s, journalists had to exercise extreme caution every day to avoid being killed as part of the Armed Islamic Group (GIA) terror campaign.

Perhaps one of the most likely targets in all of journalism, however, is the political cartoonist. Naji al-Ali, a Palestinian political cartoonist working in the London offices of *Al-Qabas*, a Kuwait newspaper, was shot outside his office on July 22, 1987. He succumbed to his injuries a few weeks later. Al-Ali negatively depicted Israel, as well as Arab regimes, in his cartoons and was often critical of the Palestinian Liberation Organization (PLO) when he viewed actions by the PLO as hypocritical. Despite his support of the Palestinian cause in many of his 40,000 published cartoons, when he was critical it resulted in threats—threats, sometimes from the PLO, that he essentially ignored, only responding via his next cartoon with an attack on PLO leader Yasser Arafat.[8] In 2015, militants attacked the offices of the satirical magazine, *Charlie Hebdo*, in France, killing ten and specifically targeting the magazine over a political cartoon depicting the Prophet Muhammad. Originally coded as a hostage-taking incident in the GTD due to the nature of the entire event, it is coded here as an assassination because the cartoonists at *Charlie Hebdo* were targeted by the militants, were not taken hostage, and were killed solely in retaliation for their work.

FRANCE—*CHARLIE HEBDO*

Just before noon local time on Wednesday, January 7, 2015, in Paris, France, ISIS militants forced their way into the offices of *Charlie Hebdo*, asking for editor Stephane Charbonnier and four cartoonists by name. All five, along with several others, were holding the first editorial meeting after a break for the Christmas holiday. The two armed men, brothers Cherif and Said Kouachi, shot and killed a maintenance worker Frederic Boisseau on their way into the building and then grabbed Corrine Rey, another *Charlie Hebdo* cartoonist, along with the subscription manager in the stairwell. The men, clad in black attire and wearing masks, held the two women at gunpoint, forcing Rey to enter the security code for the newsroom housed on the second floor. Once inside, the perpetrators killed the editor's police bodyguard, Charbonnier, the four targeted cartoonists, and four other people who were attending the meeting that morning.[9]

The building was home to several different offices and the militants encountered someone delivering mail, asking the mail carrier for the *Charlie Hebdo* office, before coming upon Rey and her colleague in the stairwell. Others in the building heard the first shot, the one that killed Boisseau, and realized something was amiss. One office, that of Premieres Lignes, realized the militants were looking for *Charlie Hebdo*, but they had no contact information for the office or staff and thus no way to warn them. The Premieres Lignes staff did all they could—barricaded their door and eventually escaped to the roof, where they were able to hear the shots being fired below in the *Charlie Hebdo* office.[10] The attack was over in minutes and with twelve people dead, the militants fled the office and took to the street, taking the life of a policewoman shortly thereafter. This initial attack and the assassination of eight journalists and four others was the beginning of a three-day manhunt that included two separate standoffs with police.

The attack came about over the magazines' publication of a Danish cartoon of the Prophet Mohammad years earlier and the terrorists' displeasure over the depiction of Islam. *Charlie Hebdo* took security measures, such as not advertising their location and having no nameplates on doors. The editor, Charbonnier, had received numerous threats and thus had the police bodyguard with him. Sadly, the precautions were not enough to prevent this attack in 2015. France, and much of the world, was shocked by these events and international debate and discussion over freedom of speech and freedom of expression ensued.

The mantra *Je Suis Charlie*, which translates to "We Are Charlie," rang out across France and parts of the world in efforts to show solidarity—supporting freedom of expression and defiance to the terrorists. Within days, marches were held in France and it is estimated that as many as 1.6 million people participated in Paris alone. Other marches were held across the country and in other major cities worldwide, such as London, Washington, and Montreal. World leaders gathered in Paris to participate in the march, including German chancellor Angela Merkel; Jordan's king, Abdullah II; Israeli prime minister Benjamin Netanyahu; and Palestinian president Mahmoud Abbas. Rough estimates are that as many as 3.7 million people participated across France in solidarity marches and the *Je Suis Charlie* motto shared millions of times across social media.

At the end of the three-day manhunt, a total of seventeen had lost their lives and France's first attack by ISIS on its home soil left much of the country shaken. *Charlie Hebdo* refused to alter its approach to publishing controversial cartoons and continued doing so in the years after the attack. A memorial is held yearly to remember the victims and in January 2020, a trial of all those involved in the planning and execution of the attack began. In total, twenty-four people are alleged to have some involvement in the attacks, but only five were captured alive and taken into custody. The remaining suspects are dead or are presumed to have fled to Syria or Iraq.[11]

This was an unusual event in France and, unfortunately, a precursor to more terror attacks in 2015. In June, a factory was attacked resulting in one death and an attack on a train from Amsterdam to Paris was thwarted by passengers in August. In November, a set of coordinated attacks on a concert, restaurants, and bars by a combination of suicide bombers and gunmen resulted in the death of 130. In total, the GTD counts thirty-seven attacks in France in 2015 including armed assaults, bombings, and hostage-taking incidents. In 2016, the number of attacks decreased to twenty-six, but increased again in 2017 to a total of forty-one.

France, for decades, has maintained societal and political stability resulting in a consistent PTS score of 9 from 1987 through 2017 and average PTS scores of 1 to 2 from 1988 through 2017. The *Charlie Hebdo* attack on political cartoonists in a stable, peaceful state indicates that no state is immune from terrorist assassinations generally, but specifically, journalists in stable, consolidated democracies are not immune from being targeted for the work they do.

In conflict zones, journalists expect more danger even (and especially) when the conflict is occurring within your home country. However, journalists typically do not expect to be targeted in the way they were targeted in Algeria in the 1990s—during what is known as the Black Decade when Islamist groups and the existing one-party governmental regime fought a brutal war which ended with some 200,000 people dead and more than 7,000 disappeared.[12]

ALGERIA—THE BLACK DECADE

Algeria emerged in 1988 from decades of one-party rule by the National Liberation Front (FLN) after years of economic decline, brought about in part by the collapse of oil prices on the world market. Economic reforms instituted by President Chadli Benjedid, including foreign investment and decentralization, led to increased corruption in the elite class and deepened societal divisions between the masses and the political elite. The reforms often provided opportunities for the elite to gain control of formerly state-owned enterprises; the elite then make use of their newfound assets to enrich themselves even further.[13] Much of the land, previously used for agriculture, was developed for other ventures resulting in less food production. By 1989, approximately two-thirds of the food for Algerians had to be imported.[14]

With the collapse of oil prices, government revenues dropped by some 40 percent, forcing the government to curb spending which included a reduction (or elimination in some cases) of government services and the removal of state subsidies and price controls. Inflation and unemployment increased with food prices doubling and unemployment rates of more than 20 percent. Protests against the government ensued, some turning violent and including the destruction of state symbols, leading to hundreds of protestor deaths in clashes with police. In October 1988, at least forty people were killed when security forces fired on a protest in Algiers' Place des Martyrs square. Violence was rampant and it is estimated that as many as 500 people were killed by security forces and 3,500 arrested in the first week of October 1988. Any remaining respect that the public held for Algeria's security forces quickly dissipated and understanding the gravity of the situation, the president gave a speech on October 10 promising substantial political reforms and a move toward democracy.

A new constitution was written, which included allowing for multiple political parties, and an immediate move to a free press. Seemingly overnight, "newspapers sprang up everywhere"[15] and Algeria's journalists embraced their new freedoms. Only twelve media publications existed in the state in 1987, but between 1989 and 1991, 103 newspapers and magazines came into existence. Television and radio remained under the control of the state, but the creation of so many press outlets greatly improved freedom of the press in a short period of time.[16]

Multiple political parties formed and participated in the first free elections for municipal and provincial seats in June 1990. The most dominant party was the Islamic Salvation Front (FIS), winning 55 percent of the popular vote—853 of the 1,539 municipal seats and 32 of 48 of the provincial seats. This win took the FLN by surprise and party leaders became concerned that FIS might gain control of the national government in the parliamentary elections scheduled for December 1991. Despite attempts to ensure an FLN victory—the party engaged, for instance, in gerrymandering and public propaganda against the FIS—voters still voted in large numbers for the FIS. Out of 231 parliamentary seats, FIS won 188 placing it in a solid position for the second round of voting and likely the dominant party in Algeria's new democratically elected government.[17]

Not willing to cede that much power to the Islamist FIS party, the FLN declared a constitutional crisis, suspending the constitution and canceling the upcoming second round of parliamentary elections. All power was transferred eventually to the Haut Comite d'Etat, of which the military was extremely influential. In what was essentially a coup, the old one-party political structure attempted to maintain power. Naturally, this led to a violent uprising that continued for a decade, opening the door for extreme tactics on both sides. Journalists were one of the many ill-fated casualties in Algeria's Black Decade.

In the decades prior to the war, Algerian media was state controlled with little freedom of expression until the 1989 reforms under the new constitution. Many turned to journalism in that brief period of press freedom and news outlets were flourishing. However, when the war broke out, much of the media was perceived as still siding with the government and the FLN. The GIA formed in the early days of the conflict and is responsible for at least 236 terror attacks in Algeria from 1994 through 2006, as counted in the GTD. Of the successful assassinations examined in this project, the GIA is responsible for sixteen journalist assassinations. It is likely this is an undercount due to insufficient data clarity common in many of these conflictual situations. International news reports suggest a much higher total count of journalist assassination—as many as ninety-four during the Black Decade. In total, this dataset counts forty-six assassinations of journalists in Algeria with all occurring from 1994 to 1997. In 1995 alone, twenty-seven of the forty-six were killed.[18]

The Black Decade stretched from 1992 to 2002, during which time journalists existed in a veritable no-man's-land in Algeria. The governmental crackdown included the media ostensibly for national security purposes and thus, the independent outlets were targeted by the state. In 1994, more than thirty journalists were jailed, newspapers were fined, and with no economic resources, they were forced to close. Those working for the pro-FLN newspaper, *El Moudjahid*, received government salaries and were allowed to live in hotels protected by police forces. In these "high-security compounds,"[19] journalists and their editors lived alongside former government leaders and generals, protected from attacks by the GIA and anyone wishing them harm.

At the beginning of the conflict, typically only journalists who criticized the GIA were targeted, but as time went on, the GIA began targeting all journalists. The first occurred on the morning of May 26, 1993—Tahar Djaout was leaving home for his office at the *Ruptures* journal (a journal he cofounded) when he was shot several times and then dragged from his car. The assassins made their getaway in his car and Djaout would lie in a coma for nearly a week before passing away. Two days later, police forces located the perpetrators just outside of Algiers killing two, but taking a third into custody. The surviving perpetrator explained the motive behind Djaout's assassination— "He was a communist and wielded a fearsome pen which could have had an effect on Islamic sectors."[20] His death was the first of many attacks on those who "wielded pens"—attacks which would also result in hundreds of journalists fleeing the war-torn state.

By 1994, news accounts reported that at least thirty journalists had been assassinated in Algeria. Sometimes the target would be forewarned, receiving assassination threats by mail or phone. In some cases fatwas were issued and lists of journalists were posted on bulletin boards in mosques. Journalists stopped using their last names in order to conceal their identities as much as possible. Most refused to sleep in their homes for fear of putting their families in danger or being easily located. On the way to and from their offices, journalists became accustomed to behaving as if they were clandestine operatives—taking cabs to work, switching cabs frequently, not getting out of the cab too close to the office, avoiding public spaces, and staying indoors as much as possible.

Essentially, journalists became "hostages of the conflict,"[21] caught in the middle between a repressive FLN government and the deadly GIA. Security forces expected the press to report only on the terrorist actions by the radicals and not on their authoritarian actions. Thus, government forces continually censored the press and jailed journalists. Those within the GIA and supporting the GIA believed that the press sided with the FLN government and thus viewed the assassinations as "settling scores"[22] with the media.[23]

By late 1994, the GIA had taken credit for many of the reported thirty-seven assassinations and by this time in the terror campaign, journalists who did not even report on the war or on politics were targeted and killed simply because they were journalists. Mekhlouf Boukzer, a sports reporter, had his throat slit and Rachida Hammadi, a television employee, was shot on her way to work, dying after ten days in a coma. Foreign publications began withdrawing their reporters and staff from Algeria over safety concerns and it is estimated that around 100 Algerian journalists fled for France by this time. Eventually, it is approximated that some 400 plus journalists would flee their homes and move abroad before the end of the Black Decade.[24]

One of Algeria's most prominent journalists, Said Mekbel, was shot and killed on December 3, 1994 as he sat in a restaurant having lunch. Mekbel was editor in chief of *Le Matin*, a publication which had only twelve of its original forty journalists remaining on staff. Reportedly none of those still lived in their homes. In order to survive, the journalists did not stay or sleep at one location for more than a few nights and made sure to develop no detectable daily routines. In late 1995, a string of journalist assassinations occurred with most taking place in or around Algiers. There were at least thirteen attacks on journalists from October 1995 through early January 1996, and all but two were successful. The targets of these attacks included a newspaper editor, a newspaper director, seven journalists, and three television journalists. It appears no branch of the media was spared. After the assassination of a journalist, most newspapers in Algeria would either cease printing temporarily or insert a blank page in the newspaper as a sign of mourning. After a journalist was imprisoned by the government, fellow journalists would strike and/or sign petitions. Thus, the surviving journalists appeared to do what they could to bring attention to their plight.[25]

Recalling the years of violence against Algerian journalists, Robert Fisk wrote in 2011 of some of the journalists who were killed, positing that these men and women are all but forgotten. He asserts that ninety-four were killed before the end of the war and writes of the victims, such as Khadija Dahmani, a young Muslim woman who choose the profession because it allowed her some liberation and freedom. Dahmani was shot and killed outside her home on December 5, 1995.[26] While Dahmani and the others discussed above constitute a small portion of the estimated 200,000 Algerians who lost their lives in this decade, this assassination campaign against journalists is unusual in its extent and scope. Sports reporters and television station employees were targeted just as the journalists who reported on the war were targeted. For simply choosing to become a journalist, individuals were forced to choose between fleeing their home country, living a clandestine existence, or being assassinated if they chose to live normal lives.

The government did eventually win the war and the Islamist insurgency quieted. Even if those outside of Algeria have forgotten the war and all the lives lost, a point alluded to by Fisk, many inside Algeria have not. The families of the disappeared still seek answers regarding their loved ones and formed the Algerian Association for the Disappeared, reportedly protesting on a weekly basis. Yet, Algerians' memories of the brutality and loss from the Black Decade are ever-present when contemplating protest movements and political issues.[27]

Algeria's stability obviously waned during the Black Decade, which is portrayed in the Polity scores and the PTS scale. In 1990, during the reform period and before the outbreak of violence, Algeria's Polity index score was

-2, indicating an authoritarian state but not fully authoritarian (which would result in a score of -10). The conflict escalated and by 1992, the Polity score fell to -7 remaining there until 1996 when it improved to -3. After the war, in 2004, the Polity score improved further to 2, indicating substantive moves toward democracy and leaving the authoritarian side of the index. As of 2017, Algeria remains at 2 on the Polity index.

The governmental repression which escalated quickly during the war, is reflected in the PTS score of 2 in 1990, indicating some repression, but not altogether repressive in nature. However, in 1991, evidence was enough to assign an average PTS score of 3, increasing again in 1992 to 4. By 1994, Algeria received an average PTS score of 5—the most repressive category on the scale. Repression did not begin to decrease until 2000, reaching an average score of 3.5 in 2007 and standing at 2.5 as of 2017.

Despite improvements, press intimidation and government corruption continue in Algeria. The state has a significant youth population—nearly 44 percent of its 43 million are under the age of twenty-four—who seek better lives for themselves. In 2019, protestors took to the streets calling for a new government, resulting in the April resignation of President Abdelaziz Bouteflika.[28] President Abdelmadjid Tebboune, elected in December 2019, is a former prime minister who promised political reforms and in the summer of 2020, he made moves to reshuffle the cabinet and pardoned the 2019 protestors, who may have been charged with a crime. It is too soon to know the direction of Algeria's future or the future of the Algerian press. Despite constitutional support of an independent media, the government was still practicing intimidation tactics in 2019 and existing television stations strongly favor the state.[29] However, should the youth movement continue to demand change, their sheer numbers may force those changes onto the existing political class. Those changes will surely include a truly independent and free press.

SURVIVAL ANALYSIS MODELS— TARGETS AND POLITICAL CHANGE

The assassination of journalists as part of a wider campaign of terrorism, whether in France or Algeria or any other state, serve to intimidate the press and even if the press continues operating while under threat, the threat may impact reporting. Thus, what are the broader repercussions of killing the messengers? Essentially, the question here is the same as those in previous chapters: Do these particular assassinations lead to significant change, or any change at all, in political institutions? The theory is the same as well in that the victim subtype matters to the likelihood of institutional change after an assassination.

The first hypothesis, then, is as follows:

H11: The likelihood of political institutional change after a terrorist assassination will vary across subtypes of journalists.

As with the previous chapters, Cox shared frailty models are utilized to test for the likelihood of Polity score change in the aftermath of a successful assassination of either a newspaper journalist, a television journalist, or online journalists. These models determine the risk of failure for each state after experiencing an assassination event, assume a gamma frailty with unknown variance, and examine the risk of failure by regime type. The authoritarian, mixed, and tumultuous regime types are measured against democracies.

For all three models, the explanatory variables included are population, employment rate, and infant mortality rate. These variables are logged with population performing best when interacted with the time variable (day). The PH violations were less robust for the logged variables of population and employment, but the other variables performed very well with no PH concerns and nearly all proved significant.

Hazard ratios are different in each category, and the category that includes online journalists suggests an important difference from the newspaper and television models. It should be noted that the number of cases differs significantly across these three second-level categories. There are 297 assassinations of newspaper journalists counted in this project, but only 61 television journalists and only 20 journalists included in the *other* category. There are 100 assassinations of radio journalists counted here, however, the model results for radio are not reported due to the similarity between radio and newspaper. Across all models—political institutional shifts, negative shifts, and positive shifts—the radio journalists category produced results very similar to that of newspaper journalists. What is most interesting from the quantitative analyses in this chapter is the notable difference across the three second-level categories—newspaper, television, and online.

Table 8.1 presents the results which support the hypothesis that the likelihood of political institutional change after the assassination of a journalist varies depending upon the type of journalist that is targeted. Authoritarian regimes face the greatest likelihood of Polity change, after the assassination of an online news journalist. These regimes are at the lowest risk for Polity change after the assassination of a newspaper journalist. Mixed regimes face the greatest risk of a political institutional change after the assassination of a newspaper journalist and the lowest risk after the assassination of an online journalist. Tumultuous regimes are the greatest risk of Polity change after the assassination of a newspaper journalist and the lowest risk after the assassination of an online journalist. In line with results in previous chapters, all regimes—authoritarian, mixed, and tumultuous—are at greater risk of institutional changes after a journalist assassination than are democracies.

Table 8.1 Journalists by Regime Type, 1977–2017

Shared Frailty Models—Political Institutional Changes
Gamma Frailty/Efron Method

	Newspaper			Television			Other/Online		
	Coefficient (SE)	Hazard Ratio (SE)	p Values	Coefficient (SE)	Hazard Ratio (SE)	p Values	Coefficient (SE)	Hazard Ratio (SE)	p Values
Authoritarian	2.93 (.21)	18.64 (3.97)	.001	3.01 (.22)	20.38 (4.47)	.001	3.08 (.30)	21.75 (6.62)	.001
Mixed	3.24 (.15)	25.52 (3.77)	.001	3.15 (.15)	23.38 (3.45)	.001	2.79 (.15)	16.34 (2.50)	.001
Tumultuous	5.30 (.23)	200.22 (46.04)	.001	5.09 (.23)	162.72 (38.23)	.001	4.40 (.25)	81.44 (20.22)	.001
Population (log)	-2.07 (.54)	.13 (.07)	.001	-2.01 (.55)	.13 (.07)	.001	-2.79 (.67)	.06 (.04)	.001
Employment (log)	1.92 (.49)	6.81 (3.33)	.001	1.91 (.50)	6.78 (3.41)	.001	2.22 (.60)	9.19 (5.53)	.001
Infant Mortality Rate (log)	-.17 (.04)	.84 (.03)	.001	-.14 (.04)	.87 (.04)	.001	-.21 (.05)	.81 (.04)	.001
Event Date	.71 (.35)	2.04 (.72)	.045	.86 (.38)	2.37 (.90)	.023	-.55 (.54)	.58 (.31)	.311
Population (log) x Day	-.01 (9.14)	.99 (9.14)	.007	-.01 (9.60)	.99 (9.60)	.002	-4.34 (.01)	.99 (.01)	.973
Theta	3.20 (.41)			3.30 (.43)			4.10 (.52)		
N Failures	592			575			492		
N Observations	157,103			154.194			134,041		
N Groups	136			136			136		

Source: Polity, GTD & Penn, 1977–2017.

All regime variables are statistically significant and it is worth reminding the reader of the large standard errors. In this survival analysis, some efficiency is lost due to the lack of baseline assumptions and while the hazard ratios are point estimates, the results are significant and instructive—differences exist across regimes and across second-level target categories.

All variables, with the exception of event date and the interaction of population and day in the *other/online* model, are statistically significant. The negatively signed coefficient for the logs of infant mortality rate and population, along with hazard ratios of less than 1, indicates a decreasing hazard risk per unit change, which is consistent across all three models. As population increases, it is expected that the hazard of experiencing a Polity change will decrease, and the measure of infant mortality rate also indicates a decreasing hazard for Polity change with negatively signed coefficients and hazard ratios below one.

The employment variable is statistically significant and suggests a hazard ratio range of 6.78 to 9.19 across the three models, all with a positively signed coefficient. Despite improving the overall model, this variable suffers some PH violation. Thus, there is less confidence in the results for this particular variable. The event date and interaction of population and date both improve the models, even though the interaction, specifically, with a .99 hazard ratio does not move the outcome one way or the other.

As in the previous chapters, to further test the overarching theory that targets matter, models for directional Polity shifts after the assassinations of journalists are presented in tables 8.2 and 8.3. The hypotheses for directional Polity shifts are as follows:

H12: Negative political institutional changes are more likely in authoritarian regimes than in mixed or democratic regimes in the aftermath of terrorist assassinations of journalists.

H13: Positive political institutional changes are more likely in mixed regimes than in authoritarian regimes in the aftermath of terrorist assassinations of journalists.

Negative Institutional Shifts

Table 8.2 provides the results of testing for negative political institutional changes. Evidence supports the hypothesis that authoritarian regimes are at greater risk for a negative Polity change after the assassination of the various second-level categories of journalists than are mixed regimes. Results indicate that the risk is greatest after the assassination of an online or "other" type of journalist. The least risk occurs after the killing of a newspaper journalist. The likelihood of a negative Polity shift in an authoritarian regime after a newspaper journalist is killed is 11,217 percent, the likelihood after a

Table 8.2   Journalists—Negative Shifts by Regime Type, 1977–2017

Shared Frailty Models—Negative Political Institutional Changes
Gamma Frailty/Efron Method

	Newspaper			Television			Other/Online		
	Coefficient (SE)	Hazard Ratio (SE)	p Values	Coefficient (SE)	Hazard Ratio (SE)	p Values	Coefficient (SE)	Hazard Ratio (SE)	p values
Authoritarian	4.73	113.17	.001	4.87	130.66	.001	3.08	161.88	.001
	(.40)	(46.20)		(.42)	(54.99)		(.30)	(90.71)	
Mixed	3.83	46.20	.001	3.79	44.38	.001	2.79	34.97	.001
	(.34)	(15.70)		(.34)	(15.29)		(.15)	(13.04)	
Tumultuous	6.01	407.75	.001	6.00	405.06	.001	4.40	211.73	.001
	(.46)	(187.48)		(.48)	(192.63)		(.25)	(106.59)	
Population (log)	-.40	.67	.085	-.30	.74	.236	-2.79	.71	.364
	(.23)	(.16)		(.25)	(.06)		(.67)	(.27)	
Infant Mortality Rate (log)	-.25	.78	.001	-.20	.82	.005	-.21	.78	.007
	(.07)	(.05)		(.07)	(.04)		(.05)	(.07)	
Event Date	.55	1.73	.358	.73	2.08	.268	-.55	3.91	.179
	(.59)	(1.03)		(.66)	(1.38)		(.54)	(3.97)	
Population (log) x Day	-6.15	.99	.682	-.01	.99	.416	-4.34	.99	.536
	(.01)	(.01)		(.01)	(9.60)		(.01)	(.01)	
Theta	2.40			2.61			2.97		
	(.42)			(.45)			(.61)		
N Failures	162			156			128		
N Observations	157,651			154.398			134,080		
N Groups	136			136			136		

Source: Polity, GTD & Penn, 1977–2017.

Table 8.3 Journalists—Positive Shifts by Regime Type, 1977–2017

Shared Frailty Models—Positive Political Institutional Changes
Gamma Frailty/Efron Method

	Newspaper			Television			Other/Online		
	Coefficient (SE)	Hazard Ratio (SE)	p Values	Coefficient (SE)	Hazard Ratio (SE)	p Values	Coefficient (SE)	Hazard Ratio (SE)	p Values
Authoritarian	2.04 (.29)	7.67 (2.26)	.001	2.06 (.30)	7.81 (2.33)	.001	1.77 (.39)	5.88 (2.31)	.001
Mixed	3.15 (.18)	23.36 (4.10)	.001	3.04 (.17)	21.06 (3.68)	.001	2.79 (.18)	16.35 (3.03)	.001
Tumultuous	-.24 (1.15)	.79 (.91)	.837	-.31 (1.15)	.73 (.84)	.784	-.46 (1.13)	.63 (.72)	.686
Population (log)	.16 (.21)	1.18 (.24)	.423	.15 (.21)	1.17 (.25)	.468	-.31 (.27)	.74 (.20)	.256
Infant Mortality Rate (log)	-.15 (.06)	.86 (.05)	.008	-.13 (.06)	.88 (.05)	.026	-.16 (.07)	.85 (.06)	.023
Event Date	1.83 (.42)	6.22 (2.61)	.001	1.74 (.45)	5.68 (2.56)	.001	-.01 (.63)	.99 (.63)	.999
Population (log) x Day	-.01 (.01)	.99 (.01)	.001	-.01 (.01)	.99 (9.60)	.001	-.01 (.01)	.99 (.01)	.292
Theta	3.27 (.46)			3.27 (.47)			3.74 (.54)		
N Failures	331			326			287		
N Observations	157,651			154,398			134,080		
N Groups	136			136			136		

Source: Polity, GTD & Penn, 1977–2017.

television journalist is killed is 12,966 percent, and the likelihood after the killing of an online/other journalist is 16,088 percent. This is in comparison with democracies.

Mixed regimes have a much lower risk of experiencing a negative Polity change across all three target types—ranging from 3,397 percent after the assassination of an online journalist to 4,520 percent after the assassination of a newspaper journalist. These regime variables are statistically significant across all three models, however, the authoritarian variable does suggest PH violations in the newspaper and television journalist models. The mixed regime variable does not exhibit PH violations across any of the models. Thus, the results are weakened a bit by the violations, but the two regime variables of interest are significant across the three models.

The explanatory variables perform similarly across the three models with negatively signed coefficients and hazard ratios less than one for population and infant mortality rate. Event date and the interaction of population and date are not significant in any of the three models, however, including these variables provided the best overall results. The tumultuous regime variable is significant across the models, but as stated in previous chapters, this variable was rarely coded for negative or positive shifts and thus is not appropriate for focus here.

Survival curves for most models in this chapter were not distinctive or particularly instructive, except for the negative institutional shifts curves. Figure 8.1 presents survival curves for the negative shifts models. The curve for mixed regimes is relatively stable and in neither model does it fall sharply below the .8 survival rate throughout the 12,000 days of the data. Thus, negative Polity shifts after an assassination of newspaper, television, or online journalists is less likely than for authoritarian regimes, but is still more likely than in democratic regimes. The trajectory of the authoritarian survival curve is similar across the models for newspaper and television journalists, but the decline is more rapid in the television journalists' model than in the newspaper journalists' model.

In the newspaper model curve, authoritarian regimes have less than .6 survival rate by the 6,000-day mark and approximately a .3 survival rate at the 8,000-day mark. Mixed regimes at 6,000 and 8,000 days are no lower than .9. In the television model curve, mixed regimes decline slowly reaching a .9 survival rate around the 8,000-day mark. However, the authoritarian regimes decline, or fail, at a faster rate reaching .6 at the 4,000-day mark and approximately .2 at the 8,000-day mark. Thus, authoritarian regimes are more likely than mixed regimes (or democracies) to experience a negative Polity shift after the assassination of either a newspaper or television journalist.

In the model for other/online news agencies, the trend for mixed regimes remains essentially the same, reaching a .9 survival rate around the 8,000-day

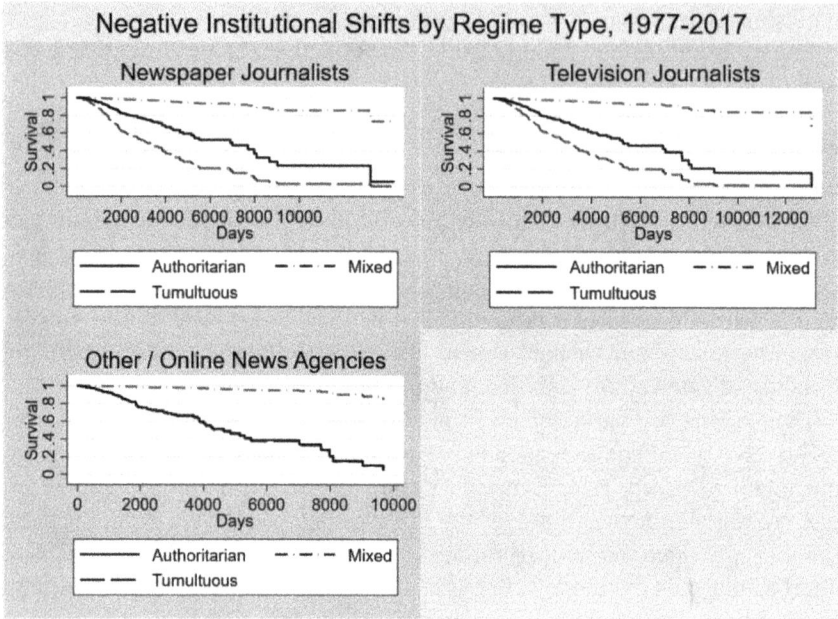

Figure 8.1   Survival Curves—Positive Regime Shifts, 1977–2017.

mark. However, the difference in this model is how closely authoritarian regimes track with tumultuous regimes. Granted, tumultuous regimes are not the focus and coding issues remain (discussed previously) yet this is an interesting deviation from the other models. Here, authoritarian regimes reach a survival rate of approximately .5 by the 4,000-day mark and .4 before the 6,000-day mark. Therefore, assassinations of online news journalists result in an authoritarian regime experiencing a negative Polity change sooner than either of the other two second-level categories. Again, newspaper journalists are targeted more often than either television or online journalists, but these survival curves yield interesting results and provide further support for the hypothesis that authoritarian states are more likely to experience negative shifts after the assassination of a journalist.

Positive Institutional Shifts

Table 8.3 presents results of the positive Polity shift models. Support is found for the hypothesis that mixed regimes are more likely to experience positive change after terrorist assassinations of journalists than are authoritarian regimes. After the assassination of a newspaper journalist, mixed regimes are 2,236 percent more likely to experience a positive change when compared to a democracy and after the assassination of a television journalist, a mixed regime is 2,006 percent more likely to experience a positive Polity shift. After the assassination of an online news journalist, a mixed regime is 1,535 percent more likely than a democracy to experience a positive institutional shift.

Authoritarian regimes are 757 percent more likely to experience a positive change in the newspaper journalists' model, 681 percent more likely in the television journalists' model, and 488 percent more likely in the online news agencies' model. These models do not exhibit any violations of the PH assumption and the authoritarian and mixed regime variables across all three models are statistically significant. The tumultuous variable is not significant and, as a reminder, few moves were coded for the tumultuous regimes and thus no extrapolations on tumultuous regimes are considered here. Statistical significance is an issue with the population variable in all three models, but the others remain strong, with the exception of the date and population/day interaction variable in the *other/online news agency* model. That said, all three models performed the best with these variables included.

CONCLUSION

The analyses of the political institutional change and the direction of said changes after the assassination of various categories of journalists provides further support to the premise of this project. Differences in outcomes across all three models—institutional change, negative institutional change, and positive institutional change—are detected in the aftermath of killings of newspaper, television, and online journalists.

Political institution changes, measured via Polity index scores, are most likely in authoritarian regimes after the assassination of an online news journalist. Mixed regimes are most likely to experience a change after the killing of a newspaper journalist. Negative institutional changes mirror the institutional changes regarding targets in that negative Polity shifts are most likely in authoritarian regimes after the killing of an online news journalist and least likely after the assassination of a newspaper journalist. Across all three models, authoritarian regimes are much more likely to experience a negative shift than mixed regimes. Positive institutional changes are most likely in mixed regimes and are the most likely after the assassination of a newspaper journalist.

These results support all three hypotheses presented here as well as the broader premise of this work. The likelihood of political institutional changes varies according to target type and even according to second-level target type. The case studies provide insight into two cases of terrorist assassinations of journalists—one that resulted in the deaths of several cartoonists and newspaper staff and began a three day national security event in France during a time of peace and another during a time of civil war that forced journalists across Algeria to live in fear of their lives for years. Much more work is needed before scholars and policymakers can begin to understand all the ramifications of attacks on journalists' and thereby, freedom of speech. A free press is critical to maintaining government accountability, transparency, and the rule of law. When journalists' are targeted as part of terror campaigns, it is an assault not only on the individual journalists' but on freedom of information across the globe.

Chapter 9

Military and Religious Leaders

Between 1977 and 2017, 217 military leaders and 319 religious leaders across the globe were killed during terror campaigns. The attacks occurred in more than forty states with military leaders killed most frequently in Libya (twenty-two assassinations) and religious leaders killed most frequently in Pakistan (thirty-five assassinations). The year 2005 was the most deadly for religious leaders (twenty-five assassinations) and 2013 the most deadly year for military leaders (fifteen assassinations).

Military leaders are often targeted due to their role as representatives of state governments and as, in many instances, an occupying foreign force. During "The Troubles" in Northern Ireland, the Irish Republican Army (IRA) often targeted British soldiers. The president of the political wing of the IRA, Gerry Adams, once stated that targeting British troops was "not only the right thing to do, but also the clever thing to do,"[1] in what the IRA perceived as its battle for the right to self-determination. The group often targeted soldiers during their off-duty hours, catching the soldiers unarmed and likely less aware of their surroundings, resulting in numerous deaths. By August 1989, twenty-seven British soldiers had been killed—twenty of those were not on duty when they were killed.[2] While many of the military deaths included in the original GTD database (discussed in detail later) are not included in the analysis here, the IRA is still responsible for fifteen of the military assassinations in this project.

The IRA is second only to the ETA in Spain in number of military leaders targeted. The ETA is responsible for seventeen military assassinations, such as the October 2000 killing of Lieutenant Colonel Antonio Munoz Carinanos in Seville, Spain. Carinanos was a high-profile military doctor known for treating Spanish celebrities. The shooting of Carinanos was one of at least three attacks in October that year—including the shooting death of a senior prosecutor on October 9 in the same Andalucia region in which Seville is located. Also in Seville in October, three military officers were targeted when bombs were placed in their cars, but failed to ignite.[3]

Based on the data here, unlike with the targeting of military leaders, it is hard to determine if any one group selectively targets religious leaders with regularity. From 1977 through 2017, religious leaders were most often targeted by the Taliban in Afghanistan (fourteen assassinations). However, the killing of religious leaders is widely distributed across groups with unknown perpetrators in 186 of the assassinations. As alluded to above, religious leaders are targeted with some frequency in certain states— Pakistan (thirty-five assassinations), Iraq (twenty-eight assassinations), India (twenty-three assassinations), and Afghanistan (nineteen assassinations) constituting nearly 33 percent of all the killings of religious leaders counted in this dataset.

The first-level categories of military leaders and religious leaders exhibit some similarities in this analysis. After cleansing the data to match the definition of assassination utilized in this project, there are no second-level categories of religious leaders and in the military category, there is only one second-level category substantial enough for examination—that of *military personnel*. Comparing these to the other first-level categories in this project, the categories of military and religious have the fewest number of assassinations and both are tested for political institutional changes in chapter 4. Thus, it is reasonable to combine military and religious into one chapter. Therefore, the structure of this chapter deviates somewhat from that of previous chapters. Here, similar to the prior chapters, the directional political institutional shifts in the aftermath of military and religious leaders are examined, but the case study approach is different. Rather than present case studies of select occurrences of assassination, I will provide a picture of contemporary assassinations of military and religious leaders before presenting the results of the directional shift models.

SECOND-LEVEL CATEGORIES OF MILITARY AND RELIGIOUS TARGETS

The GTD includes twelve second-level categories of military target types, such as *military aircraft*, *military unit/patrol/convoy*, *military recruiting station/academy*, and *military personnel (soldiers, troops, officers, forces)*. For the years 1977 through 2017, the GTD counts 1,346 terrorist assassinations of military members. After a thorough examination of these second-level categories, comparing each event to the definition of assassination in this project, most did not meet the definitional requirement.

To be included here, an individual must be targeted due to their influence, either perceived or real, in public life. A soldier—such as a Private First-Class in the U.S. Army—despite his or her role as a representative of the United States while stationed abroad does not hold the ability to influence public policy. While the targeting of military personnel, simply due to the uniforms they wear, is certainly a targeted attack, it is difficult to argue that the attack rises to the level of a terrorist assassination. Thus, the military category was cleansed significantly from the original GTD count of 1,346 assassinations. The result is a count of 219 terrorist assassinations of military leaders—ranging, for instance, from captains to lieutenant colonels to generals.

In the first-level category of religious figures, three second-level target categories are included—*religious figure*, *place of worship*, and *affiliated institution*. Of these, *religious figure* is the only one meeting the assassinations' definition. The original GTD count included the assassinations of 380 *religious figures*, 10 *places of worship*, and 37 *affiliated institutions*. These are often coded due to, for instance, an attack on a place of worship that resulted in deaths of religious leaders. After cleansing this category, there are 319 attacks meeting the applied assassination criteria, including religious clerics and at least one Christian missionary with a local leadership role. Specific examples of successful assassinations of both of these target categories—military and religious—are provided below.

ASSASSINATIONS OF MILITARY LEADERS

Attacks on military personnel have occurred in Afghanistan, Argentina, Colombia, Iraq, Libya, Peru, Spain, the UK, and Yemen among many others. Sri Lanka's chief of Northern Command, Colonel A. Ariyaperuma, was killed in November 1984 and in Santiago, Chile, Brigadier General Miquel Concha Martinez was shot and killed in June 1990. A grisly assassination occurred in September 2000 in Kosovo when the commander of the Kosovo Protection Corps, Skender Gashi (also a former commander in the Kosovo Liberation Army), was shot multiple times after which the perpetrators cut off his hands.

In Libya, attacks on the military began in the post–Arab Spring era with the greatest number occurring in 2013. In late 2012, the National Security Chief of the Armed Forces of Libya, Faraj Mohammed al-Dursi, was shot and killed when returning home in Benghazi City. Al-Dursi, a former member of the deposed Gadhafi regime, had defected from the regime to join the revolt during the Arab Spring. As with the majority of the attacks on military leaders in Libya, no group claimed responsibility for al-Dursi's shooting and thus the true motivation is unknown.[4]

Libya proved a dangerous state for military members in 2013, when as many as twelve military leaders were assassinated, again, by unknown perpetrators. An Army intelligence officer, Major Busaifi Mabrouk al-Moughrabi, was killed when a bomb underneath his car exploded in November that year.[5] Another car bomb exploded in Benghazi City (same city as al-Moughrabi's attack) a few months earlier in August, killing Alaa al-Fitouri, a colonel in the special forces.[6] Nineteen of the twenty-two assassinations in Libya included in this dataset occurred in Benghazi, with two in Derna and one in Sirte. For example, in July 2013, Colonel Fathi al-Omami of the Search and Rescue Bureau in the Libyan Air Force was shot and killed at a store in Derna[7] and in Sirte, the head of the local military council and a former rebel leader, Makhluf al-Ferjani, was shot and killed in March 2014.[8]

Other attacks on the African continent include the killing of Malian Army captain Hamata Ag Hantafaye in Timbuktu in July 2016 and as with so many of the Libyan attacks, no group claimed responsibility for Hantafaye's killing.[9] In Sierra Leone on December 22, 2016, former Chief of Defense, Lieutenant Colonel Samuel Omar Williams was shot and killed at his home in Devil Hole.

Military leaders are targeted in other parts of the world as well, such as Afghanistan and Colombia. In Afghanistan, General Khan Agha Achakzai of the Afghan National Army (ANA) was shot and killed as he left a mosque in Kandahar on March 24, 2016. The Taliban claimed responsibility for the assassination and both of the perpetrators were killed when the general's bodyguards returned fire. The Taliban also claimed responsibility for an April 2017 attack on the vehicle of ANA general Abdul Hai Atahai in Kunduz, which killed the general and injured another officer.[10]

In Colombia, attacks on the military are not as recent as those in Libya and Afghanistan and are concentrated in the 1980s with six of the ten assassinations occurring from 1981 to 1988. On March 11, 1983, General Jose Marie Gomez Jauregui of the Colombian Air Force was killed at his home in Bogota with no group taking responsibility for the attack. Retired Colombian Navy vice admiral Eduardo Melendez Ramirez was shot and killed in April 1986 in Chigorodo and Colombian Army lieutenant Juan Jesus Cuellar was shot and killed in February 1987 in Medellin. No group claimed responsibility for Cuellar's killing, but sources attributed the vice admiral's killing to the Popular Liberation Army.[11]

While the events above are only a small sample of the attacks on military leaders around the world, they do paint a picture of the assassinations that occurred from 1977 through 2017. However, many more attacks on military personnel occur—from bombings to armed assaults—resulting in the killings of significant numbers of soldiers, airmen, and other members of the military. In Libya, for instance, more recent attacks have involved the abduction of military leaders by groups, such as the abduction and execution of a Libyan Army captain in Sirte on May 1, 2016.[12] Members of the military, particularly when stationed in a foreign state or during times of significant unrest in their home state, are subject to attack from terrorist actors. The number of attacks and deaths are not in dispute, but in compiling the data for this analysis, the issue discovered is that only approximately 16 percent of the attacks on the military counted in the GTD as an assassination actually meets the definition of assassination utilized in this project.

ASSASSINATIONS OF RELIGIOUS LEADERS

In the review of religious leader assassinations, the data is much less complicated. As stated above, 319 of the 440 assassinations in the religious category meet the assassination definition utilized in this project—72.5 percent. Forty-nine states experienced at least one assassination of a religious leader during the forty years examined here with twenty-five (approximately 7.8% of the total) assassinations occurring in 2005. Religious leader killings also occurred with some frequency in the years 1989, 1992, 2012, and 2014. Each of these years saw at least 16 leaders killed and when combining these five years—1989, 1992, 2005, 2012, and 2014—nearly 29 percent of the 319 assassinations occurred in those five years. Roughly 43 percent of the killings of religious leaders in this dataset occurred during the last seventeen years, from 2000 to 2017. Few groups claim responsibility for the killings of these religious leaders and thus, over 58 percent of the perpetrators are unknown.

In Iraq, however, we know that many killings of religious leaders are driven by sectarian violence, particularly in the years since the toppling of Saddam Hussein's regime in 2002. In July 2005, a cleric with ties to the top Shia leader, Grand Ayatollah Ali Sistani, was assassinated on his way to Friday prayers at the al-Doreen Mosque in Bagdad.[13] Al-Qaeda took responsibility for the killing and suspicion at the time is that this was part of an escalation of violence, intent on sparking a sectarian civil war. On the same day of the assassination, a car bomb exploded outside the party offices of the Shia prime minister. Shia clerics around the city called for calm in light of these events, but Iraq would suffer more assassinations and more violence in the years that followed, such as the 2010 assassination of an imam who was killed as he left the al-Hasanayn Mosque in Baghdad after evening prayers.[14] Iraq accounts for nearly 9 percent of all killings of religious leaders in this dataset. Only Pakistan accounts for more assassinations of religious leaders—some 11 percent of the 319 assassinations occurred in Pakistan.

For instance, Christian missionary and director of the Full Gospel Assemblies of Pakistan church, Birgitta Almby, was shot in December 2012 in Lahore.

Almby was taken to the hospital and then transferred to a hospital in Sweden, succumbing to her injuries a few days later. The perpetrators, suspected Punjabi Taliban militants, shot Almby from a motorcycle as she stood outside her home.[15] Pakistani Taliban militants claimed responsibility for killing a Shi'ite cleric in Lahore a year later in December 2013. As with the Almby shooting, the perpetrators shot the cleric from a motorcycle—in this case as he drove home on a Sunday evening. The cleric, Allama Nasir Abbas, died en route to the hospital and the Pakistani Taliban publicly stated that his killing was retaliatory—in response to an attack on Sunnis' a month earlier in Rawalpindi in which eight were killed. The group stated that Abbas was directly involved in the Rawalpindi incident and that their intention was to kill even more Shia.[16]

Moderate clerics and/or those who speak out against radical terror groups often find themselves in the crosshairs of terrorists. In June 2014, a Kenyan cleric, Sheikh Mohammed Idris, who was chairman of the Council of Imams and Preachers of Kenya was targeted and killed in Mombasa. Idris had received threats on his life due to his attempts to stop religious extremism and radicalization of the youth in Kenya. A prominent critic of Al-Shabaab, it was suspected that the group was behind his killing.[17]

In Algeria, Abu-Hafs al-Jaza'iri, an imam who called for an end to violent extremism and who moderated between the Salafist Group for Preaching and Fighting (GSPC) and Algerian government forces, was shot and killed in at attack at his mosque in March 2004.[18] In 2007, an attack on a mosque in Kano, Nigeria, left three people dead, including Sheikh Jafar Adam who was the target of the attack, and Imam Abdul Karim Ssentamu was shot and killed on a street in Kampala, Uganda, in April 2012. In Bangladesh, a Sufi leader, Mohammad Shahidullah, was hacked to death in May 2016.[19] The Islamic State of Bangladesh is suspected in that attack, although the group did not publicly claim responsibility. The following year, another Sufi leader and his daughter were shot and then hacked to death, likely by Islamist extremists (possibly again the Islamic State of Bangladesh), despite governmental claims that the Islamic State has no presence in the state.[20]

Although not included in the data analysis here due to the unsuccessful outcome of the attack, a Saudi Arabian cleric was shot in the Philippines in March 2016 as he left an Islamic forum held in a school auditorium. The cleric, Ayed al-Qarni, was shot but not killed by a perpetrator who was quickly shot and killed by the cleric's security detail. Qarni reportedly has a social media presence and over twelve million followers on Twitter and is a pro-government cleric. Qarni was listed on an Islamic State hit list due to his ties to the Saudi government, which the Islamic State group viewed as apostates over its relationships with various Western governments.[21]

A spate of cleric killings began in Yemen in 2017, and thus, only one in this string of assassinations is included in this data analysis. However, as many as twenty-seven assassinations of clerics in Yemen are reported from 2017 through 2018, including that of Sheikh Adel Shehri who was shot and killed in Aden on October 28, 2017.[22] Neither group claimed responsibility for this attack nor were there any claims in the killings that followed. Many of the killings have occurred in and around Aden and are typically drive-by shootings, some near the mosques of the clerics.

One of the attacks in March 2018 in Tarim, Yemen, which killed an imam, is attributed to Al-Qaeda in the Arabian Peninsula.[23] Speculation abounds since Yemen is wracked by violence both from its civil war and its status as a proxy battle between Saudi Arabia, Iran via the Houthi. Motivations are unclear, but the clerics may have been targeted due to their political positions regarding the war and/or the amount of influence wielded by these clerics.[24]

Nevertheless, the qualitative data discussed herein highlights the use of assassination in sectarian-related terrorist violence. This project contributes to the political violence and terrorism literature by providing baseline insight into the likelihood of political institutional change after the assassination of a religious leader (see chapter 4) and in this chapter, the likelihood of the type of institutional change—moves toward either authoritarianism or democracy after the assassination of a religious leader.

SURVIVAL ANALYSIS MODELS— TARGETS AND POLITICAL CHANGE

Examining the assassinations of military and religious leaders requires some deviation from the approach taken with other targets and chapters in this book. Government officials, the politically active, law enforcement, and journalists all had at least two second-level categories with an adequate number of cases for both qualitative and quantitative study. Military and religious targets are fewer in number and each has only one category with substantial numbers, thereby necessitating a slightly difference approach.

That said, the categories are substantial enough to still allow for testing of political institutional shifts. The results presented in chapter 4 show the comparison of the first-level military and religious categories regarding the likelihood for any political institutional changes. Across all regime types, the analysis indicates that the hazard of experiencing a Polity change is greater after a military target is assassinated versus after a religious leader is assassinated. Here, the same first-level categories of military and religious leaders are tested for the direction of those shifts. Thus, the hypotheses are as follows:

H14: Negative political institutional changes are more likely in authoritarian regimes than in mixed or democratic regimes in the aftermath of terrorist assassinations of military and religious leaders.

H15: Positive political institutional changes are more likely in mixed regimes than in authoritarian regimes in the aftermath of terrorist assassinations of military and religious leaders.

As with the previous chapters, Cox shared frailty models are used to test for the likelihood of either negative or positive Polity score changes in the aftermath of a successful assassination of either a military or religious leader. These models determine the risk of failure for each state after experiencing an assassination event, assume a gamma frailty with unknown variance, and examine the risk of failure by regime type. The authoritarian, mixed, and tumultuous regime types are measured against democracies.

For all models, the explanatory variables included are population and infant mortality rate. These variables are logged with population performing best when interacted with the time variable (day). In the negative shifts' models, PH violations are present in the authoritarian regime variable and the tumultuous regime variable, but the others perform quite well. In the positive shifts' models, all variables perform well and there are no significant PH violations.

Negative Institutional Shifts

Table 9.1 provides the results of testing for both negative and positive political institutional changes after assassinations of military and religious leaders. Evidence supports the hypothesis that authoritarian regimes are at greater risk for a negative Polity change after the assassinations of either military or religious leaders. However, results are mixed due to existing PH violations and loss of efficiency in the models with large standard errors. Both relevant regime variables, however, are statistically significant in both models.

Results suggest that the assassination of a religious leader places authoritarian regimes at greater risk for a negative institutional change than the killing of a military leader. The hazard ratio for an authoritarian regime after the killing of a religious leader is 11,718 percent while the hazard ratio after the killing of a military leader is 11,217 percent. Mixed regimes have a hazard of 4,419 percent and 4,520 percent respectively. Thus, a mixed regime is slightly more likely to experience a negative shift after the assassination of a military leader versus that of a religious leader, and in both models an authoritarian regime is much more likely to experience a negative Polity shift than either a democracy or a mixed regime after the assassination of a military or religious leader.

Table 9.1 Military and Religious Leaders—Negative and Positive Shifts, 1977–2017

Shared Frailty Models—Political Institutional Changes
Gamma Frailty/Efron Method

	Military Leaders						Religious Leaders					
	Negative Shifts			Positive Shifts			Negative Shifts			Positive Shifts		
	Coefficient (SE)	Hazard Ratio (SE)	p Values	Coefficient (SE)	Hazard Ratio (SE)	p Values	Coefficient (SE)	Hazard Ratio (SE)	p Values	Coefficient (SE)	Hazard Ratio (SE)	p values
Authoritarian	4.73 (.40)	113.17 (45.46)	.001	2.04 (.29)	7.67 (2.26)	.001	4.77 (.41)	118.18 (48.16)	.001	2.03 (.29)	7.59 (2.23)	.001
Mixed	3.83 (.34)	46.20 (15.70)	.001	3.15 (.18)	23.36 (4.10)	.001	3.81 (.34)	45.19 (15.42)	.001	3.14 (.18)	23.17 (4.07)	.001
Tumultuous	6.01 (.46)	407.74 (187.48)	.001	-.24 (1.15)	.79 (.91)	.837	6.08 (.47)	438.62 (205.37)	.001	-.26 (1.15)	.77 (.89)	.823
Population (log)	-.40 (.23)	.67 (.16)	.085	.16 (.21)	1.18 (.24)	.423	-.41 (.24)	.67 (.16)	.086	.16 (.21)	1.17 (.24)	.448
Population (log) x Day (log)	-6.15 (.01)	.99 (.01)	.682	-.01 (.01)	.99 (.01)	.001	-5.28 (.01)	.99 (.01)	.730	-.01 (.01)	.99 (.01)	.001
Infant Mortality Rate (log)	-.25 (.07)	.78 (.05)	.001	-.15 (.06)	.86 (.05)	.008	-.26 (.07)	.83 (.03)	.001	-.15 (.06)	.86 (.05)	.007
Day (log)	.55 (.60)	1.73 (1.03)	.358	1.83 (.42)	6.22 (2.62)	.001	.01 (.01)	1.78 (1.09)	.340	1.74 (.42)	5.72 (2.43)	.001
Theta	2.40 (.42)			3.27 (.46)			2.52 (.44)			3.28 (.47)		
N Failures	162			331			160			331		
N Observations	157,651			157,651			156,914			156,914		
N Groups	136			136			136			136		

Source: Polity, GTD & Penn, 1977–2017.

The explanatory variables perform similarly across the negative models with negatively signed coefficients and hazard ratios less than one for population and infant mortality rate. The event date and the interaction of population and date are not significant in either negative model. The tumultuous regime variable is significant in the negative models, but as stated in previous chapters, this variable was rarely coded for negative or positive shifts and thus is not relevant in this analysis.

Survival curves for the negative shifts' models reflect the trend in the shared frailty models and in previously reported survival curves when testing for negative institutional changes. Mixed regimes, after the assassination of either a military or religious leader, were most likely to survive the longest, and failed at only a slightly faster rate after a military leader assassination than after a religious leader assassination. Authoritarian regimes failed at a much faster rate in both models than mixed regimes, with the military model failing slightly faster than the religious model—suggesting that the interpretation of the hazard ratio estimates should be considered carefully when comparing military versus religious leader assassinations. The survival curves do provide further support for the theory that authoritarian regimes are at greater risk of experiencing a negative Polity shift than a mixed regime after the assassinations of either military or religious leaders.

Positive Institutional Shifts

Testing for the likelihood of positive Polity shifts finds support for the theory that mixed regimes are more likely to experience positive institutional changes after terrorist assassinations of military and religious leaders than are authoritarian regimes. After the assassination of a military leader, mixed regimes are 2,236 percent more likely to experience a positive change when compared to a democracy and after the assassination of a religious leader, a mixed regime is 2,217 percent more likely to experience a positive Polity shift.

Authoritarian regimes are 757 percent more likely to experience a positive change in the military model and 749 percent more likely in the religious leaders' model. These models do not exhibit any violations of the PH assumption and the authoritarian and mixed regime variables across both models are statistically significant. The tumultuous variable is not significant and, again, few moves were coded for the tumultuous regimes and thus no extrapolations on tumultuous regimes are appropriate. Statistical significance is an issue with the population variable in both models, but the other explanatory variables remain solid.

Survival curves for the positive shifts mimic results in previous models with the survival rates for mixed and authoritarian regimes closely tracking one another and beginning to fail (i.e., experience a positive shift) around the 3,000-day mark, reaching a survival rate of .7 around the 5,000-day mark. By the 10,000-day mark, after the assassination of a military or religious leader, the failure rate reaches .1 for both mixed and authoritarian regimes.

CONCLUSION

The analyses of the directional political institutional changes after the assassination of either a military or religious leader supports at least two key themes of this project. First, the overall premise that the target matters. Differences, however slight, in the likelihood of negative and positive Polity shifts are detected between the two targets here. Second, the hypotheses that authoritarian regimes are more likely to experience negative changes and that mixed regimes are more likely to experience positive changes are supported here.

The case sketches of the assassinations of both military and religious leaders are intended to paint a picture of these attacks. The qualitative data suggests that sectarian violence may increase the likelihood of the targeting of religious leaders, but no trend is identified in the cases of military leader assassinations. What the examination of military assassinations data does suggest is that clarification of what constitutes an assassination of military personnel is necessary. In order to provide robust analyses of terror attacks on military targets, the tactic or type of attack must be delineated. Targeting a military general in an armed assault is altogether different from a bombing of military barracks and thus, the outcomes (not to mention the motivations and goals) may also be different.

Chapter 10

Understanding Terrorist Assassinations

As indicated by the data and as this study has established, terrorists engage in assassination frequently. Yet, there is a dearth in our understanding of the *who*, *what*, *when*, *where*, and *why* of this phenomenon. There is also a lack of understanding regarding *how* terrorist assassinations affect political or societal institutions. The aim of this book is to address the *who* and *how* gaps in the literature and to offer qualitative context, furthering our understanding of both the environments within which terrorist assassinations occur and the aftermath of these events. In doing so, this study is also able to address, on the periphery at least, some of the *when*, *where*, and *why* questions.

Thus, this chapter offers a summary of the quantitative findings and discusses what the qualitative data suggest about terrorist assassinations. Deduced from the findings here, a framework is then suggested for enhancing our understanding of these events. This framework may further motivational explanations for choosing terrorist assassination as a tactic in campaigns of violence (essentially, the *why* question). Finally, suggestions for future research are proffered.

QUANTITATIVE FINDINGS

Successful assassinations are more likely to lead to political institutional changes in authoritarian, mixed, and tumultuous regimes than in democracies regardless of the type of target chosen. The premise of the book is that the types of target chosen for assassination are important to the outcomes and support is found for this argument. While trends are certainly similar, differences exist across first- and second-level target types.

Across all target types, tumultuous regimes are the most likely to experience an institutional change, but the hazard ratios and survival curves differ according to the target category. For example, assassinations of religious leaders result in lower hazard rates for tumultuous regimes than after the assassination of law enforcement officials. In the second-level target categories, political changes are least likely in tumultuous regimes after the assassination of international peacekeepers and/or online journalists, and most likely after the assassination of politicians, court officials, and police security forces.

Mixed regimes are more likely than democracies, across target types, to experience a political institutional change in the aftermath of terrorist assassinations. Hazard ratios differ slightly here, but the targeting and killing of law enforcement officials portends the greatest hazard for mixed regimes. The assassinations of religious leaders have the lowest hazard rate for these regimes. In the second-level target categories, the killing of politicians is the most likely to result in institutional changes and the killing of international peacekeepers or online journalists are the least likely to result in political changes.

In authoritarian regimes, the likelihood of political institutional changes is the greatest after the terrorist assassination of law enforcement officials and the least likely after the killing of politicians, journalists, or military leaders. The second-level category models show that the targeting and killing of diplomats, intelligence officials, or heads of state result in the least likelihood for political change, while the assassinations of international peacekeepers portend the greatest likelihood for institutional change in authoritarian regimes.

The survival curves presented throughout this text provide insight into the estimated length of time before changes begin to occur. These curves suggest that authoritarian regimes do fail faster than mixed regimes, indicating that future research may be useful in further delineating the differences. The curves also suggest that political institutions do not see enough cumulative change (enough to result in a Polity score change) in mixed or authoritarian regimes until at least 2,000 days after the terrorist assassination (thus, at least five to five-and-a-half years). Regimes in a stage of tumult experience institutional changes at considerably faster rates.

The examinations of directional shifts throughout the study yields insight into the types of political changes after terrorist assassinations. The analyses focused solely on the mixed and authoritarian regime categories, in comparison with democracies, and found that negative shifts (i.e., moves toward authoritarianism) are most likely in authoritarian regimes after the assassinations of international peacekeepers. Thus, it suggests that authoritarian regimes become even more entrenched after terrorists assassinate members of international organizations. The results also suggest that the killings of online journalists lead to further authoritarian moves in an already authoritarian state. Mixed regimes are much less likely, regardless of target, to experience negative shifts toward authoritarianism after assassinations, but are still more likely than democracies to experience such changes. The greatest likelihood for moves toward authoritarianism for mixed regimes occurs when court officials or police security forces are assassinated.

The survival curves for the negative Polity shifts largely support the hazard estimates. Authoritarian regimes fail (i.e., experience negative changes) at faster rates than mixed regimes, with noticeable survival rate changes by the 2,000-day mark across the models. In fact, in the international peacekeepers model, the survival rate is already at .8 around the 1,000-day mark for authoritarian regimes. Across all the models, mixed regimes are relatively steady with only minor curve declines and therefore are unlikely to experience significant negative shifts.

Mixed regimes are, however, more likely than authoritarian ones to experience positive shifts (i.e., moves toward democracy) after terror assassinations. Positive institutional shifts are most likely in mixed regimes after the killing of court personnel or police security forces, but hazard ratios are very similar after the assassinations of heads of state, newspaper journalists, diplomats, and politicians. The second-level targets that are least likely to result in positive moves in mixed regimes are online journalists and international peacekeepers. The greatest likelihood for authoritarian regimes to make moves toward democracy occurs after the assassinations of television journalists, with court officials, police security forces, and government personnel assassinations suggesting a greater likelihood than other target categories.

Survival curves for positive Polity shifts suggest that mixed and authoritarian regimes track closely. The failure rates are much slower in these models compared to previous ones with no significant declines occurring until after the 4,000-day mark and in some cases after the 6,000-day mark. Still, both mixed and authoritarian regimes are more likely to experience positive changes after terrorist assassinations than are democracies. Thus, the quantitative analyses indicate that terrorist assassinations result in different outcomes across target types and that the impact of these killings is different in authoritarian, mixed, and democratic regimes. Democracies are much less likely to experience changes, either positive or negative, after an assassination than are authoritarian or mixed regimes.

Lastly, assassinations targets do matter. Of the multiple models tested in this project, it was rare for any of the second-level targets to share the same hazard ratios or survival curves and in the first-level categories only three of six target categories share the same hazard ratios. It is interesting that the categories of online journalists and international peacekeepers often fall into the "most likely" or "least likely" parameters and, therefore, suggests that attacks on journalists and international workers/peacekeepers deserve more in-depth analysis.

QUALITATIVE FINDINGS

Chapter 2 presented an important quandary regarding the use of terrorist assassinations. If campaigns of terror are indiscriminate and wish to instill as much chaos, intimidation, and fear as is possible to entire communities and states, then why selectively target certain leaders? Would not a bombing of a crowded shopping mall create more widespread fear than the selective targeting of a mayor or a journalist or a religious leader? These mass casualty bombings certainly occur, as do other tactics of terrorism, but why do terror groups spend the additional time and resources necessary to carry out an assassination, which targets a specific individual? It is difficult to extrapolate any potential explanations for this based on the quantitative findings, but the case studies offer some insight.

First, the use of assassinations in terror campaigns is intended to intimidate and instill fear in the wider population. This matches one of the consensus criteria in terrorism definitions. But more specifically, the intent of assassination in certain circumstances is to intimidate and instill enough fear so that people alter certain behaviors—not just general behavior. The case of the Shining Path's 1989 campaign in Peru discussed in chapter 6 supports this assertion.

Assassinations of candidates for local office, politicians, and others already serving in office may be intended to deter others from putting forth their names as political candidates. If the previous three mayors of a town have been assassinated, it certainly would lead any rational individual to question the worth of running for mayor in that town. Attacks on candidates and on election officials may deter citizens from voting in elections thereby preventing democratic processes from occurring or at the least ensuring the status quo. Status quo in some locales may include political and/or societal instability and this may suit the needs of the terror group.

Second, terror groups may expend the time and resources to target certain public officials for retaliatory purposes. Three of the case studies discussed in this book support this contention. Indira Gandhi was killed in retaliation for the massacre at the Golden Temple, Judge Chuvashov in Russia was killed allegedly in retaliation for harsh sentences he handed down previously, and the journalists at the *Charlie Hebdo* magazine in France were killed in retaliation for the printing of political cartoons.

A FRAMEWORK

While four qualitative case studies do not offer a foundation adequate for theory development, the studies here do suggest that this may be a theoretical avenue worth taking. This is an unintended finding of this project.

As discussed in chapter 2, motivations (and thus, one approach to the *why* question) for assassinations often vary widely and may be hard to determine in some cases. The aim at the onset was to establish that the type of target chosen for assassination was important to resultant outcomes and to determine the political repercussions to the various regime types. To that extent, the project was successful. The risk of political institutional change after a terrorist assassination does vary by target type and across regimes. The type of change also varies—mixed regimes are more likely to experience moves toward democracy and authoritarian regimes are more likely to become more deeply entrenched in authoritarianism after terrorist assassinations. The degree of these likelihoods varies according to the category of public official who is targeted. For instance, assassinations of international peacekeepers in authoritarian regimes pose the greatest risk for negative change to that regime.

That said, an interesting result from the qualitative examinations is the identification of two potential trends that may help to explain the *why* of terrorist assassinations—deterrence and retaliation. The Shining Path campaign in October and November of 1989 was intended to disrupt elections and deter in two ways. First, the violence was intended to deter individuals from running for office and second, to deter citizens from voting. Information suggests that this campaign by the Shining Path was at least minimally successful. It can be argued as well that the targeting of journalists in Algeria also served as a deterrent for media members since many left the profession or left the country.

Retaliation was a known motive in at least two of the case studies here and likely three, possibly four. Prime Minister Gandhi was assassinated by Sikhs in retaliation for the government attack at the Golden Temple and the *Charlie Hebdo* attack was in retaliation for the publishing of religious/political cartoons. It is likely that Judge Chuvashov was killed over sentences he had previously handed down and it is possible that former prime minister Rafik Hariri was killed because of his refusal to tow Syria's line in Lebanon.

It is an ambitious task to set out to establish a theory explaining *why* assassinations occur—be they terrorist or otherwise. Tactically, are there operational situations that indicate to the terrorists that an assassination will inflict the damage they seek? Strategically, are there motivational reasons that achieve some greater goal, such as revenge for previous acts or decisions by the targeted official? This work does not and cannot assert that all terrorist assassination decisions are made based on deterrence or retaliation as discussed above. However, this is most assuredly an avenue for further development and research. Therefore, from this project a framework for understanding terrorist assassinations may be drawn based on the following data and positions in seeking to address the *who, when, where, why,* and *how* of terrorist assassinations (*what*).

Terrorists engage in assassinations frequently with nearly 10,000 individuals assassinated during terror campaigns from 1977 through 2017. Government officials, politicians, and police security forces are the ones most often targeted in these terror campaigns. Most of these assassinations occur in democracies—some 51.8 percent. Thirty percent occur in mixed regimes, 13.1 percent in tumultuous regimes, and only 5.1 percent of terrorist assassinations occur in authoritarian regimes. Thus, we know where these attacks are most likely to occur and we know that they are much less likely to significantly impact political institutions in democratic states. We now know that there is a greater likelihood for authoritarian regimes to become more entrenched in its authoritarianism when terror assassinations do occur. The analyses here also indicate that mixed regimes are more likely to make moves toward democracy as opposed to authoritarian moves in the aftermath of terrorist assassinations.

Thus, we have answers to *where* terrorist assassinations occur (at least broadly speaking) and *who* is most often targeted. While some questions regarding *when* are less clear from this study (for instance, are these assassinations more likely near election-time?) and therefore should be a subject in future investigations, descriptive data discussed in chapter 3 does provide some insight into the annual trends. For instance, the three years at the end of the Cold War witnessed slightly more than 16 percent of all the assassinations counted in this project.

Next, this project begins to answer the question of *how* these attacks affect political institutions and *how* the difference in target affects the political changes. Democracies remain stable after terrorist assassinations, but these events do result in political changes in authoritarian, mixed, and tumultuous regimes and there is variation across target types.

Finally, this study yields unintended but welcome insight into *why* assassination may be chosen as a tactic in terrorist campaigns—reasons relating to deterrence and/or retaliation. A complete framework for understanding terrorist assassination requires the five W's of investigation along with insight into how these events impact politics and society. This study provides the beginning of such a framework with insight into three of the five W's along with the how.

FUTURE RESEARCH

Empirical inquiry is a process that does not truly ever reach an end point—it only deepens and expands once initial answers are achieved. The political violence literature lacks answers to an array of questions regarding assassination and terrorism, among other aspects of political violence. This project focuses on a particular category of assassination—terrorist assassination—that has not received adequate scholarly attention. The results here certainly move the ball forward, but limitations exist, and much work is still needed.

The limitations of this study include the significant span of time from a terrorist assassination to a political institutional change and thus require closer examination. If it is three years or more before Polity changes occur, what happens in the interim? What other variables are present that may speed or delay political changes? The quantitative method utilized does result in some loss of efficiency, but yields interesting insights and does not require any baseline assumptions. This work would also benefit from combining data sources as opposed to using data from only the GTD, yet as discussed in chapter 2, significant definitional challenges exist in trying to combine data from the various datasets that contain assassination event counts.

Terrorist assassinations occur in volatile and dangerous environments and the correlations with other terrorist tactics need unpacking. For instance, are assassinations strategically coordinated with the bombing of a marketplace the day after or before an assassination? Additionally, as with many conflict studies, omitted variables may create bias.

However, this study is novel in that the target categories were cleansed to ensure the events met the definitional criteria of a terrorist assassination. This improves upon the work of GTD researchers and contributes to two important subfields of political violence—assassination studies (although currently underdeveloped) and terrorism studies. The mixed methods approach provides insight that is not achieved in a strictly quantitative study.

Future studies of terrorist assassinations should focus on correlations with other tactics of terrorism, the timing of assassinations, the motivations for these acts, and further examining the repercussions of these attacks. The motivations detected in the case studies here suggest that further exploration of deterrence and retaliation as motives is worthwhile. The case studies also suggest that these assassinations may spur other types of political violence. The case of India highlighted the massive anti-Sikh violence in the aftermath of Gandhi's assassination. In Lebanon, some anti-Syrian violence occurred but more importantly, the Cedar Revolution protests altered the political landscape of the state by demanding (and receiving) the return of its sovereignty from Syria. In Spain, the assassination of police chief, Joseba Pagazaurtundua, generated anti-ETA protests, although with less significant results when compared to the Hariri assassination.

Outside of political violence, are there other repercussions from terrorist assassinations? The assassination in Greece appears to be the trigger that led to the downfall of the 17N group. In what circumstances does an assassination lead to government repression? Are there types of repression that are more prevalent after terrorist assassinations and if so, does this vary according to the assassination target?

Many questions are yet to be answered regarding terrorist assassination, but here, the *where* was able to be answered, at least in part, and the *how* of the political institutional impact is now better understood. Investigating the *when* and *why* of these attacks as discussed above should prove fruitful and can potentially lead one to inform the other. This project establishes a solid understanding of *who* is targeted for assassination by terrorists and begins addressing *how* these attacks affect political institutions. Further research into the *when*, *where*, and *why* of this tactic of terrorism, along with more studies of *how* these attacks affect politics and society, will allow scholars to continue to build a solid framework for understanding contemporary assassinations.

Notes

CHAPTER 1

1. The United Nations Office on Drugs and Crime, *Global Study on Homicide*, 2019. https://www.unodc.org/documents/data-and-analysis/gsh/Booklet1.pdf.

2. Salahuddin, Sayed, "U.S. Commander in Afghanistan Survives Deadly Attack at Governor's Compound that Kills Top Afghan Police General," *The Washington Post*, October 18, 2018. https://www.washingtonpost.com/world/asia_pacific/gunfire-erupts-in-afghan-governors-compound-after-meeting-with-us-commander/2018/10/18/109fc5e0-d2ce-11e8-b2d2-f397227b43f0_story.html (accessed August 12, 2019).

3. *All Africa*, "Somalia: Gunmen Kill a Prominent Somali Elder in Bardere Town," December 6, 2017. https://allafrica.com/stories/201712060425.html (accessed September 7, 2020).

4. Franklin L. Ford, *Political Murder: From Tyrannicide to Terrorism* (Cambridge: Harvard University Press, 1985), 103.

5. Ford, *Political Murder*, 102.

6. *Organization of African Unity Charter*, 1963. https://au.int/sites/default/files/treaties/7759-file-oau_charter_1963.pdf (accessed August 10, 2019); and United Nations Treaty Collection, *1977 Convention on the Prevention and Punishment of Crimes against Internationally Protected Persons, Including Diplomatic Agents*. https://treaties.un.org/pages/ViewDetails.aspx?src=TREATY&mtdsg_no=XVIII-7&chapter=18&clang=_en (accessed August 10, 2019).

7. Federal Register, *Executive Order 12333–United States Intelligence Activities*. https://www.archives.gov/federal-register/codification/executive-order/12333.html.

8. It should be noted that this coincides with an increase in both frequency and lethality of all terror tactics during this time period.

9. History of the Vietnam War on Microfilm, the Fulbright Hearings transcript, from the Texas Tech University Vietnam Center & Sam Johnson Vietnam Archive. https://www.vietnam.ttu.edu/virtualarchive/.

10. See GTD Case IDs 199406290003, 200906250012, 201401120001, 201712100043, 201203060031, 201711060006, and 200311270007.

11. This is discussed in more detail in chapter 3.

12. Daniel J. Milton, "Dangerous Work: Terrorism against U.S. Diplomats," *Contemporary Security Policy*, 38, No. 3 (2017), 345–370.

13. Milton, "Dangerous Work," 361.

CHAPTER 2

1. Richard Bach Jenson, *The Battle against Anarchist Terrorism: An International History, 1878–1934* (Cambridge, UK: Cambridge University Press, 2015), 186–244.

2. Murray Clark Havens, Carl Leiden, and Karl M. Schmitt, *The Politics of Assassination* (New Jersey: Prentice-Hall, Inc., 1970), 3–4.

3. William Crotty, "Assassination and Their Interpretation within the American Context," in *Assassinations and the Political Order*, ed. William Crotty (New York: Harper & Row Publishers, 1971), 8.

4. H. H. A. Cooper, *On Assassination* (Boulder, CO: Paladin Press, 1984), 2.

5. Haig Katchadourian, "Is Political Assassination Ever Morally Justified?" in *Assassination*, ed. Harold Zellner (Cambridge, UK: Schenkman Publishing Company, 1974), 41.

6. Zaryb Iqbal and Christopher Zorn. "Sic Semper Tyrannis? Power, Repression and Assassination since the Second World War," *The Journal of Politics*, 68, No. 3 (2006), 489–501, and "The Political Consequences of Assassination," *The Journal of Conflict Resolution*, 52, No. 3 (2008), 385–400.

7. Arie Perliger, "The Rationale of Political Assassinations," *Combatting Terrorism Center at West Point* (2015), 21. https://ctc.usma.edu/the-rationale-of-political-assassinations/.

8. Perliger, "Rationale," 22.

9. Cooper, *On Assassination*, 2.

10. Thomas Snitch, "Terrorism and Political Assassinations: A Transnational Assessment, 1968–80," *Annals of the American Academy of Political and Social Science*, 463 (1982), 54–68.

11. Daniel L. Premo, "Political Assassination in Guatemala: A Case of Institutionalized Terror," *Journal of Interamerican Studies and World Affairs*, 23, No. 4 (November 1981), 429.

12. Premo, "Political Assassination."

13. David George, "Distinguishing Classical Tyrannicide from Modern Terrorism," *The Review of Politics*, 50, No. 3 (1988), 390–419.

14. George, "Distinguishing," 391.

15. H. Edward Price, "The Strategy and Tactics of Revolutionary Terrorism," *Comparative Studies in Society and History*, 19, No. 1 (1977), 52–66.

16. Walter Enders and Todd Sandler, "Is Transnational Terrorism Becoming More Threatening? A Time-Series Investigation," *Journal of Conflict Resolution*, 44, No. 3 (2000), 307–332.

17. Martha Crenshaw, "The Causes of Terrorism," *Comparative Politics*, 13, No. 4 (1981), 379–399.

18. Bruce Hoffman, *Inside Terrorism* (New York: Columbia University Press, 2006), 40–41.

19. For an excellent discussion on the state of terrorism studies and how to advance/improve research see Joseph K. Young, "Measuring Terrorism," *Terrorism and Political Violence*, 31, No. 3 (2016), 323–345.

20. See START publication "Background Report: Global Terrorism in 2017," https://www.start.umd.edu/pubs/START_GTD_Overview2017_July2018.pdf

21. Global Terrorism Database, National Consortium for the Study of Terrorism and Responses to Terrorism (START), University of Maryland, https://www.start .umd.edu/gtd/.

22. Andrew H. Kydd and Barbara F. Walter, "Strategies of Terrorism," *International Security*, 31, No. 1 (Summer 2006), 49–80.

23. Kydd and Walter, "Strategies," 51.

24. See, for instance, Section 140(d)(2) of the U.S. Foreign Relations Authorization Act, Fiscal Years 1988 and 1989 which defines "terrorism" as "premeditated, politically motivated violence perpetrated against noncombatant targets by subnational groups or clandestine agents."

25. J. Bowyer Bell, "Assassination in International Politics," *International Studies Quarterly*, 16, No. 1 (March 1972), 59–82.

26. In an interview with Joanna Saidel in 1993, Yitzak Shamir (a former Israeli prime minister and former member of the Lehi Group in the 1940s) stated that Lord Moyne was targeted because the group was fighting against the British and Moyne was the highest ranking British officer in the Middle East. See Joanna Saidel, "Yitzak Shamir: Why We Killed Lord Moyne," *The Times of Israel*, July 5, 2012. https://ww w.timesofisrael.com/yitzhak-shamir-why-we-killed-lord-moyne/ (accessed March 30, 2020).

27. Snitch, "Terrorism and Political Assassination."

28. Price, "Strategy and Tactics."

29. George, "Distinguishing."

30. George, "Distinguishing."

31. Marco Pinfari, "Exploring the Terrorist Nature of Political Assassinations: A Reinterpretation of the Orsini Attentat," *Terrorism and Political Violence*, 21, No. 4 (2009), 580–594.

32. Pinfari, "Exploring," 589.

33. Marissa Mandala, "Assassination as a Terrorist Tactic: A Global Analysis," *Dynamics of Asymmetric Conflict*, 10, No. 1 (2017): 14–39.

34. Marissa Mandala and Joshua D. Freilich, "Disrupting Terrorist Assassinations Through Situational Crime Prevention," *Crime & Delinquency*, 64, No. 12 (2018): 1515–1537.

35. Perliger, "Rationale."

36. Perliger, "Rationale," 34.

37. I utilized this definition in earlier work. See Bell, "Terrorist Assassination and Target Selection," *Studies in Conflict & Terrorism*, 40, No. 2 (2017), 157–171.

38. Margaret A. Wilson, Angela Scholes, and Elizabeth Brocklehurst. "A Behavioural Analysis of Terrorist Action," *British Journal of Criminology*, 50, No. 4 (2010), 690–707.

39. For more, see George (1988), and Benjamin F. Jones and Benjamin A. Olken, "Hit or Miss? The Effect of Assassinations on Institutions and War," *American Economic Journal: Macroeconomics*, 1, No. 2 (2009), 55–87.

40. Henk E. Goemans, Kristian S. Gleditsch, and Giacomo Chiozza. "Introducing Archigos: A Dataset of Political Leaders," *Journal of Peace Research*, 46, No. 2 (2009), 269–283.

41. See SPEED Definitions of Destabilizing Events, p. 10, https://uofi.app.box .com/s/xdgimrspyjhuli3pa191zccwas3ueiqf.

42. Typically, domestic terrorism is terrorism that does not in some way "cross a border." For instance, if the terrorist attacks their own government and the terrorist is a member of a domestic terror group, this terror event would typically be considered a domestic terror event. However, if a terrorist in one state crosses a border to attack a government of another state, this would be considered an act of transnational or international terrorism. See work by Walter Enders and Todd Sandler, such as "Transnational Terrorism 1968–2000: Thresholds, Persistence, and Forecasts," *Southern Economic Journal*, 71, No. 3 (2005), 467–483.

43. Patrick T. Brandt and Todd Sandler. "What Do Transnational Terrorists Target? Has It Changed? Are We Safer?" *Journal of Conflict Resolution*, 54, No. 2 (2010), 214–236.

44. Zahra Ali, "After Several High-Profile Murders in Iraq, Here's What Headlines Missed About Their Cause," *The Washington Post*, October 15, 2018. https://www .washingtonpost.com/news/monkey-cage/wp/2018/10/15/after-several-high-profile -murders-in-iraq-heres-what-headlines-missed-about-their-cause/?utm_term=.e82 53dda78fe (accessed April 5, 2020).

45. Sudarsan Raghavan, "Who Is Killing Yemen's Clerics? Mystery Murders Are Sending a Chill Through the Mosques," *The Washington Post*, August 28, 2018. https://www.washingtonpost.com/world/middle_east/who-is-killing-yemens-clerics -mystery-murders-are-sending-a-chill-through-the-mosques/2018/08/27/10b7da3c- ce0f-49e2-ad8e-d4adf05ef885_story.html?utm_term=.7e64c5a414cb (accessed April 10, 2020).

46. Kevin Sieff, "36 Local Candidates Have Been Assassinated in Mexico. And the Election Is Still 2 Months Away," *The Washington Post*, May 20, 2018. https://www.washingtonpost.com/news/worldviews/wp/2018/05/20/36-local-candi dates-have-been-assassinated-in-mexico-and-the-election-is-still-2-months-away/ (accessed April 8, 2020).

47. See the Committee to Protect Journalists, https://cpj.org.

CHAPTER 3

1. For more, see Stathis N. Kalyvas, "The Ontology of "Political Violence": Action and Identity in Civil Wars," *Perspectives on Politics*, 1, No. 3 (2003), 475–494.

2. William Booth, "Was Yasser Arafat Killed by Polonium Poisoning?" *The Washington Post*, November 6, 2013. https://www.washingtonpost.com/world/middle_east/was-yasser-arafat-killed-by-polonium-poisoning/2013/11/06/bada9e82-472c-11e3-95a9-3f15b5618ba8_story.html (accessed April 16, 2020).

3. For a more detailed account, see The White House Historical Association. https://www.whitehousehistory.org/spies-lies-and-disguise-abraham-lincoln-and-the-baltimore-plot (accessed April 10, 2020).

4. For more detail on the GTD, see "About the GTD," https://www.start.umd.edu/gtd/about/.

5. See the *Global Terrorism Database Codebook: Inclusion Criteria and Variables*, July 2018, The University of Maryland, 10.

6. For more on this event, see the discussion in chapter 6.

7. Lone actor attacks (i.e., those not attributed to a group) are not coded in these variables. For more, see the 2018 GTD Codebook, 45–46.

8. 2018 GTD Codebook, 24.

9. See the GTD Database, Case ID 201505030012.

10. See the 2018 GTD Codebook for the full list, along with subtype, 32–40.

11. From this point forward, the only data or descriptive statistics used will be taken from the cleansed GTD dataset for this project, consisting of 9,932 terrorist assassinations. All references are to this set of attacks. Examples in this chapter are the exception and may or may not be counted in the cleansed dataset.

12. See the GTD Database, Case ID 201305310028.

13. See the GTD Database, Case ID 201410010099.

14. See the GTD Database, Case ID 19970422001.

15. James Bargent, "Police Bullets Used in Paraguay Rancher Murder," *InSight Crime*, June 21, 2013. https://www.insightcrime.org/news/brief/police-bullets-used-in-paraguay-rancher-murder/ (accessed April 12, 2020).

16. See the GTD Database, Case ID 200505100010.

17. See the GTD Database, Case ID 200010160001.

18. See the GTD Database, Case ID 201409220110.

19. The remaining second-level/sub-target exclusions are *religion identified, student, race/ethnicity identified, farmer, vehicles/transportation, marketplace/plaza/square, village/city/town/suburb, house/apartment/residence, procession/gathering (funeral, wedding, birthday, religious), public areas (e.g., public garden, parking lot, garage, beach, public buildings, camp), memorial/cemetery/monument, museum/cultural center/cultural house, places of worship, religiously affiliated institutions*. See the 2018 GTD Codebook on target types and sub-target types for more information (32–40). Note: Although the telecommunications category was excluded,

one assassination of a state-run TV chief from this category was included as an assassination.

20. Of the suicide attacks in GTD from 1977 through 2017, 6,154 are bombings.

21. Smaller categories were examined on a case-by-case basis and these target and sub-target categories are as follows: *abortion clinics*, *airports/aircraft*, *educational institutions*, *place of worship*, *telecommunications*, and *military* (military is discussed in chapter 9). The *success* variable was also examined case by case.

22. Monty G. Marshall, Ted Robert Gurr, and Keith Jaggers, *Polity IV Project: Political Regime Characteristics and Transitions,1800–2010*, Societal-Systems Research, Inc. and the Center for Systemic Peace, University of Colorado and University of Maryland. (2016). http://www.systemicpeace.org/inscrdata.html.

23. For an excellent discussion of state repression, see Christian Davenport, "State Repression and the Tyrannical Peace," *Journal of Peace Research*, 44, No. 4 (2007), 485–504, and/or Christian Davenport and Molly Inman, "The State of State Repression Research Since the 1990s," *Terrorism and Political Violence*, 24, No. 4 (2012), 619–634.

24. Mark Gibney, Linda Cornett, Reed Wood, Peter Haschke, Daniel Arnon, and Attilio Pisano. (2018). See http://www.politicalterrorscale.org.

25. See the full explanation of the PTS repression levels at http://www.political terrorscale.org/Data/Documentation.html.

26. It should be noted that most of the 170 states in the dataset experienced at least one terrorist assassination attempt between 1977 and 2017. Benin, Bhutan, Djibouti, and Finland are four states that experienced terror attacks but no terrorist assassinations in this time period.

27. See, for example, Erica Chenoweth, "Terrorism and Democracy," *Annual Review of Political Science*, 16 (2013), 355–378; Khusrav Gaibullov, James A. Piazza, and Todd Sandler, "Regime Types and Terrorism," *International Organization*, 71 (2017), 491–522; and James A. Piazza, "Regime Age and Terrorism: Are New Democracies Prone to Terrorism?" *International Interactions*, 39, No. 2 (2013), 246–263.

CHAPTER 4

1. Laura N. Bell, "Terrorist Assassinations and Target Selection," *Studies in Conflict & Terrorism*, 40, No. 2 (2017), 157–171. The original research note also includes five models of second-level targets not included in this chapter.

2. Ronen Yitzhak, "The Assassination of King Abdallah: The First Political Assassination in Jordan: Did It Truly Threaten the Hashemite Kingdom of Jordan?" *Diplomacy & Statecraft*, 21 (2010), 68–86.

3. Zaryab Iqbal and Christopher Zorn, "Sic Semper Tyrannis? Power, Repression and Assassination since the Second World War," *The Journal of Politics*, 68, No. 3 (2006), 489–501; Zaryab Iqbal and Christopher Zorn, "The Political Consequences of Assassination," *The Journal of Conflict Resolution*, 52, No. 3 (2008), 385–400; and Benjamin F. Jones and Benjamin A. Olken, "Hit or Miss? The Effect of Assassinations

on Institutions and War," *American Economic Journal: Macroeconomics*, 1, No. 2 (2009), 55–87.

4. Asaf Zussman and Noam Zussman, "Assassinations: Evaluating the Effectiveness of an Israeli Counterterrorism Policy Using Stock Market Data," *The Journal of Economic Perspectives*, 20, No. 2 (2006), 193–206.

5. Thomas H. Snitch, "Terrorism and Political Assassinations: A Transnational Assessment, 1968–80," *Annals of the American Academy of Political and Social Science*, 463 (1982), 54–68.

6. Patrick T. Brandt and Todd Sandler, "What Do Transnational Terrorists Target? Has It Changed? Are We Safer?" *Journal of Conflict Resolution*, 54, No. 2 (2010), 214–236.

7. C. J. M. Drake, "The Role of Ideology in Terrorists' Target Selection," *Terrorism and Political Violence*, 10, No. 2 (1998), 53–85.

8. Victor H. Asal, R. Karl Rethemeyer, Ian Anderson, Allyson Stein, Jeffrey Rizzo, and Matthe Rozea, "The Softest of Targets: A Study on Terrorist Target Selection," *Journal of Applied Security Research*, 4, No. 3 (2009), 258–278.

9. Ranya Ahmed, "Terrorist Group Types and Tactic Choice," *Journal of Applied Security Research*, 13, No. 1 (2018), 89–110.

10. Zussman and Zussman, "Assassinations."

11. Zoe Marchment and Paul Gill, "Spatial Decision Making of Terrorist Target Selection: Introducing the TRACK Framework," *Studies in Conflict and Terrorism*, (2020) DOI:10.1080/1057610X.2020.1711588.

12. Ronald Clarke and Graeme R. Newman, *Outsmarting the Terrorists* (Westport, CT: Praeger Security International, 2006).

13. Monty G. Marshall, Ted Gurr, and Keith Jaggers. *Polity IV Project: Political Regime Characteristics and Transitions, 1800–2010* (2013) Societal-Systems Research, Inc. and the Center for Systemic Peace, University of Colorado, and University of Maryland.

14. Janet Box-Steffensmeier and Bradford S. Jones, *Event History Modeling: A Guide for Social Scientists* (New York: Cambridge University Press, 2004).

15. Paul D. Allison, *Event History and Survival Analysis*, Second Edition (Los Angeles: SAGE Publications, 2014).

CHAPTER 5

1. See GTD Case ID 200403020002 and 201712030024.

2. Ibrahim Barzak, "Arafat Advisor Murdered in Gaza City," *The Washington Post*, March 1, 2004. https://www.washingtonpost.com/wp-dyn/articles/A20570 -2004Mar1.html?sections=http://www.washingtonpost.com/wp-dyn/world/issues (accessed July 15, 2020).

3. See GTD Case ID198710070008 and "Gunman and Accomplice Assassinate Syrian Diplomat," *United Press International*, October 7, 1987. https://www.upi

.com/Archives/1987/10/07/Gunman-and-accomplice-assassinate-Syrian-diplomat/ 7058560577600/ (accessed June 15, 2020).

4. Yemen accounts for nearly 31 percent of these attacks. Afghanistan accounts for 21.7 percent, Somalia accounts for nearly 14 percent, and Iraq accounts for 9.6 percent of attacks on intelligence officials around the globe.

5. See GTD Case ID 200705140003.

6. Robin Wright, "New President of Lebanon Killed by a Massive Blast," *The Los Angeles Times*, November 23, 1989. https://www.latimes.com/archives/la-xpm-1989-11-23-mn-247-story.html (accessed June 18, 2020).

7. Pranay Gupte, *Vengeance: India after the Assassination of Indira Gandhi* (New York: W.W. Norton & Company, 1985), 49.

8. Madhuparna Gupta. *Women, Power and Leadership: Case Studies of Indira Gandhi, Margaret Thatcher and Golda Meir* (India: Partridge, 2015), 49–115.

9. Gupte, *Vengeance*, 27.

10. Gupte, *Vengeance*, 96.

11. Gupte, *Vengeance*, 100.

12. M. R. Narayan Swarmy. "When Death Ruled the Streets of Delhi," *News India Times, ViewPoints*, November 7, 2014, 2–6.

13. Tarun Basu, "Recalling the Assassination of Indira," *News India Times, ViewPoints*, November 7, 2014, 2–6.

14. Directorate of Intelligence, *India and the Sikh Challenge: A Research Paper*, Office of Near Eastern and South Asia Analysis, March 1987, sanitized declassified report released May 11, 2012.

15. Refer to chapter 4 for a refresher on the PTS.

16. "Group Says It Ambushed Briton as Retribution," *Chicago Tribune, Tribune News Services*, June 10, 2000. https://www.chicagotribune.com/news/ct-xpm-2000-06-10-0006100144-story.html (accessed June 21, 2020).

17. "Prison Leave for Guerilla Who Blew up Attaché," *The Times*, London, November 10, 2017. https://www.thetimes.co.uk/article/guerrilla-who-blew-up-british-attach-brigadier-stephen-saunders-given-leave-from-greek-jail-23b2jzjw0 (accessed July 21, 2020).

18. Janet Box-Steffensmeier and Bradford S. Jones, *Event History Modeling: A Guide for Social Scientists* (New York: Cambridge University Press, 2004), 131–132.

19. Laura N. Bell, "Terrorist Assassination and Institutional Change in Repressive Regimes," *Terrorism and Political Violence*, 31, No. 4 (2019), 853–875.

CHAPTER 6

1. See GTD Case ID 198910240002.

2. James F. Smith, "Politicians Become Target in Peru's Bloody October," *The Los Angeles Times*, October 17, 1989, 1–A22.

3. See GTD Case ID 199710190006.

4. See GTD Case ID 201404210012.

5. Aaron Brooks, "Another Opposition Leader Killed in Burundi," *The East Africa Monitor*, October 2, 2015, https://eastafricamonitor.com/another-opposition-leader-killed-in-burundi/ and GTD Case ID 201509290053.

6. Nicholas Blanford, *Killing Mr. Lebanon: The Assassination of Rafik Hariri and its Impact on the Middle East* (New York: I.B. Tauris, 2006), 1–2.

7. Azadeh Moaveni and Soraya Sarhaddi Nelson, "Bomb Kills Former Prime Minister—Islamist Group Claims Responsibility, But Victim's Supporters Blame Syria," *Lexington-Herald Leader* (KY), February 15, 2005, A3.

8. Blanford, *Killing Mr. Lebanon*, 3.

9. Lebanon's is a parliamentary republic utilizing a proportional list system of voting. Recent reforms of the electoral system were made in 2018.

10. Blanford, *Killing Mr. Lebanon*, 10.

11. Nicholas Blanford. "Major Assassination Rocks Lebanon: Beirut Car Blast Kills Ex-Prime Minister, a Foe of Syrian Presence," *Chicago Sun-Times* (IL), February 15, 2005, 3.

12. Associated Press. "Hariri Funeral Turns into Anti-Syrian Rally," *Anniston Star* (AL), February 16, 2005. *NewsBank: America's News.* https://infoweb-newsbank-com.databases.wtamu.edu/apps/news/document-view?p=NewsBank&docref=news/10CD1BC3B584E5B0 (accessed July 22, 2020).

13. Karim Knio, "Is Political Stability Sustainable in Post-'Cedar Revolution' Lebanon?" *Mediterranean Politics*, 13, No. 3 (November 2008), 445–451.

14. See GTD Case ID 200506210002 and 200611210002.

15. This evidence is also supported by intelligence regarding Hezbollah. U.S. officials believe that a hit squad exists within Hezbollah's ranks, designed to carry out assassinations of those Hezbollah deems a problem. For more on this, see Souad Mekhennet, "Man Convicted in 2005 Assassination of Former Lebanese Prime Minister Was Part of a Hezbollah Hit Squad, Officials Say," *The Washington Post*, August 25, 2020. https://www.washingtonpost.com/national-security/man-convicted-in-2005-assassination-of-former-lebanese-prime-minister-was-part-of-a-hezbollah-hit-squad-officials-say/2020/08/25/543cbf1a-e6e0-11ea-bc79-834454439a44_story.html (accessed August 27, 2020).

16. Associated Press, "Missile Hit Near Convoy of Ex-Lebanon PM Hariri, Report Says," https://www.abccolumbia.com/2020/06/29/missile-hit-near-convoy-of-ex-lebanon-pm-hariri-report-says/ (accessed July 23, 2020).

17. Jason Heeg. "The Shining Path's Employment of Psychological Warfare during Its Terrorism Campaign in Peru, 1970–1992," *Special Operations Journal*, 3, No. 2 (2017): 111–126.

18. See the Big, Allied, and Dangerous database, hosted by the University of Maryland, for an information sheet on the group. https://www.start.umd.edu/baad/narratives/shining-path-sl.

19. Associated Press. "Leftists' Bomb Injures 10 Near Peruvian Congress Hall," *San Jose Mercury News (CA)*, October 3, 1989, 10A.

20. James F. Smith, "Politicians Become Target in Peru's Bloody October," *The Los Angeles Times*, October 17, 1989, A23.

21. James F. Smith, "Politicians Targeted by Peruvian Maoists," *The Los Angeles Times*, October 17, 1989, A22–23.

22. Smith, "Politicians Targeted."

23. Roger Atwood, "Rebels Kill 15 in Attacks in Peru Towns," *Philadelphia Inquirer, The* (PA), October 12, 1989, A17. *NewsBank: America's News.* https://infoweb-newsbank-com.databases.wtamu.edu/apps/news/document-view?p=NewsBank&docref=news/0EB95FE208D32971 (accessed July 22, 2020).

24. Associated Press, "Leftists' Bomb."

25. James F. Smith, "Maoists Take Aim at Democracy in Peru. Shining Path's Red October' Casts Dark Cloud Over National Life, Institutions," *Houston Chronicle*, October 17, 1989, 16.

26. Reuters, "Peru Suspends Civil Liberties," *Sun-Sentinel*, October 25, 1989, 11A.

27. Associated Press, "Maoist Rebels Suspected in Embassy Blasts in Peru," *San Jose Mercury News (CA)*, October 26, 1989, 14A.

28. Wire Services, "Shining Path Kills 2 Warns USSR, China," *San Jose Mercury News (CA)*, October 31, 1989, 9A.

29. New York Times News Service, "Rebels Threaten Peru Elections," *The Dallas Morning News*, October 29, 1989, 14A.

30. "Peruvians United in Anti-Guerilla March" *The Desert News (Salt Lake City, UT)*, November 4, 1989, A4.

31. Associated Press, "Rebel Attacks Leave 17 Dead in Peru," *Austin American-Statesman*, November 11, 1989, A16.

32. "Peru Rebels Step Up Terror Campaign before Vote," *Houston Chronicle*, November 11, 1989, A19.

33. Associated Press, "Peruvians Vote despite Bloodshed: Rebels Kill Politicians, Dynamite 2 Buildings," *Austin American-Statesman*, November 13, 1989, A3 and James Brooke, "Peru Votes for President Today; Polls see a Runoff," *New York Times*, April 8, 1990. Late edition.

34. Associated Press, "Peruvians Vote." and Associated Press, "Election Officials Slain by Rebels," *San Jose Mercury News (CA)*, November 14, 1989, 15A.

35. Brooke, "Peru Votes."

36. Jeronimo Rios, "Narratives about Political Violence and Reconciliation in Peru," *Latin American Perspectives*, Issue 228, 46, No. 5 (September 2019): 44–58. And *The Economist*, "Looking Back on Peru's Shining Path," May 16, 2020. https://www.economist.com/the-americas/2020/05/16/looking-back-on-perus-shining-path (accessed July 31, 2020).

37. For a refresher on the *tumultuous* category coding for negative and positive Polity shifts, see chapter 5.

38. Models were tested for the impact of repressive regimes in the likelihood of Polity change, but as with the government officials' category, no significance was found in any of the models tested, including stratified models.

CHAPTER 7

1. See GTD Case No. 201506290011.

2. BBC News, "Egypt Prosecutor Hisham Barakat Killed in Cairo Attack," June 29, 2015. https://www.bbc.com/news/world-middle-east-33308518 (accessed July 30, 2020).

3. Amina Ismail, "Egypt Executes Nine Over Public Prosecutor's Killing," *Reuters*, February 20, 2019. https://www.reuters.com/article/us-egypt-execution/egypt-executes-nine-men-over-killing-of-public-prosecutor-prison-source-lawyer-idUSKCN1Q9125 (accessed August 1, 2020).

4. Erin M. Kearns, Brendan Conlon, and Joseph K. Young, "Lying About Terrorism," *Studies in Conflict & Terrorism*, 37, No. 5 (2014), 422–439. DOI: 10.1080/1057610X.2014.893480.

5. See GTD ID 201501250033.

6. Jose de Cordoba, "Mexico Launches Raids After Assassination Attempt of Police Chief," *BBC News*, June 26, 2020. https://www.bbc.com/news/world-latin-america-53207372 (accessed August 2, 2020).

7. Shamsudin Bokov, "Russian Judge Slain While Taking Her Children to School," *Toronto Star (Ontario)*, June 11, 2009. P. A14. And Philip A. Pan, "Judge Assassinated in Russia's Caucasus; 2nd Killing in a Week," *Washington Post*, June 11, 2009, p. A12.

8. Pan, "Judge Assassinated."

9. Associated Press News Service, "A Glance at Other Recent Attacks in Ingushetia," August 17, 2009. *NewsBank: America's News*. https://infoweb-newsbank-com.databases.wtamu.edu/apps/news/document-view?p=NewsBank&docref=news/141454B2b92DB5E8.

10. See GTD Case ID 201004120010.

11. Interfax America, Inc., "Baklagin, Isayev Charged with Murder of Judge Chuvashov—Investigative Committee," *Russia & CIS Military Newswire*, June 28, 2012; Interfax America, Inc., "Serbia, Ukraine Arrest Russian Radicals Accused of Murder," *Ukraine General Newswire*, May 13, 2013; and *BBC News*, "Russian Nationalist Jailed for Life Over Hate Crimes," July 24, 2015. https://www.bbc.com/news/world-europe-33657409 (accessed August 2, 2020).

12. Ivan Nechepurenko, "Russian Ultranationalists Get Life Sentences for Slew of Hate Killings," *The Moscow Times*, April 21, 2015. https://www.themoscowtimes.com/2015/04/21/russian-ultranationalists-get-life-sentences-for-slew-of-hate-killings-a45981 (accessed August 8, 2020).

13. See GTD Case ID 201503310015.

14. Andrew Gardner, "Can Turkey Open a Fresh Chapter Following the Death of Berkin Elvan?" *Amnesty International*, March 13, 2014. https://www.amnesty.org/en/latest/campaigns/2014/03/can-turkey-open-a-fresh-chapter-following-the-death-of-berkin-elvan/ (accessed August 6, 2020).

15. See GTD Case ID 200302080005.

16. "Basque Group is Protested," *New York Times*, February 10, 2003, Late edition (East Coast).

17. "Vigils Mark Assassination Blamed on Eta," *Independent [London, England]*, February 11, 2003.

18. See short bio posted by Concordia at https://www.concordia.net/community/maite-pagazaurtundua/.

19. Teresa Whitfield, *Endgame for ETA: Elusive Peace in the Basque Country* (New York: Oxford University Press, 2014).

20. Associated Press, "The Latest: Relatives of ETA Victims Skeptical of Statement," *Associated Press News Service*, May 2, 2018.

21. The survival curves for the models in this chapter are similar in trend to previous survival models and thus are only discussed, not displayed, in the interest of space.

CHAPTER 8

1. Josh Halliday, "Egypt Protests: BBC, CNN and al-Jazeera Journalists Attacked," *The Guardian*, February 3, 2011. https://www.theguardian.com/media/2011/feb/03/journalists-attacked-in-egypt-protests (accessed July 20, 2020).

2. Dan Rivers, "UK Journalist Assaulted in Tahrir Square: 'Please Make It Stop,'" *CNN*, June 28, 2012. https://www.cnn.com/2012/06/27/world/meast/egypt-journalist-assaulted/index.html (accessed July 30, 2020).

3. Simon Cottle, Richard Sambrook, and Nick Mosdell, *Reporting Dangerously: Journalist Killings, Intimidation, and Security* (London: Palgrave Macmillan, 2016).

4. "Reporter Daniel Pearl Is Dead, Killed by His Captors in Pakistan," *Wall Street Journal*, February 24, 2002. https://online.wsj.com/public/resources/documents/pearl-022102.htm (accessed July 21, 2020).

5. "Kate Peyton, BBC, Killed in Mogadishu, Somalia, February 9, 2005," Committee to Protect Journalists. https://cpj.org/data/people/kate-peyton/ (accessed July 25, 2020).

6. "Turkey: 3 Arrested Over the Killing of a Syrian Journalist," *Associated Press*, January 10, 2016. https://apnews.com/a74bf8f3995149a5993371f43290bdf5 (accessed July 10, 2020), and GTD Case ID 201512270005.

7. See GTD Case ID 201508070060 and 201505120071.

8. Rupert Hawksley, "Naji al-Ali: Remembering One of the Middle East's Most Important Cartoonists," *The National*, August 28, 2018.

9. *BBC News*, "Charlie Hebdo Attack: Three Days of Terror," January 14, 2015. https://www.bbc.com/news/world-europe-30708237 (accessed August 1, 2020).

10. *Three Days of Terror: The Charlie Hebdo Attacks*. directed by Dan Reed, 60 min. (HBO Documentary, 2016).

11. "Charlie Hebdo Trial Opens in Paris with Most Suspects Dead or Presumed Dead," *France24*, June 1, 2020. https://www.france24.com/en/20200106-charlie-hebdo-trial-opens-in-paris-with-most-suspects-dead-or-presumed-dead-1 (accessed August 1, 2020).

12. The government has officially admitted to 7,000 disappeared during the Black Decade, but some estimate the number to be as high as 17,000. See the International

Center for Transitional Justice (ICTJ) for more. https://www.ictj.org/news/algeria-w omen-disappeared-truth.

13. Eleanor Beardsley, "Algeria's 'Black Decade' Still Weighs Heavily," *NPR*, April 25, 2011. https://www.npr.org/2011/04/25/135376589/algerias-black-decade-st ill-weighs-heavily (accessed July 10, 2020).

14. Jeremy Keenan. *The Dark Sahara: America's War on Terror in Africa* (New York: Pluto Press, 2009), 134.

15. Keenan, *The Dark Sahara*, 136.

16. Nancy J. Woodhull and Robert W. Snyder, eds., *Journalists in Peril* (New Brunswick: Transaction Publishers, 1998).

17. Keenan, *The Dark Sahara*, 138–139.

18. As a reminder, GTD does not contain information on attacks for 1993. This is a partial explanation for the lower assassination count here.

19. Jonathan Randal, "Most News Is Bad News for Algerian Journalists: Assassinations, Restrictions Plague Press," *The Washington Post*, June 8, 1994, A31.

20. Eric Sellin, "Tahar Dajourt (1954–1993)," *World Literature Review*, 68, No. 1 (Winter 1994), 71–73.

21. Woodhull and Snyder, *Journalists in Peril*, 86.

22. Woodhull and Snyder, *Journalists in Peril* and Randal, "Most News."

23. Woodhull and Snyder, *Journalists in Peril* and Randal, "Most News."

24. Michael Balter, "Killing the Messengers: Thirty-Seven Murdered Journalists— and Counting." *Columbia Journalism Review*, 34, No. 1 (1995): 17. *Gale Academic OneFile* (accessed August 17, 2020); Randal, "Most News," Woodhull and Snyder, *Journalists in Peril*.

25. Balter, "Killing the Messengers," Woodhull and Snyder, *Journalists in Peril*.

26. Robert Fisk. "The Forgotten Martyrdom of Algeria's Reporters," *The Independent* [London, England], January 8, 2011, p. 38. *Gale OneFile: News* (accessed August 12, 2020).

27. Beardsley, "Algeria's 'Black Decade.'"

28. Orla Guerin, "Algeria's Protest: Youth Lead the Movement for Change," *BBC News*, April 14, 2019. https://www.bbc.com/news/world-africa-47927296 (accessed August 6, 2020).

29. Guerin, "Algeria's Protest."

CHAPTER 9

1. Steve Lohr, "I.R.A. Shifts Tactics, and the Results are Deadly," *The New York Times*, August 23, 1989, A3.

2. Lohr, "I.R.A Shifts Tactics."

3. See GTD Case ID 200010160001 and *BBC News*, "Spanish Military Doctor Shot Dead," October 17, 2000. http://news.bbc.co.uk/2/hi/europe/975554.stm (accessed July 2, 2020).

4. See GTD Case ID 201211210007.

5. See GTD Case ID 201311060022.

6. See GTD Case ID 201308310006.

7. See GTD Case ID 201307160027.

8. See GTD Case ID 201403010007.

9. See GTD Case ID 201607310062.

10. See GTD Case ID 201603240013 and 201704170002.

11. See GTD Case ID 198604230015 and 198702260014.

12. See GTD Case ID 201605010051.

13. See GTD Case ID 200507010002.

14. Andy Mosher, "Aide to Cleric Killed in Baghdad: Objective Thought to Tempt Civil War," *The Washington Post*, July 3, 2005. https://www.washingtonpost.com /archive/politics/2005/07/03/aide-to-cleric-killed-in-baghdad/49cc4b7b-b7dd-45fa -bea1-a34a0cf13a5c/ (accessed August 19, 2020).

15. See GTD Case ID 201212030001; John Asher, "Swedish Woman Shot in Lahore Passes Away in Sweden," *Pakistan Today*, December 13, 2012. https://ww w.pakistantoday.com.pk/2012/12/13/swedish-woman-shot-in-lahore-passes-away-in -sweden/ (accessed August 17, 2020).

16. Syed Raza Hassan, "Pakistani Shi'ite Cleric Shot Dead in Reprisal Attack," *Reuters*, December 15, 2013. https://www.reuters.com/article/us-pakistan-sectar ian/pakistani-shiite-cleric-shot-dead-in-reprisal-attack-idUSBRE9BF03620131216 (accessed August 16, 2020).

17. *BBC News*, "Kenya Cleric Sheikh Mohammed Idris Shot Dead in Mombasa," June 10, 2014. https://www.bbc.com/news/world-africa-27776743 (accessed August 17, 2020).

18. GTD Case ID 200403100002.

19. GTD Case ID 201605060022.

20. Associated Press News, "Sufi Leader Shot, Hacked to Death in Bangladesh," March 17, 2017. https://apnews.com/2b00b207f12a4798ad806d761f176fcc/Sufi-lea der-shot,-hacked-to-death-in-Bangladesh (accessed August 19, 2020).

21. Reuters, "Prominent Saudi Cleric Injured in Philippines Shooting," March 1, 2016. https://www.reuters.com/article/us-philippines-saudi-idUSKCN0W358X (accessed August 17, 2020).

22. See GTD Case ID 201710280017.

23. See GTD Case ID 201803020019.

24. Sudarsan Raghavan, "Who Is Killing Yemen's Clerics? Mystery Murders Are Sending a Chill Through the Mosques," *The Washington Post*, August 28, 2018. https://www.washingtonpost.com/world/middle_east/who-is-killing-yemens-clerics -mystery-murders-are-sending-a-chill-through-the-mosques/2018/08/27/10b7da3c- ce0f-49e2-ad8e-d4adf05ef885_story.html (accessed August 1, 2020); Ahmed al-Haj, "Unidentified Assailants Kill Well Known Cleric in Yemen," *Associated Press News*, July 22, 2018. https://apnews.com/e70e324e2567420ba7d4dbeb01ed1a1 5/Unidentified-assailants-kill-well-known-cleric-in-Yemen (accessed August 19, 2020).

Bibliography

Ahmed, Ranya. "Terrorist Group Types and Tactic Choice." *Journal of Applied Security Research* 13, No. 1 (2018): 89–110.

"Algerian Journalists' Toll Nears 30: [Evening Update, C Edition]." *Chicago Tribune (Pre-1997 Fulltext)*, December 1, 1994.

Al-Haj, Ahmed. "Unidentified Assailants Kill Well Known Cleric in Yemen." *Associated Press News*, July 22, 2018. https://apnews.com/e70e324e2567420ba7d4dbeb01ed1a15/Unidentified-assailants-kill-well-known-cleric-in-Yemen

Ali, Zahra. "After Several High-Profile Murders in Iraq, Here's What Headlines Missed about their Cause." *The Washington Post*, October 15, 2018. https://www.washingtonpost.com/news/monkey-cage/wp/2018/10/15/after-several-high-profile-murders-in-iraq-heres-what-headlines-missed-about-their-cause/?utm_term=.e8253dda78fe

All Africa. "Somalia: Gunmen Kill a Prominent Somali Elder in Bardere Town." *Shabelle Media Network*, December 6, 2017. https://allafrica.com/stories/201712060425.html

Allison, Paul D. *Event History and Survival Analysis, Second Edition*. Los Angeles: SAGE Publications, 2014.

Alzuro, Blair. "Missile Hit Near Convoy of Ex-Lebanon PM Hariri, Report Says." *ABC Columbia (SC)*, June 29, 2020. https://www.abccolumbia.com/wireap_af6c3369915d4b278afb2259eecf7764_16x9_992/

Appleton, Sheldon. "Trends: Assassinations." *The Public Opinion Quarterly* 64, No. 4 (2000): 495–522.

Asal, Victor H., R. Karl Rethemeyer, Ian Anderson, Allyson Stein, Jeffrey Rizzo, and Matthe Rozea. "The Softest of Targets: A Study on Terrorist Target Selection." *Journal of Applied Security Research* 4, No. 3 (2009): 258–78.

Asher, John. "Swedish Woman Shot in Lahore Passes Away in Sweden." *Pakistan Today*, December 13, 2012. https://www.pakistantoday.com.pk/2012/12/13/swedish-woman-shot-in-lahore-passes-away-in-sweden/

Associated Press. "Election Officials Slain by Rebels." *San Jose Mercury News (CA)*, November 14, 1989.

Associated Press. "Hariri Funeral Turns into Anti-Syrian Rally." *Anniston Star* (AL), February 16, 2005. *NewsBank: America's News*. https://infoweb-newsbank-com .databases.wtamu.edu/apps/news/document-view?p=NewsBank&docref=news /10CD1BC3B584E5B0

Associated Press. "Leftists' Bomb Injures 10 Near Peruvian Congress Hall." *San Jose Mercury News (CA)*, October 3, 1989.

Associated Press. "Maoist Rebels Suspected in Embassy Blasts in Peru." *San Jose Mercury News (CA)*, October 26, 1989.

Associated Press. "Rebel Attacks Leave 17 Dead in Peru." *Austin American-Statesman (TX)*, November 11, 1989.

Associated Press. "Peruvians Vote Despite Bloodshed: Rebels Kill Politicians, Dynamite 2 Buildings." *Austin American-Statesman (TX)*, November 13, 1989.

Associated Press News Service. "A Glance at Other Recent Attacks in Ingushetia." *NewsBank: America's News*, August 17, 2009. https://infoweb-newsbank-com.d atabases.wtamu.edu/apps/news/document-view?p=NewsBank&docref=news/1414 54B2b92DB5E8

Associated Press News Service. "Sufi Leader Shot, Hacked to Death in Bangladesh." *AP News*, March 17, 2017. https://apnews.com/2b00b207f12a4798ad806d761f 176fcc/Sufi-leader-shot,-hacked-to-death-in-Bangladesh

Associated Press News Service. "The Latest: Relatives of ETA Victims Skeptical of Statement." *Fox News*, May 2, 2018. https://www.foxnews.com/world/the-latest -relatives-of-eta-victims-skeptical-of-statement

Atwood, Roger. "Rebels Kill 15 in Attacks in Peru Towns." *Philadelphia Inquirer, The (PA)*, October 12, 1989. *NewsBank: America's News*. https://infoweb-news bank-com.databases.wtamu.edu/apps/news/document-view?p=NewsBank&docref =news/0EB95FE208D32971

Balter, Michael. "Killing the Messengers: Thirty-Seven Murdered Journalists—and Counting." *Columbia Journalism Review* 34, No. 1 (1995): 17. *Gale Academic OneFile*.

Banks, Arthur S., Wilson, Kenneth A. "Cross-National Time-Series Data Archive." Databanks International. Jerusalem, Israel. (2020). https://www.cntsdata.com/

Bargent, James. "Police Bullets Used in Paraguay Rancher Murder." *InSight Crime*, June 21, 2013. https://www.insightcrime.org/news/brief/police-bullets-used-in-pa raguay-rancher-murder/

Barzak, Ibrahim. "Arafat Advisor Murdered in Gaza City." *The Washington Post*, March 1, 2004. https://www.washingtonpost.com/wp-dyn/articles/A20570 -2004Mar1.html?sections=http://www.washingtonpost.com/wp-dyn/world/issues

"Basque Group is Protested." *New York Times Late Edition (East Coast)*, February 10, 2003.

Basu, Tarun. "Recalling the Assassination of Indira." *News India Times*, *ViewPoints*, November 7, 2014.

Beardsley, Eleanor. "Algeria's 'Black Decade' Still Weighs Heavily." *NPR*, April 25, 2011. https://www.npr.org/2011/04/25/135376589/algerias-black-decade-still -weighs-heavily

Bell, J. Bowyer. "Assassination in International Politics." *International Studies Quarterly* 16, No. 1 (March 1972): 59–82.

Bell, Laura N. "Terrorist Assassination and Institutional Change in Repressive Regimes." *Terrorism and Political Violence* 31, No. 4 (2019): 853–75.

Bell, Laura N. "Terrorist Assassinations and Target Selection." *Studies in Conflict & Terrorism* 40, No. 2 (2017): 157–71.

Blanford, Nicholas. *Killing Mr. Lebanon: The Assassination of Rafik Hariri and Its Impact on the Middle East.* New York: I.B. Tauris & Co. Ltd., 2006.

Blanford, Nicholas. "Major Assassination Rocks Lebanon: Beirut Car Blast Kills Ex-Prime Minister, a Foe of Syrian Presence." *Chicago Sun-Times (IL)*, February 15, 2005.

Bokov, Shamsudin. "Russian Judge Slain while Taking Her Children to School." *Toronto Star (Ontario)*, June 11, 2009.

Booth, William. "Was Yasser Arafat Killed by Polonium Poisoning?" *The Washington Post*, November 6, 2013. https://www.washingtonpost.com/world/middle_east/was-yasser-arafat-killed-by-polonium-poisoning/2013/11/06/bada9e82-472c-11e3-95a9-3f15b5618ba8_story.html

Bosco, Robert M. "The Assassination of Rafik Hariri: Foreign Policy Perspectives." *International Political Science Review* 30 (2009): 349–61.

Box-Steffensmeier, Janet and Bradford S. Jones. *Event History Modeling: A Guide for Social Scientists.* New York: Cambridge University Press, 2004.

Brandt, Patrick T. and Todd Sandler. "What Do Transnational Terrorists Target? Has It Changed? Are We Safer?" *Journal of Conflict Resolution* 54, No. 2 (2010): 214–36.

Brooke, James. "Peru Votes for President Today; Polls See a Runoff." *New York Times Late Edition*, April 8, 1990.

Brooks, Aaron. "Another Opposition Leader Killed in Burundi." *The East Africa Monitor*, October 2, 2015. https://eastafricamonitor.com/another-opposition-leader-killed-in-burundi/

Central Intelligence Agency, Directorate of Intelligence. *India and the Sikh Challenge: A Research Paper*, Office of Near Eastern and South Asia Analysis, March 1987, sanitized declassified report released May 11, 2012.

"Charlie Hebdo Attack: Three Days of Terror." *BBC News*, January 14, 2015. https://www.bbc.com/news/world-europe-30708237

"Charlie Hebdo Trial Opens in Paris with Most Suspects Dead or Presumed Dead." *France24*, June 1, 2020. https://www.france24.com/en/20200106-charlie-hebdo-trial-opens-in-paris-with-most-suspects-dead-or-presumed-dead-1

Chenoweth, Erica. "Terrorism and Democracy." *Annual Review of Political Science* 16 (2013): 355–78.

Clarke, Ronald and Graeme R. Newman. *Outsmarting the Terrorists.* Westport, CT: Praeger Security International, 2006.

Cooper, H. H. A. *On Assassination.* Boulder, CO: Paladin Press, 1984.

Cottle, Simon, Richard Sambrook, and Nick Mosdell. *Reporting Dangerously: Journalist Killings, Intimidation, and Security.* London: Palgrave Macmillan, 2016.

Crenshaw, Martha. "The Causes of Terrorism." *Comparative Politics* 13, No. 4 (1981): 379–99.

Crotty, William. "Assassination and Their Interpretation within the American Context." In *Assassinations and the Political Order*, edited by William Crotty, 3–53. New York: Harper & Row Publishers, 1971.

Davenport, Christian. "State Repression and the Tyrannical Peace." *Journal of Peace Research* 44, No. 4 (2007): 485–504.

Davenport, Christian and Molly Inman. "The State of State Repression Research Since the 1990s." *Terrorism and Political Violence* 24, No. 4 (2012): 619–34.

De Cordoba, Jose. "Mexico Launches Raids after Assassination Attempt of Police Chief." *BBC News*, June 26, 2020. https://www.bbc.com/news/world-latin-ame rica-53207372

Drake, C. J. M. "The Role of Ideology in Terrorists' Target Selection." *Terrorism and Political Violence* 10, No. 2 (1998): 53–85.

"Egypt Prosecutor Hisham Barakat Killed in Cairo Attack." *BBC News*, June 29, 2015. https://www.bbc.com/news/world-middle-east-33308518

Enders, Walter and Todd Sandler. "Is Transnational Terrorism Becoming More Threatening? A Time-Series Investigation." *Journal of Conflict Resolution* 44, No. 3 (2000): 307–32.

Enders, Walter and Todd Sandler. "Transnational Terrorism 1968–2000: Thresholds, Persistence, and Forecasts." *Southern Economic Journal* 71, No. 3 (2005): 467–83.

Fisk, Robert. "The Forgotten Martyrdom of Algeria's Reporters." *The Independent [London, England]*, January 8, 2011. *Gale OneFile: News*.

Feenstra, Robert C., Robert Inklaar, and Marcel P. Timmer. "The Next Generation of the Penn World Table." *American Economic Review* 105, No. 10 (2015): 3150–82. www.ggdc.net/pwt

Foerstel, Herbert N. *Killing the Messenger: Journalists at Risk in Modern Warfare*. Westport, CT: Praeger Publishers, 2006.

Ford, Franklin L. *Political Murder: From Tyrannicide to Terrorism*. Cambridge: Harvard University Press, 1985.

Frey, Bruno S. "Why Kill Politicians? A Rational Choice Analysis of Political Assassinations." (May 2007). http://dx.doi.org/10.2139/ssrn.990275

Gaibullov, Khusrav, James A. Piazza, and Todd Sandler. "Regime Types and Terrorism." *International Organization* 71 (2017): 491–522.

Gardner, Andrew. "Can Turkey Open a Fresh Chapter following the Death of Berkin Elvan?" *Amnesty International*, March 13, 2014. https://www.amnesty.org/en/ latest/campaigns/2014/03/can-turkey-open-a-fresh-chapter-following-the-death-of -berkin-elvan/

George, David. "Distinguishing Classical Tyrannicide from Modern Terrorism." *The Review of Politics* 50, No. 3 (1988): 390–419.

Gibney, Mark, Linda Cornett, Reed Wood, Peter Haschke, Daniel Arnon, Attilio Pisanò, and Gray Barrett. "The Political Terror Scale 1976–2018." (2019). http:// www.politicalterrorscale.org

Goemans, Henk E., Kristian S. Gleditsch, and Giacomo Chiozza. "Introducing Archigos: A Dataset of Political Leaders." *Journal of Peace Research* 46, No. 2 (2009): 269–83.

Graham, Bradley. "Peruvian Rebels, in Policy Shift, Extend List of Assassination Targets." *The Washington Post*, April 14, 1987.

"Group Says it Ambushed Briton as Retribution." *Chicago Tribune, Tribune News Services*, June 10, 2000. https://www.chicagotribune.com/news/ct-xpm-2000-06 -10-0006100144-story.html

Guerin, Orla. "Algeria's Protest: Youth Lead the Movement for Change." *BBC News*, April 14, 2019. https://www.bbc.com/news/world-africa-47927296

"Gunman and Accomplice Assassinate Syrian Diplomat." *United Press International*, October 7, 1987. https://www.upi.com/Archives/1987/10/07/Gunman-and-acco mplice-assassinate-Syrian-diplomat/7058560577600/

Gupta, Madhuparna. *Women, Power and Leadership: Case Studies of Indira Gandhi, Margaret Thatcher and Golda Meir*. India: Partridge Publishing, 2015.

Gupte, Pranay. *Vengeance: India after the Assassination of Indira Gandhi*. New York: W.W. Norton & Company, 1985.

Halliday, Josh. "Egypt Protests: BBC, CNN and al-Jazeera journalists Attacked." *The Guardian*, February 3, 2011. https://www.theguardian.com/media/2011/feb/03/ journalists-attacked-in-egypt-protests

Hardgrave, Robert L. Jr. "India in 1984: Confrontation, Assassination, and Succession." *Asian Survey (A Survey of Asia in 1984 Part II)* 25, No. 2 (1985): 131–44.

Hassan, Syed Raza. "Pakistani Shi'ite Cleric Shot Dead in Reprisal Attack." *Reuters*, December 15, 2013. https://www.reuters.com/article/us-pakistan-sectarian/pakist ani-shiite-cleric-shot-dead-in-reprisal-attack-idUSBRE9BF03620131216

Havens, Murray Clark, Carl Leiden, and Karl M. Schmitt. *The Politics of Assassination*. New Jersey: Prentice-Hall, Inc., 1970.

Hawksley, Rupert. "Naji al-Ali: Remembering One of the Middle East's Most Important Cartoonists." *The National*, August 28, 2018. https://www.thenational .ae/arts-culture/naji-al-ali-remembering-one-of-the-middle-east-s-most-important -cartoonists-1.764543

Heeg, Jason. "The Shining Path's Employment of Psychological Warfare During Its Terrorism Campaign in Peru, 1970–1992." *Special Operations Journal* 3, No. 2 (2017): 111–26.

Hoffman, Aaron M. "Voice and Silence: Why Groups Take Credit for Acts of Terror." *Journal of Peace Research* 47, No. 5 (2010): 615–26.

Hoffman, Bruce. *Inside Terrorism*. New York: Columbia University Press, 2006.

Iqbal, Zaryab and Christopher Zorn. "Sic Semper Tyrannis? Power, Repression and Assassination Since the Second World War." *The Journal of Politics* 68, No. 3 (2006): 489–501.

Iqbal, Zaryab and Christopher Zorn. "The Political Consequences of Assassination." *The Journal of Conflict Resolution* 52, No. 3 (2008): 385–400.

Interfax America, Inc. "Baklagin, Isayev Charged with Murder of Judge Chuvashov— Investigative Committee." *Russia & CIS Military Newswire*, June 28, 2012.

Interfax America, Inc. "Serbia, Ukraine Arrest Russian Radicals Accused of Murder." *Ukraine General Newswire*, May 13, 2013.

"Iraqi Clerics Urge Restraint Amid Growing Violence: Militants' Threat Shocked Imams." *Edmonton Journal* (Alberta). September 17, 2005.

Ismail, Amina. "Egypt Executes Nine over Public Prosecutor's Killing." *Reuters*, February 20, 2019. https://www.reuters.com/article/us-egypt-execution/egypt-executes-nine-men-over-killing-of-public-prosecutor-prison-source-lawyer-idUSKCN1Q9125

Jaszi, Oscar. "The Stream of Political Murder." *American Journal of Economics and Sociology (Essays in Memory of Franz Oppenheimer, 1864–1943)* 3 (1944): 335–55.

Jenson, Richard Bach. *The Battle against Anarchist Terrorism: An International History, 1878–1933.* Cambridge, UK: Cambridge University Press, 2015.

Jones, Benjamin F. and Benjamin A. Olken. "Hit or Miss? The Effect of Assassinations on Institutions and War." *American Economic Journal: Macroeconomics* 1, No. 2 (2009): 55–87.

Kalyvas, Stathis N. "The Ontology of "Political Violence": Action and Identity in Civil Wars." *Perspectives on Politics* 1, No. 3 (2003): 475–94.

Kassimeris, George. *Inside Greek Terrorism.* New York: Oxford University Press, 2013.

Kassimeris, George. "Last Act in a Violent Drama? The Trial of Greece's Revolutionary Organization 17 November." *Terrorism and Political Violence* 18, No. 1 (2006): 137–57.

Kassimeris, George. "Why Greek Terrorists Give Up: Analyzing Individual Exit from the Revolutionary Organization 17 November." *Studies in Conflict & Terrorism* 34 (2011): 556–71.

Katchadourian, Haig. "Is Political Assassination Ever Morally Justified?" In *Assassination*, edited by Harold Zellner, 41–56. Cambridge, UK: Schenkman Publishing Company, 1974.

"Kate Peyton, BBC, Killed in Mogadishu, Somalia, February 9, 2005." *Committee to Protect Journalists.* https://cpj.org/data/people/kate-peyton/

Kearns, Erin M., Brenda Conlon, and Joseph K. Young. "Lying About Terrorism." *Studies in Conflict & Terrorism* 37, No. 5 (2014): 422–39.

Keenan, Jeremy. *The Dark Sahara: America's War on Terror in Africa.* New York: Pluto Press, 2009.

"Kenya Cleric Sheikh Mohammed Idris Shot Dead in Mombasa." *BBC News*, June 10, 2014. https://www.bbc.com/news/world-africa-27776743

Knio, Karim. "Is Political Stability Sustainable in Post-Cedar Revolution Lebanon?" *Mediterranean Politics* 13, No. 3 (2008): 445–51.

Knudsen, Are and Michael Kerr (eds). *Lebanon: After the Cedar Revolution.* New York: Oxford University Press, 2013.

Kydd, Andrew H. and Barbara Walter. "Strategies of Terrorism." *International Security* 31, No. 1 (Summer 2006): 49–80.

Lentz, Harris M. III. *Assassinations and Executions: An Encyclopedia of Political Violence, 1900 through 2000 Revised Edition.* North Carolina: McFarland & Company, Inc., 2002.

Lohr, Steve. "I.R.A. Shifts Tactics, and the Results are Deadly." *The New York Times*, August 23, 1989.

"Looking Back on Peru's Shining Path." *The Economist*, May 16, 2020. https://www.economist.com/the-americas/2020/05/16/looking-back-on-perus-shining-path

Mandala, Marissa. "Assassination as a Terrorist Tactic: A Global Analysis." *Dynamics of Asymmetric Conflict* 10, No. 1 (2017): 14–39.

Mandala, Marissa and Joshua D. Freilich. "Disrupting Terrorist Assassinations Through Situational Crime Prevention." *Crime & Delinquency* 64, No. 12 (2018): 1515–37.

Marchment, Zoe and Paul Gill. "Spatial Decision Making of Terrorist Target Selection: Introducing the TRACK Framework." *Studies in Conflict and Terrorism* (2020): 1–19. DOI:10.1080/1057610X.2020.1711588.

Marshall, Monty G., Ted Gurr, and Keith Jaggers. "Polity IV Project: Political Regime Characteristics and Transitions, 1800–2018." Societal-Systems Research, Inc. and the Center for Systemic Peace, University of Colorado and University of Maryland, 2019. https://www.systemicpeace.org/inscrdata.html

Marvick, Dwaine and Elizabeth Wirth Marvick. "The Political Consequences of Assassination." In *Assassinations and the Political Order*, edited by William Crotty, 489–543. New York: Harper & Row Publishers, 1971.

Mazrui, Ali A. "Thoughts on Assassination in Africa." *Political Science Quarterly* 83, No. 1 (March 1968): 40–58.

Mekhennet, Souad. "Man Convicted in 2005 Assassination of Former Lebanese Prime Minister was Part of a Hezbollah Hit Squad, Officials Say." *The Washington Post*, August 25, 2020. https://www.washingtonpost.com/national-security/m an-convicted-in-2005-assassination-of-former-lebanese-prime-minister-was-part -of-a-hezbollah-hit-squad-officials-say/2020/08/25/543cbf1a-e6e0-11ea-bc79-834 454439a44_story.html

Mickolus, Edward F., Todd Sandler, Jean M. Murdock, Peter A. Flemming. "International Terrorism: Attributes of Terrorist Events (ITERATE), 1968–2010." 2011. https://vinyardsoftware.com/research-projects/

Milton, Daniel J. "Dangerous Work: Terrorism against U.S. Diplomats." *Contemporary Security Policy* 38, No. 3 (2017): 345–70.

Moaveni, Azadeh and Soraya Sarhaddi Nelson. "Bomb Kills Former Prime Minister—Islamist Group Claims Responsibility, But Victim's Supporters Blame Syria." *Lexington-Herald Leader (KY)*, February 15, 2005.

Morris, Loveday and Robyn Dixon. "Germany Links Russian Agents to Berlin Assassination, Expels Diplomats." *The Washington Post*, December 4, 2019. https ://www.washingtonpost.com/world/europe/germany-links-russian-agents-to-berl in-assassination-expels-diplomats/2019/12/04/7b1ccb40-168c-11ea-80d6-d0ca70 07273f_story.html

Mosher, Andy. "Aide to Cleric Killed in Baghdad: Objective Thought to Tempt Civil War." *The Washington Post*, July 3, 2005. https://www.washingtonpost.com /archive/politics/2005/07/03/aide-to-cleric-killed-in-baghdad/49cc4b7b-b7dd-45fa -bea1-a34a0cf13a5c/

Nechepurenko, Ivan. "Russian Ultranationalists Get Life Sentences for Slew of Hate Killings." *The Moscow Times*, April 21, 2015. https://www.themoscowtimes.com/2015 /04/21/russian-ultranationalists-get-life-sentences-for-slew-of-hate-killings-a45981

New York Times News Service. "Rebels Threaten Peru Elections." *The Dallas Morning News*, October 29, 1989.

Organization of African Unity Charter. 1963. https://au.int/sites/default/files/treaties /7759-file-oau_charter_1963.pdf

Pan, Philip A. "Judge Assassinated in Russia's Caucasus; 2nd killing in a week." *The Washington Post*, June 11, 2009.

Peri, Yoram, ed. *The Assassination of Yitzhak Rabin*. Stanford, CA: Stanford University Press, 2000.

Perliger, Arie. "The Rationale of Political Assassinations." *Combatting Terrorism Center at West Point*, (2015). https://ctc.usma.edu/the-rationale-of-political-assassinations/

"Peru Rebels Step Up Terror Campaign Before Vote." *Houston Chronicle*, November 11, 1989.

"Peruvians United in Anti-Guerilla March." *The Desert News (Salt Lake City, UT)*, November 4, 1989.

Piazza, James A. "Regime Age and Terrorism: Are New Democracies Prone to Terrorism?" *International Interactions* 39, No. 2 (2013): 246–63.

Piazza, James A. and James Igoe Walsh. "Physical Integrity Rights and Terrorism." *PS: Political Science and Politics* 43, No. 3 (2010): 411–14.

Pinfari, Marcus. "Exploring the Terrorist Nature of Political Assassinations: A Reinterpretation of the Orsini Attentat." *Terrorism and Political Violence* 21, No. 4 (2009): 580–94.

Premo, Daniel L. "Political Assassination in Guatemala: A Case of Institutionalized Terror." *Journal of Interamerican Studies and World Affairs* 23, No. 4 (November 1981): 429–56.

Price, H. Edward Jr. "The Strategy and Tactics of Revolutionary Terrorism." *Comparative Studies in Society and History* 19, No. 1 (1977): 52–66.

"Prison Leave for Guerilla Who Blew up Attaché." *The Times*, London, November 10, 2017. https://www.thetimes.co.uk/article/guerrilla-who-blew-up-british-attach-brigadier-stephen-saunders-given-leave-from-greek-jail-23b2jzjw0

Raghavan, Sudarsan. "Who is Killing Yemen's Clerics? Mystery Murders are Sending a Chill through the Mosques." *The Washington Post*, August 28, 2018. https://www.washingtonpost.com/world/middle_east/who-is-killing-yemens-clerics-mystery-murders-are-sending-a-chill-through-the-mosques/2018/08/27/10b7da3c-ce0f-49e2-ad8e-d4adf05ef885_story.html?utm_term=.7e64c5a414cb.

Randal, Jonathan. "Most News is Bad News for Algerian Journalists: Assassinations, Restrictions Plague Press." *The Washington Post*, June 8, 1994.

RAND National Defense Research Institute Project. "Database of Worldwide Terrorism Incidents." 2013. http://www.rand.org/nsrd/projects/terrorism-incidents.html

Raviv, Amiram, Avi Sadeh, Alona Raviv, Ora Silberstein, and Orna Diver. "Young Israeli's Reactions to National Trauma: The Rabin Assassination and Terror Attacks." *Political Psychology* 21, No. 2 (2000): 299–322.

Reid, Donald M. "Political Assassinations in Egypt, 1910–1954." *The International Journal of African Historical Studies* 15, No. 4 (1982): 625–51.

"Reporter Daniel Pearl Is Dead, Killed by His Captors in Pakistan." *Wall Street Journal*, February 24, 2002. https://online.wsj.com/public/resources/documents/pearl-022102.htm

Reuters. "Peru Suspends Civil Liberties." *Sun-Sentinel*, October 25, 1989.

Reuters. "Prominent Saudi Cleric Injured in Philippines Shooting." March 1, 2016. https://www.reuters.com/article/us-philippines-saudi-idUSKCN0W358X

Rios, Jeronimo. "Narratives about Political Violence and Reconciliation in Peru." *Latin American Perspectives* Issue 228, 46 No. 5 (2019): 44–58.

Rivers, Dan. "UK Journalist Assaulted in Tahrir Square: 'Please Make It Stop'." *CNN*, June 28, 2012. https://www.cnn.com/2012/06/27/world/meast/egypt-journalist-assaulted/index.html

"Russian Nationalist Jailed for Life over Hate Crimes." *BBC News*, July 24, 2015. https://www.bbc.com/news/world-europe-33657409

Saidel, Joanna. "Yitzak Shamir: Why We Killed Lord Moyne." *The Times of Israel*, July 5, 2012. https://www.timesofisrael.com/yitzhak-shamir-why-we-killed-lord-moyne/

Salahuddin, Sayed. "U.S. Commander in Afghanistan Survives Deadly Attack at Governor's Compound that Kills Top Afghan Police General." *The Washington Post*, October 18, 2018.

Sellin, Eric. "Tahar Dajourt (1954–1993)." *World Literature Review* 68, No. 1 (Winter 1994): 71–3.

Sieff, Kevin. "36 Local Candidates Have Been Assassinated in Mexico. And the Election is Still 2 Months Away." *The Washington Post*, May 20, 2018. https://www.washingtonpost.com/news/worldviews/wp/2018/05/20/36-local-candidates-have-been-assassinated-in-mexico-and-the-election-is-still-2-months-away/

Smith, James F. "Politicians Become Target in Peru's Bloody October." *The Los Angeles Times*, October 17, 1989.

Smith, James F. "Politicians Targeted by Peruvian Maoists." *The Los Angeles Times*, October 17, 1989.

Smith, James F. "Maoists Take Aim at Democracy in Peru. Shining Path's Red October' Casts Dark Cloud over National Life, Institutions." *Houston Chronicle*, October 17, 1989.

Snitch, Thomas H. "Terrorism and Political Assassinations: A Transnational Assessment, 1968–80." *Annals of the American Academy of Political and Social Science* 463 (1982): 54–68.

"Spanish Military Doctor Shot Dead." *BBC News*, October 17, 2000. http://news.bbc.co.uk/2/hi/europe/975554.stm

Stanley, Alessandra. "British Attaché is Assassinated on Greek Street." *The New York Times*, June 9, 2000.

Swarmy, M. R. Narayan. "When Death Ruled the Streets of Delhi." *News India Times*, *ViewPoints*, November 7, 2014.

Texas Tech University. "History of the Vietnam War on Microfilm, the Fulbright Hearings Transcript from The Vietnam Center and Sam Johnson Vietnam Archive." https://www.vietnam.ttu.edu/virtualarchive/

Thomas, Ward. "Norms and Security: The Case of International Assassination." *International Security* 25, No. 1 (2000): 105–33.

"Three Days of Terror: The Charlie Hebdo Attacks." *HBO Documentary*, 59 (2016). https://www.hbo.com/documentaries/three-days-of-terror-the-charlie-hebdo-attack

"Turkey: 3 Arrested Over the Killing of a Syrian Journalist." *Associated Press*, January 10, 2016. https://apnews.com/a74bf8f3995149a5993371f43290bdf5

United Nations Office on Drugs and Crime. "Global Study on Homicide." 2019. https://www.unodc.org/documents/data-and-analysis/gsh/Booklet1.pdf

United Nations Treaty Collection. "1977 Convention on the Prevention and Punishment of Crimes against Internationally Protected Persons, Including Diplomatic Agents." https://treaties.un.org/pages/ViewDetails.aspx?src=TREATY&mtdsg_no=XVIII-7&chapter=18&clang=_en

United States Federal Register. "Executive Order 12333—United States Intelligence Activities." https://www.archives.gov/federal-register/codification/executive-order/12333.html

University of Illinois. Cline Center for Advanced Social Research. "Social, Political and Economic Events Database." 2014. https://clinecenter.illinois.edu/what-we-do/resources-and-assets

University of Maryland. "Big, Allied and Dangerous (BAAD) Database." 2016. https://www.start.umd.edu/baad/narratives/shining-path-sl

University of Maryland. "National Consortium for the Study of Terrorism and Responses to Terrorism (START)." *Global Terrorism Database*, 2019. [Data file]. http://www.start.umd.edu/gtd

"Vigils Mark Assassination Blamed on Eta." *Independent [London, England]*, February 11, 2003.

West, Nigel. *Encyclopedia of Political Assassinations*. Lanham, MD: Rowman & Littlefield, 2017.

Whitfield, Teresa. *Endgame for ETA: Elusive Peace in the Basque Country*. New York: Oxford University Press, 2014.

Wilson, Margaret A., Angela Scholes, and Elizabeth Brocklehurst. "A Behavioural Analysis of Terrorist Action." *British Journal of Criminology* 50, No. 4 (2010): 690–707.

Wire Services. "Shining Path Kills 2 Warns USSR, China." *San Jose Mercury News (CA)*, October 31, 1989.

Woodhull, Nancy J. and Robert W. Snyder. *Journalists in Peril*. New Brunswick: Transaction Publishers, 1998.

Wright, Robin. "New President of Lebanon Killed by a Massive Blast." *The Los Angeles Times*, November 23, 1989. https://www.latimes.com/archives/la-xpm-1989-11-23-mn-247-story.html

Yitzhak, Ronen. "The Assassination of King Abdallah: The First Political Assassination in Jordan: Did It Truly Threaten the Hashemite Kingdom of Jordan?" *Diplomacy & Statecraft* 21 (2010): 68–86.

Young, Joseph K. "Measuring Terrorism." *Terrorism and Political Violence* 31, No. 3 (2016): 323–45.

Zussman, Asaf and Noam Zussman. "Assassinations: Evaluating the Effectiveness of an Israeli Counterterrorism Policy Using Stock Market Data." *The Journal of Economic Perspectives* 20, No. 2 (2006): 193–206.

Index

About the Author

Laura N. Bell is an assistant professor of Political Science at West Texas A&M University. Dr. Bell's past and current research focuses on assassination as a tactic of terrorism and its impact upon political institutions and society. She is now expanding her research focus to state-sponsored assassinations and accountability mechanisms for perpetrators of assassination under international law. Dr. Bell's research has been published in peer-reviewed journals, such as *Studies in Conflict & Terrorism* and *Terrorism and Political Violence*, and she has contributed articles to *Political Animal Magazine*.

Dr. Bell teaches courses in American National Security, Comparative Politics, International Law & Organization, Middle Eastern Politics, and Terrorism. From 2018 through 2020, she served as assistant dean of Undergraduate Studies for the College of Education and Social Sciences. Dr. Bell holds a Bachelor of Science degree in Political Science and a Master's in Public Administration from the University of Texas at Tyler, and a PhD in Political Science from the University of Texas at Dallas.

www.ingramcontent.com/pod-product-compliance
Lightning Source LLC
Chambersburg PA
CBHW050447280326
41932CB00013BA/2273